APPROACHING
THE BUDDHIST PATH

THE LIBRARY OF WISDOM AND COMPASSION

The Library of Wisdom and Compassion is a special multivolume series in which His Holiness the Dalai Lama shares the Buddha's teachings on the complete path to full awakening that he himself has practiced his entire life. The topics are arranged especially for people not born in a Buddhist culture and are peppered with the Dalai Lama's own unique outlook. Assisted by his longterm disciple, the American nun Thubten Chodron, the Dalai Lama sets the context for practicing the Buddha's teachings in modern times and then unveils the path of wisdom and compassion that leads to a meaningful life and a sense of personal fulfillment. This series is an important bridge from introductory to profound topics for those seeking an in-depth explanation in contemporary language.

APPROACHING THE BUDDHIST PATH

Bhikṣu Tenzin Gyatso,
the Fourteenth Dalai Lama

and

Bhikṣuṇī Thubten Chodron

Wisdom Publications
199 Elm Street
Somerville, MA 02144 USA
wisdompubs.org

Library of Congress Cataloging-in-Publication Data
Names: Bstan-'dzin-rgya-mtsho, Dalai Lama XIV, 1935– author. | Thubten Chodron, 1950–
Title: Approaching the Buddhist path / Bhikṣu Tenzin Gyatso, the Fourteenth Dalai
Lama and Bhikṣuṇī Thubten Chodron.
Description: Somerville, MA: Wisdom Publications, 2017. | Series: The library of wisdom
and compassion; Volume 1 | Includes bibliographical references and index.
Identifiers: LCCN 2016053409 print) | LCCN 2017017596 (ebook) | ISBN
9781614294412 (pbk.: alk. paper) | ISBN 1614294410 (pbk.: alk. paper) | ISBN
9781614294573 (ebook)
Subjects: LCSH: Buddhism—Doctrines.
Classification: LCC BQ7935.B774 A77 2017 (ebook) | LCC BQ7935.B774 (print) |
DDC 294.3—dc23
LC record available at https://lccn.loc.gov/2017017596

ISBN 978-1-61429-441-2   EBOOK ISBN 978-1-61429-457-3

21 20 19
5 4 3

Cover and interior design by Gopa & Ted2, Inc. Set in Diacritical Garamond Pro 11/14.6.
Photo credits: p. xii, Stephen Cysewski; pp. 16, 146, Olivier Adam; p. 170, Konstantin
Sutyagin; p. 190 (top), Dennis Jarvis; p. 190 (bottom), Zhong Feng; p. 230, Roberto
Dutesco; p. 246, Kevin K. Cheung. All photos reprinted with permission.

This book was produced with environmental mindfulness. For more information, please
visit wisdompubs.org/wisdom-environment.

Wisdom Publications' books are printed on acid-free paper and meet the guidelines for
permanence and durability of the Production Guidelines for Book Longevity of the Council on Library Resources.

Printed in the United States of America.

Publisher's Acknowledgment

The publisher gratefully acknowledges the generous help of the Hershey Family Foundation in sponsoring the production of this book.

Contents

Prologue

THE WORLD WE LIVE IN is very different from the world at the Buddha's time, yet we human beings have the same afflictions and still experience physical and mental suffering. While the truth of the Buddha's teachings transcends historical eras, the way they are presented to practitioners in a given time is influenced by the specific culture, environment, and economic and political challenges. I encourage us to become twenty-first-century Buddhists—people whose view is rooted in the Buddha's message of compassion and wisdom and who also have a broad understanding of many fields, such as science—especially neurology, psychology, and physics—and other religions.

Our Buddhist knowledge must be expansive, not limited to just one topic, practice, or Buddhist tradition. We should try to learn about the teachings and practices of other Buddhist traditions and understand how they suit the particular dispositions and interests of the people who practice them. We may also include some of these teachings in our own practice. In this way, we will better appreciate the Buddha's skill as a teacher, which will reduce the sectarianism that limits us Buddhists from acting together to contribute to the welfare of all peoples and environments on our planet. We should also understand the full path to awakening and how different teachings can be practiced by the same individual at different points of his or her spiritual journey. This will clarify our personal practice as well as increase our respect for all Buddhist traditions and other religions.

To grow these understandings in ourselves, reciting prayers and mantras is not sufficient. While perhaps increasing our devotion, these activities alone do not bring wisdom. In the modern world, we need to be realistic and practical, and for this, knowledge is essential. All of us want happiness, not suffering. Since both happiness and suffering arise in dependence on causes and conditions, we must know the causes of each so that we can train our minds to create the causes for happiness and abandon the causes for suffering.

All of us want a harmonious society. Since society consists of individuals, to bring about peace each individual must cultivate peace in his or her own heart and mind. Of course the ultimate aim of the Buddha's teachings goes beyond world peace to liberation from all rebirth in cyclic existence (*saṃsāra*), but the teachings can help us to create a more peaceful society while we are still in cyclic existence.

The material in this series accords with the general presentation of the Indian sages of the Nālandā tradition, who are held in esteem by all four Buddhist traditions in Tibet as well as Buddhist traditions in China. Most of the quoted passages come from these Indian sources, and in terms of the *method* aspect of the path—renunciation, bodhicitta, and the perfections of generosity, ethical conduct, fortitude, joyous effort, and meditative stability—there is little difference among them. Tibetan traditions follow Nāgārjuna and speak of the noncontradictory nature of emptiness and dependent arising as the essence of the *wisdom* aspect of the path, here we will emphasize Tsongkhapa's presentation of emptiness and sometimes mention teachings from the Nyingma, Kagyu, and Sakya traditions. Because the Pāli tradition emphasizes the Fundamental Vehicle which is common to all Buddhist traditions, we also cite passages from it.

In general, my teaching style does not follow the approach of the traditional *lamrim* (stages of the path) teachings. I like to speak a lot about emptiness and show its relationship to other aspects of the path; this way of presenting the teachings also flourished in ancient India. Many years ago, His Eminence Geshe Lungrik Namgyal, the Gaden Tripa at that time, said to his friends, "Understanding His Holiness the Dalai Lama's teachings is challenging because his way of presenting the material is special. He touches on this point and that, but we are unable to integrate everything into the traditional framework of the teachings." I wonder if this is praise or criticism. In any case, please think deeply about the various topics in the manner explained. Contemplate how these topics relate to one another and to your life.

Bhikṣu Tenzin Gyatso, the Fourteenth Dalai Lama
Thekchen Choling

Preface

The Purpose of This Series

EVERYTHING COMES ABOUT due to causes and conditions, and this series is no exception. Explaining some of its causes and conditions will help you understand the purpose of this series. Its ultimate purpose is to lead you, the reader, and other sentient beings to full awakening. Although many excellent works on the stages of the path, the lamrim, already exist, there is a need for this unique series. To explain why, I will share a little of my personal story, which is typical of the first generation of Westerners encountering Tibetan Buddhism.

Born in the United States, I grew up in a Judeo-Christian culture. I tried to believe in God, but that worldview didn't work for me. There were too many unanswered questions. When I was twenty-four, I attended a three-week Dharma course taught by two Tibetan lamas. One of the first things they said was, "You don't have to believe anything we say. You are intelligent people. Examine these teachings using reasoning. Practice them and see through your own experience if they work. Then decide if you want to adopt them." The attitude of *ehipaśyika*, or "come and see," that the Buddha spoke about in the sūtras attracted me. Studying, contemplating, and practicing the Buddha's teachings over time, I became convinced that this path made sense and would help me if I practiced it sincerely.

Like many young Westerners in the 1970s, I steeped myself in studying and practicing Tibetan Buddhism as best I could, considering that I didn't know the Tibetan language or much about Tibetan culture. Our Dharma education commenced with the lamrim—a genre of texts that lead readers through the progressive stages of the path to awakening. Here it is helpful to look at the place of Tibetan lamrim works within the tradition. After the Buddha's awakening, he taught across India for forty-five years. Sensitive to the needs, interests, and dispositions of the various audiences, he gave teachings that were appropriate for them at that moment. After his passing (*parinirvāṇa*), the great Indian sages organized the material in the sūtras by topic points and wrote treatises and commentaries explaining these. After the Dharma spread to Tibet, Tibetan masters also wrote treatises and commentaries, of which lamrim literature is one type.

Tibetans see this development of treatises, commentaries, and commentaries on commentaries as a demonstration of the sages' kindness. The fortunate ones who were direct disciples of the Buddha had great merit and could attain realizations of the path without needing lengthy teachings. Since those of future generations had less merit, their minds were not as sharp, and they required more detailed explanations to dispel their doubts, generate the correct views, and attain realizations. Since people's minds are even more obscured and they have less merit now, new commentaries are needed. Our teachers thus said the sūtras are like freshly picked cotton, the Indian treatises and commentaries like woven cloth, and the lamrim texts like ready-made clothes. When the first generation of Westerners were introduced to the lamrim, we were told that everything we needed to know was in these texts, and that all we had to do to gain awakening was study and practice them correctly over time.

However, things didn't turn out to be that simple. From the very beginning of the lamrim, we had doubts about topics that for our Tibetan teachers were obvious. Precious human life, one of the initial meditations of the lamrim, speaks of our fortune being born as human beings, not as hell beings, hungry ghosts, or animals. Tibetans, raised in a culture that believes in rebirth and various realms of existence, accept this without question. However, for those of us raised in Christian, Jewish, or secular cultures that respect science, this is not the case.

Furthermore, while our Tibetan teachers talked about all phenomena being empty of true existence, we were wondering, "Does God exist?" When they taught selflessness, we were trying to find our souls or our true selves. When they explained dependent arising, we were seeking the one absolute truth independent from all else. Philosophically, our views did not coincide.

The traditional presentation of the teachings assumed that the audience had faith in the Buddha, Dharma, and Saṅgha and was free from doubts about religious institutions and issues around authority. The teachings were directed toward people who could separate their emotional needs from their spiritual practice and who would correctly understand the teachings. For example, they assumed we would not be overwhelmed with guilt when reflecting on our harmful actions; we would not harshly criticize ourselves when contemplating the disadvantages of self-centeredness; and we would not succumb to our culture's tendency to idolize the charismatic.

From our side, we Westerners assumed that all Tibetan teachers were buddhas and that the values we grew up holding—democracy, gender equality, care for the environment, and so on—would be perfectly embodied in Tibetan society.

All these assumptions on both sides were incorrect, and after a while many Westerners began to have difficulties with their Dharma studies and practices. The cultural difference was difficult for us and for our spiritual mentors, who were doing their best to teach people whose perspective on life was totally new to them. It took many years for all of us to realize that Westerners require pre-lamrim teachings. For us to grow in the Dharma, the stages of the path need to commence with material that meets our dispositions.

His Holiness the Dalai Lama understood this and adjusted his teachings in the West accordingly. Instead of beginning with a reliance upon a spiritual mentor elevated to the status of a buddha, he started with the two truths—how things appear to exist and how they actually exist. Rather than tell us that reciting a certain mantra a few times would protect us from rebirth in the hells, he explained the four truths of the *āryas*—those who nonconceptually perceive ultimate reality. Instead of saying that drinking blessed water would purify eons of destructive karma, he taught us about the nature of mind, the workings of the mental afflictions, and the possibility of attaining liberation. Diving into the philosophy that underlies the Buddhist worldview, he asked us to think deeply about it. He challenged us to doubt our anger and to open our hearts with compassion for all sentient beings. His was a no-nonsense approach, and when he learned that, contrary to Buddhist scriptures, the earth was not flat and revolved around the sun, he was quick to say that if science conclusively proves something, we should accept it and not adhere to scriptural pronouncements to the contrary.

In this environment, in 1993, I requested an interview with His Holiness. The interview did not happen for another two years due to His Holiness's full schedule. During the interview, I humbly requested him to write a short lamrim text designed for non-Tibetans. A text that Tibetan geshes could use to teach Westerners, it would present the topics in an order suitable for people who did not grow up Buddhist and would deal with doubts and issues that non-Tibetans had about the Dharma. His Holiness agreed with the idea, but he immediately stipulated that a larger commentary should be written first and then points extracted from it to make a root text. He asked me to speak to senior Dharma students about the topics to include, gave me a transcript of a lamrim teaching he had recently given to use as a foundation, and asked me to begin. I spoke with many senior Western practitioners and assembled a list of questions, topics, issues, and doubts that they would like His Holiness to address.

Over the ensuing years, I met with His Holiness several times to address these topics and to show him the work I had done so far on the manuscript. In our time together, he taught specific subjects upon my request, offered deeper explanations of others, and answered the many questions that I had accumulated. He seemed to thoroughly enjoy these sessions and usually invited other geshes and his brother to come. I would ask a question, and they discussed the answer animatedly in Tibetan, with His Holiness asking the geshes what they thought, bringing up points they had not considered. After some time, the translator gave me the conclusion of the discussion.

As I continued to add more material from many of His Holiness's oral teachings and from our interviews, the manuscript became larger and larger. I came to see that the purpose of this series was to fill the gap between the short lamrim texts with teachings lamas gave in the West and the long philosophical treatises translated into English by scholars. Western practitioners needed a concise presentation in their own language of the major topics in the philosophical texts that could also be the basis for an analytical meditation on the lamrim.

In 2003, I began to read the manuscript aloud for His Holiness so he could check it. We soon realized that this would be a lengthy process that his schedule did not permit. In 2004, he asked his translator Geshe Dorje

Damdul to go through the manuscript with me. Geshela and I worked methodically until 2010 doing this.

His Holiness also clarified that this series was not meant solely for Westerners, but for all those who have interest in Buddhism—particularly the Nālandā tradition—and are keen to study and practice but need a new approach to it. Here he included Tibetans born in the Tibetan diaspora who have a modern education, as well as Asians from Taiwan, Korea, Vietnam, and so forth who are attending his teachings in Dharamsala, India, with increasing frequency and interest.

This series chiefly contains the teachings of the Nālandā tradition, the classical Indian Buddhist tradition stemming from the great monastic universities such as Nālandā, Odantapurī, and Vikramaśīla. This is the Buddhist tradition the Tibetans and to some extent East Asians inherited from classical India. However, His Holiness clearly stated that this series must be unique—it must not be limited to the Nālandā tradition but must also include information about and teachings from other Buddhist traditions. It was time, he said, that followers of Tibetan Buddhism learned more about diverse Buddhist traditions and their teachings. As he began to speak more and more in public talks about being a twenty-first-century Buddhist, I came to understand his wish to dispel wrong conceptions and stereotypes that practitioners of various Buddhist traditions had about one another and bring them closer together. For this purpose, he asked me to visit other Asian countries to learn about how they practiced the Dharma. I stayed in a monastery in Thailand and also visited Taiwan to learn from scholars and practitioners there. I continued intra-Buddhist dialogues with Buddhist monastics in the West at our annual Western Buddhist Monastic Gatherings and became familiar with the teachings of their Asian teachers. These were very rich experiences.

In the 2011 series of interviews, His Holiness clarified that to fulfill the above purpose, he wanted a book explaining the similarities and differences between the Pāli and Sanskrit traditions. While most books that introduce the many forms of Buddhism deal with more superficial topics such as altar layout, forms of worship, and so forth, this book was to deal with doctrine. He wanted people to think deeply about the Buddha's teachings and his skill in addressing the various dispositions and interests of his disciples. By this time the manuscript was too large to be a single volume. To fulfill His

Holiness's wish, I extracted and abbreviated portions of it to form *Buddhism: One Teacher, Many Traditions*, published by Wisdom Publications in 2014.

The present series, which will be published in several volumes, explains the path to buddhahood as set forth in the Nālandā tradition as practiced in the Tibetan Buddhist tradition. In some sections, it brings in teachings from other Buddhist traditions to enrich our understanding and give us a broader view of a topic. The series also incorporates several other purposes: it links study to daily life and formal meditation practice; it serves as a bridge for both new and seasoned practitioners from the short lamrim texts to the lengthy philosophical treatises; and it exposes the reader to the tenets and practices of other Buddhist traditions. Because some of the topics have already been explained in *Buddhism: One Teacher, Many Traditions*, we will sometimes refer you to that book.

Overview of the Entire Series

We begin by laying the groundwork for the Buddha's teachings. The need for pre-lamrim material is evinced in a comment His Holiness made when we began working on the series: "The lamrim assumes that someone is already a practitioner with full faith in the Buddha. The main audience for the lamrim texts in all the Tibetan traditions is someone who already has some knowledge of rebirth and karma, the Three Jewels, reliable cognizers and their objects (Buddhist epistemology), and so on. We need to add introductory material to this series so the students are properly prepared." Also covered here are the meaning of faith, balancing faith and wisdom, seeking out a qualified spiritual mentor, relying on that person properly, and developing the qualities of a receptive student. These will help you to approach the Dharma as a twenty-first-century Buddhist.

Then we set the foundation for learning and meditating by explaining how to structure a meditation session on the lamrim. After again reflecting on the possibility that the continuity of our mindstream does not end at death but will take another body in another life, we look at the precious opportunity our present human life offers us and how to set our priorities. This leads us to reflect on the eight worldly concerns—ways in which we get distracted from making our lives meaningful—and karma (volitional actions) and their effects, for the first step to having a meaningful life is to abandon harming others. In this way, we will know the causes for happiness and the causes of suffering so we can go about creating the former and abandoning the latter. The topic of karma is vast and of great interest to many people, so that is covered in depth.

We then proceed to explore the four truths of the āryas, those beings who directly realize the ultimate mode of existence. These four form the basic framework of the Buddha's teachings. The first two truths—true *duḥkha* and true origins—lay out our present unsatisfactory situation in cyclic existence and its causes, the afflictions that torment our minds and lie behind our suffering. We look at the twelve links of dependent origination—the process by which afflictions and polluted karma propel our rebirth in cyclic existence and the way we can free ourselves from it. This section delves into the psychology behind wrong views and disturbing emotions.

At this point we realize that we need the guidance of the Three Jewels—the Buddha, Dharma, and Saṅgha—who will teach us and show us the path to liberation through the example of their lives. Learning about the potential of our mind, the possibility to attain liberation, and our buddha nature increases our confidence that we can succeed in freeing ourselves from saṃsāra and attain nirvāṇa, a state of genuine peace. This is explained in the latter two of the four truths—true cessation and true paths—the state of liberation and the method leading to it. Included in true paths are the three higher trainings, the four establishments of mindfulness, and the thirty-seven aids to awakening—topics that are oriented toward practice in both daily life and meditation sessions. Through these we will calm our daily behavior, deepen our concentration, and gain wisdom, thus beginning to actualize our great potential.

But freeing ourselves alone is limited, considering that others suffer just as we do and they have been amazingly kind to us. To free ourselves from the prison of self-centeredness, we learn how to cultivate immeasurable love, compassion, joy, and equanimity, as well as *bodhicitta*—the intention to attain full awakening in order to most effectively benefit all sentient beings. Then we learn how to train in the perfections (*pāramitās*)—practices that enable us to bring our bodhicitta motivation to fruition by practicing generosity, ethical conduct, fortitude, joyous effort, meditative stability, and wisdom. Imagine the kind of person you will become when all those wonderful qualities have become second nature to you.

Having generated the altruistic intention to attain full awakening, we now want to cultivate the wisdom realizing the nature of reality, the only counterforce that will completely and irreversibly eradicate all the afflictions and their latencies from our mindstreams. Here we learn the tenets of the various Buddhist philosophical systems, which have diverse views about the ultimate truth. Our job is to sort through them with the aid of the past great sages and discern the most accurate view, that of the Prāsaṅgika Madhyamaka tenet system.

This leads us to discuss the two truths—veil and ultimate. Veil truths are objects that appear true to a mind affected by ignorance, and ultimate truth is their actual mode of existence, their emptiness. After further reflection, we come to see the uniqueness of the Prāsaṅgika Madhyamaka view of emptiness as well as how to unite the concentrated mind of serenity (*samatha*) and the analytic mind of insight (*vipaśyanā*) to realize the ultimate nature. Here we will also touch on the view of selflessness as understood in the Pāli and Chinese Traditions.

The Buddha also set out the paths and stages that practitioners traverse to attain their particular goals—liberation from saṃsāra or the full awakening of buddhahood. Learning these gives us a roadmap to follow on our spiritual journey and we come to understand the various qualities and realizations that are gradually developed on the path. They also enable us to check our meditative experiences with the generally accepted sequence of development.

We then learn about the pure land practice found in both the Tibetan and Chinese traditions, and this leads us to a discussion of Vajrayāna, which is a branch of the general Mahāyāna. The work concludes with an epilogue from His Holiness containing personal advice for his students.

This work is designed not simply to give you information about Buddhism, but to enrich your Dharma practice. To this end, most chapters contain summaries of the main points so that you can easily remember and reflect on them. Please take advantage of these to deepen your practice by contemplating what you read. The work would have become too long had reflections been inserted for every section, so where they are missing, please review what you read and write out the main points for contemplation. This will help you to apply what you learn to your own experience and integrate the Dharma into your life.

The volumes of this work will be published one at a time. This way you can spend some time learning, contemplating, and meditating on the material in one volume, which will prepare you for the material in the following volume. The stages of the path are presented in a particular order in this series of volumes for the purpose of allowing you to grow into the more advanced and complex stages. Nevertheless, each volume stands alone as an explanation of its unique topic.

When giving public teachings to audiences of people with very different backgrounds and degrees of understanding, His Holiness doesn't shy away from introducing profound topics. Although he doesn't give a full explanation, he brings in advanced concepts and vocabulary in a concise manner. He doesn't expect everyone to understand these topics but is planting seeds for newer students to one day learn and understand the more complex teachings. He often will weave back and forth between general topics that most people can easily understand and difficult topics that only the learned will comprehend. Don't get discouraged if you don't understand everything all at once. The concepts and terms introduced in earlier volumes will be fleshed out in later ones.

This series is written in a similar style, although I tried to edit the material so that the reader is led from easier topics to more difficult ones. If you do not completely understand a topic the first or even second time, don't worry; the series is meant to be a resource for you on the path, a text to which you will repeatedly refer to deepen your understanding of the Dharma. Each time you read it, you will understand more due to the merit and wisdom you accumulated in the intervening time.

By learning the entire path from beginning to end, you will come to see the relationships between the various topics, which will enrich your practice. Although the stages are presented in a linear fashion, the knowledge and experience obtained from later stages will inform your meditation on earlier stages. As you continue to delve into the Buddha's teachings, you will find new ways to relate different points to each other in a creative and thought-provoking way. One of His Holiness's unique qualities as a teacher is his ability to draw threads from seemingly different topics together to make a tapestry that continually draws us into more profound understandings.

Overview of Volume I

This first volume and part of the second cover topics that form the basic approach of the Nālandā tradition. In the curriculum at a Tibetan monastery, many of these are embedded in larger texts and others are learned in public teachings. Here we extracted the most important points and incorporated them in one volume, so that people who did not grow up in a Buddhist culture or in a monastery will have the background that supports the study of the stages of the path.

Chapter 1 explores the role of Buddhism in the world: the purpose of our lives, the middle way between theistic religions and scientific reductionism, Buddhism's relationship with the other great world religions, and the meaning of being a spiritual practitioner in the modern world.

Chapter 2 delves into the Buddhist view of life: the explanation of the mind and its relationship to body, rebirth, and the self. The four truths of the āryas lay out the essential framework of the path, and to understand these more deeply, we investigate dependent arising and emptiness and the possibility of ending duḥkha—our unsatisfactory situation in cyclic existence.

Chapter 3 explores our minds and emotions, and furnishes some practical strategies for calming our minds as well as for developing a confident and optimistic attitude for approaching life and spiritual practice.

Chapter 4 is a brief survey of the historical development of the Buddhadharma: the early Buddhist schools in the Indian subcontinent, Sri Lanka, and Central Asia; the Buddhist canons; and the philosophical tenet systems that began to form in India. More detailed information has been included in footnotes for those readers who are interested.

This leads to an examination in chapter 5 of the three turnings of the Dharma wheel—one schema for organizing the Buddha's teachings—as well as the authenticity of the Mahāyāna scriptures. This chapter concludes with an introduction to Tibetan Buddhism as the continuation of the Nālandā tradition in India.

Chapter 6 investigates the teachings, first by discerning reliable teachings and differentiating them from exaggerated statements given to encourage a particular type of disciple, and then by ensuring we understand the correct point of the teachings we study.

Chapter 7 discusses cultivating a proper motivation for spiritual practice, since this is crucial to prevent fooling ourselves, getting sidetracked, or becoming hypocritical. This chapter brings us back to our inner heart and encourages us to cultivate the sincere wish to free both ourselves and others from cyclic existence and to attain full awakening. His Holiness also illustrates a practical way to cultivate and maintain a compassionate motivation.

Chapter 8 deals with how to progress along the path to full awakening as an initial, intermediate, and advanced level practitioner. This provides the framework for knowing where each topic the Buddha taught fits into the entire path, so we can practice the path in a step-by-step manner without undue confusion.

Chapter 9 speaks of the mental tools we will need to progress along the path, such as faith and wisdom. Here we'll understand the role of prayers and rituals as well as memorization and debate in cultivating the three wisdoms: the wisdom arising from learning, reflecting on the teachings, and meditating on them.

Chapter 10 anticipates some common challenges that practitioners could encounter and offers ways to overcome them.

In chapter 11, His Holiness shares some of his personal reflections and experiences practicing the path, so we can see how a genuine practitioner uses the Dharma in daily life.

Chapter 12 shifts our focus from personal practice to using Buddhist principles to guide our work in and for the world. The Buddha taught the Dharma not only for spiritual transcendence, but also as a method to create a healthier and more just society. Here we apply Buddhist ideas and practices to politics, business, consumerism, the media, the arts, science, gender equality, and respect for other religions as well as for other Buddhist traditions.

Please Note

While this series is coauthored, the vast majority is in His Holiness's voice. I wrote the chapter on Buddhist history, all parts pertaining to the Pāli tradition, and some paragraphs here and there.

Pāli and Sanskrit terms are usually given in parentheses only for the first usage of a word. Unless otherwise noted with "P" or "T," indicating Pāli or Tibetan respectively, the italicized terms are Sanskrit. In most cases, Dharma terms and scriptural titles are in English, but when Sanskrit or Pāli terms are well known, those are used, for example Prajñāpāramitā for Perfection of Wisdom, and *jhāna* or *dhyāna*, the Pāli and Sanskrit names respectively for meditative stabilization. Sanskrit or Pāli spellings are used in sections concerning their respective traditions and in quotations from each tradition's scriptures. For ease of reading, most honorifics have been omitted, although that does not diminish the great respect we have for these most excellent sages. Because it is awkward to gloss every new term when it first appears, a glossary is included at the end of the book. Unless otherwise noted, the personal pronoun "I" refers to His Holiness.

Acknowledgments and Appreciation

I bow to Śākyamuni Buddha and all the buddhas, bodhisattvas, and arhats who embody the Dharma and share it with others. I also bow to all the realized lineage masters of all Buddhist traditions through whose kindness the Dharma still exists in our world.

Since this series will appear in consecutive volumes, I will express my appreciation of those involved in that particular volume. This first volume is due to the talent and efforts of His Holiness's translators—Geshe Lhakdor, Geshe Dorje Damdul, and Geshe Thupten Jinpa—and of Samdhong Rinpoche and Geshe Sonam Rinchen for their clarification of important points. I also thank Geshe Dadul Namgyal for checking the manuscript; the staff at the Private Office of His Holiness for facilitating the interviews; the communities of Sravasti Abbey and Dharma Friendship Foundation for supporting me while writing this series; and David Kittelstrom for his skillful editing. I am grateful to everyone at Wisdom Publications who contributed to the successful production of this series. All errors are my own.

Bhikṣuṇī Thubten Chodron
Sravasti Abbey

Abbreviations

TRANSLATIONS USED IN THIS volume, unless noted otherwise, are as cited here. Some terminology has been modified for consistency with the present work.

AN   Aṅguttara Nikāya. Translated by Bhikkhu Bodhi in *The Numerical Discourses of the Buddha* (Boston: Wisdom Publications, 2012).

AKC   *Advice to Kunzang Chogyal*, by Dza Patrul Rinpoche, translated by Karen Lilienberg. http://vajracakra.com/viewtopic.php?f=57& t=3287.

BCA   *Engaging in the Bodhisattva's Deeds* (*Bodhicaryāvatāra*) by Śāntideva. Translated by Stephen Batchelor in *A Guide to the Bodhisattva's Way of Life* (Dharamsala, India: Library of Tibetan Works and Archive, 2007).

CŚ   *The Four Hundred* (*Catuḥśataka*), by Āryadeva.

LC   *The Great Treatise on the Stages of the Path* (Tib. *Lam rim chen mo*) by Tsongkhapa, 3 vols. Translated by Joshua Cutler et al. (Ithaca: Snow Lion Publications, 2000–2004).

MN   Majjhima Nikāya. Translated by Bhikkhu Ñāṇamoli and Bhikkhu Bodhi in *The Middle-Length Discourses of the Buddha* (Boston: Wisdom Publications, 1995).

RA   *Precious Garland* (*Ratnāvalī*) by Nāgārjuna. Translated by John Dunne and Sara McClintock in *The Precious Garland: An Epistle to a King* (Boston: Wisdom Publications, 1997).

SN   Saṃyutta Nikāya. Translated by Bhikkhu Bodhi in *The Connected Discourses of the Buddha* (Boston: Wisdom Publications, 2000).

Vism   *Path of Purification (Visuddhimagga)* of Buddhaghosa. Translated by Bhikkhu Ñāṇamoli in *The Path of Purification* (Kandy: Buddhist Publication Society, 1991).

Approaching
the Buddhist Path

1 | Exploring Buddhism

A SPIRITUAL PATH IS ESSENTIAL to human life. Although advances in medicine, science, and technology have done much to improve the quality of human life, they have not been able to free us from all suffering and bring us secure and lasting happiness. In fact, in many cases, they have brought new problems that we did not face in the past, such as environmental pollution and the threat of nuclear war. Therefore, external improvements in our world are not sufficient to bring the happiness and peace that we all desire. For this, internal transformation through spiritual development is essential. For this transformation to occur, we need to follow a spiritual path.

Spiritual practice involves transforming our mind. Although our body is important, satisfying it does not bring lasting happiness. We must look inside ourselves, examining our attitudes and emotions to understand how profoundly they influence and shape our experiences. The Buddha comments (SN 1.62):

> The world is led by mind and drawn along by mind. All phenomena are controlled by one phenomenon, mind.

The mind includes not only our intellect, but also all our cognitions, emotions, and other mental factors. The Sanskrit word for "mind," *citta*, can also be translated as "heart." It refers to all our consciousnesses—sensory and mental—and to the variety of mental states we experience. By subduing the afflicted aspects of our mind, our experience of the world is transformed, whereas if we seek to change only the external environment and the people in it, we continually meet with frustration and disappointment because we cannot control the external world. It is only by developing the great potential of our mind/heart that we will be able to find a way out of our suffering and to truly benefit others as well.

In Buddhism, therefore, the obstacles we aim to eliminate are not external, but are afflictive mental states—distorted attitudes and disturbing emotions. The tools we use to counteract them are also mental—compassion, wisdom, and other realistic and beneficial attitudes and emotions that we consciously cultivate. The Buddha's teachings, or Buddhadharma—what is commonly known as Buddhism—help us to differentiate realistic and beneficial attitudes, views, and emotions that accord with the way things are. The teachings also give us instructions regarding what to practice and what to abandon on the spiritual path. The Buddha taught from his own experience, and we are free to accept or reject his teachings, using valid reasons as well as our own experience as criteria.

The Purpose of Existence and the Meaning of Life

The Buddha says (MN 46.2):

> For the most part, beings have this wish, desire, and longing: "If only unwished for, undesired, disagreeable things would diminish and wished for, desired, agreeable things would increase!" Yet although beings have this wish, desire, and longing, unwished for, undesired, disagreeable things increase for them, and wished for, desired, agreeable things diminish.

What the Buddha says above is confirmed by our own experience. All of us want happiness and no one wants misery. Yet, despite our sincere wish, the opposite comes about. I believe the meaning and purpose of our life has to do with eradicating the causes of pain and increasing the causes of happiness, so that this deepest wish in the heart of each and every living being can be fulfilled.

I do not know of an overarching purpose for the existence of this world, and from the Buddhist viewpoint, there is not a clear explanation. We simply say that the existence of the world is due to causes and conditions, to nature. The existence of this universe is a fact. How existence came into being and the possibility of ending suffering are quite different issues. We do not need to know how the world began in order to stop our suffering.

Everyone wants to be happy and peaceful and to avoid suffering. Even a person who doesn't know the purpose for the existence of the universe doesn't want to suffer. Such a person would never think, "Because there is no plan or big purpose, I will let myself suffer." Our body exists, and feelings of happiness and unhappiness exist. Whether our intellect understands the reason for our existence or not, we are concerned about the happiness of ourselves and others. By seeking to bring about this happiness, we give purpose and meaning to our lives.

The purpose of our life is happiness and peace, an internal feeling of well-being. To bring that about, we need material development and proper education. We also need spiritual development. By spirituality, I do not mean religious belief or rituals. For me, spirituality refers to the basic good qualities of human beings, such as compassion, affection, gentleness, and humility. When these qualities are well established in our hearts, we will have more peace of mind and will contribute to the happiness of others. Someone can be happy without religious beliefs but not without these basic good qualities.

Sentient beings—all beings with minds that are not fully awakened—experience two types of happiness and suffering: physical happiness and suffering (which occur at the level of our senses) and mental or emotional happiness and suffering (which occur at the mental level). As human beings, we are not different from animals, insects, and other beings with bodies; we are all basically the same in terms of seeking physical comfort and avoiding pain. But in terms of mental and emotional happiness and suffering, we human beings are very different from other species. We have human intelligence and thus have more capacity to think, remember, explain, and examine. For example, unlike animals, human beings may suffer mentally when they remember injustices their ancestors experienced. We may speculate about the future and become anxious or furious about situations that haven't occurred yet. Due to our imagination, we are much more sensitive on a mental level and experience so much joy and misery that is created by our mind. Because mental suffering is created by the conceptions in our mind, countermeasures that are likewise mental are important. Toward this end, human beings have developed various religions, philosophies, psychological theories, and scientific hypotheses.

A Middle Way between Theistic Religions and Scientific Reductionism

The more than seven billion human beings on our planet can be divided into three general groups: those who are not interested in religion, those who believe and practice a religion, and those who are actively hostile to religion. The first group, those who are not very interested in religion, is the largest. These people are concerned principally with their day-to-day lives, especially with financial security and material prosperity. Among this group there are two types. The first consists of people who have ethical principles and use them to guide their lives. The second values money, prestige, and pleasure above all else. Those guided by ethical principles are, in general, happier. Those who lack ethical restraint may gain more temporary benefit, but in the end, they do not feel good inside themselves about what they have done. Afraid that their devious means will be found out, they lack genuine self-confidence and inner peace. Many of our global problems are due to such a lack of ethical principles, which comes about when people do not know or care about the moral consequences of their actions. Without such knowledge and the restraint it produces, greed has free reign. We can see that many of our global problems would be solved if people lived with a sense of responsibility that comes from valuing ethical principles.

Of the other two groups, those who sincerely believe in a religion and practice it and those who are hostile to religion, the former also uses ethical principles and compassion to guide their lives, while the latter intentionally opposes religious ideas. Some people in the latter group say religion is the instrument through which the ruling class exploits others; others say that religion is just superstition or a cause of ignorance.

People in these three groups are the same in that they all seek happiness. There is no difference among them in this regard. The difference occurs in terms of what each group believes will lead to happiness. Except for those in the first group who privilege ethical values above personal gain, the rest trust principally in money and material comfort; the second affirms that happiness comes primarily through ethical conduct as well as religious and spiritual practice; the third believes not only that happiness lies in the material world but also that religious ideas are irrelevant, make-believe, and counter to human happiness. Of these three groups, Buddhist practitioners belong to the second.

From one perspective, Buddhism is a religion and a spiritual discipline. Because Buddhist precepts and meditation are directly linked to mental training, it is also a science of mind. From another viewpoint, since Buddhism does not accept an external creator, it is not a theistic religion but a philosophy. Depending on how we look at Buddhism, we may describe it as a religion, a science of mind, or a philosophy. We do not need to say it is one and not the others, for Buddhism embraces aspects of all three.

We also see radical materialists who deny the existence of mind as an immaterial phenomenon, as well as religious believers who assert an external creator. We see people who stress logical reasoning and others who emphasize uncritical faith. It seems Buddhism does not fit in any of these categories. In contrast to religions that oppose critical investigation, Buddhism emphasizes that we should be skeptical, even of the Buddha's words. We have to investigate whether scriptural passages are reliable and true or not. If we find contradictory evidence, including scientific findings, we should follow what can be proven rather than what the Buddha said. The Buddha himself stated that his followers should not accept his teaching out of respect but after investigation and personal experiment. We have the liberty to examine and test the Buddha's teachings.

On the other hand, while Buddhism shares respect for logic and experimental proof, it doesn't deny the value of having faith and confidence in spiritually realized beings. Since our five senses are limited in what they are capable of knowing, scientific tools are not amenable to investigating many existent phenomena. So it seems that Buddhism is in between science and theistic religions. In the future, perhaps Buddhism may become a bridge between religion and science, bringing the two closer together.

I have met many times with people of other faiths as well as with scientists. Sometimes my Buddhist explanations have helped my Christian brothers and sisters practice their own faith. Other times, scientists in the fields of cosmology, biology, physics, and modern psychology have found common points between Buddhism and their disciplines. Some of these scientists began our meetings thinking, "This will be a waste of time because Buddhism is a religion and religion doesn't have much in common with science." But after a few sessions, they were eager to learn about the Buddhist concepts of subtle particles or our explanation of the relation between the mind and the brain. This demonstrates the possibility of mutual understanding with practitioners of other religions and with scientists.

Buddhadharma and Other Religions

There are two aspects to each religion: one is transformation of the mind or heart, and the other is the philosophy that supports that transformation. I believe that in terms of transforming human beings' minds and hearts, all religions are in general agreement. They all teach love, compassion, forgiveness, nonharm, contentment, self-discipline, and generosity. No matter the religion, a person who practices it sincerely will develop these qualities. In every religion, we see many examples of ethical and warm-hearted people who benefit others.

The difference among religions occurs mainly in the area of philosophy. Theistic religions—Judaism, Christianity, Islam, and many branches of Hinduism—believe in a supreme being who created the universe and the living beings in it. Theistic philosophy supplies the reasons for the adherents of these religions to transform their hearts and minds. For them, all existence depends on the creator. The creator created us and loves us, and so in return, with gratitude we love the creator. Because we love the creator, we then must love the creations—other sentient beings—and treat them respectfully. This is the reason for our Jewish, Christian, Hindu, and Muslim brothers and sisters to be kind and ethical people.

Buddhism, on the other hand, speaks not of an external creator but of the law of causality. Our actions create the causes for what we will experience in the future. If we want happiness—be it temporal happiness or happiness that comes through spiritual realizations—we must abandon destructive actions and practice love, compassion, tolerance, forgiveness, and generosity.

While big differences exist among their philosophies, all religions agree on the good qualities for human beings to develop. For some people, the

Buddhist philosophy is more effective in cultivating these qualities. For others, the doctrine of another religion is more helpful. Therefore, from the viewpoint of an individual, each person will see one philosophy as true and one religion as best for him or her. But looking at all of society, we must accept the diversity and plurality of religions and of views of truth. These two perspectives—what is best for a given individual and what is best for society—do not contradict each other.

Even within Buddhism, our teacher, the Buddha, taught different philosophies to different people because he understood that due to each individual's disposition and interest, what is suitable for one person is not necessarily effective for another. Thus the Buddha respects individual views, be they within Buddhadharma itself or among individuals from various religions.

This series is written mainly for Buddhist practitioners, so some philosophical explanations naturally will not agree with people of other religions. However, as Buddhists we do not criticize those religions or the people who practice them. From a Buddhist viewpoint, the plurality of religions in the world is beneficial, for each individual must find a belief system that is suited to his or her disposition and interests. Although the philosophy of another faith may not be correct from a Buddhist viewpoint, we must respect it if it benefits others.

Whether we accept religion or not is an individual choice. But if we accept a religion, we should be serious in following it and make our way of life concordant with its teachings. If the teachings become part of our lives, we receive true value. In politics and business, hypocrisy and deception are commonplace and regrettable, but in religion they are totally deplorable. We must be sincere and cultivate a kind heart and tolerance no matter which religion we choose.

Once I met a Chilean scientist who told me that he reminds himself not to be attached to his particular scientific field. I think the same is true regarding religion because attachment leads to bias, which in turn brings a fundamentalist attitude that clings to a single absolute truth. While I was still young and lived in Tibet, I was a little biased against other faiths. However, upon coming to India, I met Thomas Merton, Mother Teresa, and people from many other religions. Seeing that the practice of other religions can produce wonderful people, I developed respect for other religions.

When my non-Buddhist brothers and sisters come to learn the Buddha-dharma, I usually recommend that they do not think of becoming Buddhists. Buddhism does not proselytize or seek to convert others. You should first explore the religion of your family, and if that meets your spiritual needs, practice that rather than taking on Buddhism. In that way, you will avoid the difficulties of practicing a religion that exists within a culture foreign to your own and whose scriptures are written in languages that you do not understand. However, if your family's religion does not meet your needs and the Buddhadharma suits your disposition better, then of course you are free to become a Buddhist or to adopt some practices from Buddhism while retaining your previous religion.

The reason I advise people to first investigate their family's religion is that some people become confused when they change religions. A case in point is the family of a Tibetan lay official who fled Tibet in the early 1960s after the uprising against the Chinese occupation and became refugees in India. After the father passed away, one of the many Christian missionary groups who kindly helped refugees aided his wife and children. After some years, the wife came to see me and told me her story, saying that the Christians helped her a lot and gave her children an education, so for this life she is a Christian. But in the next life she will be a Buddhist!

To practice and benefit from the Buddha's teachings, you do not need to be a Buddhist. If certain teachings make sense to you, help you to get along better with others, and enable your mind and heart to be clearer and more peaceful, practice those teachings within the context of your own life. The Buddha's teachings on subduing anger and cultivating patience may be practiced by Christians, Jews, Muslims, Hindus, and those who do not follow any religion. Buddhist instructions on how to develop concentration and focused attention can be used by anyone who meditates, no matter what religion or philosophy they follow.

If you are interested in following the Buddhist path, I recommend that you first understand the Buddhist worldview. Take your time and learn how the Buddha describes our present state, the causes of our difficulties, our potential, and the path to actualize it. Explore the ideas of rebirth, karma and its effects, emptiness, awakening, and so on. Then, when you have some conviction arising from thoughtful reflection, you can consider following the Buddhist path.

Religion in the Modern World

Once we adopt a religion, we should practice it sincerely. If we truly believe in Buddha, God, Allah, Śiva, and so forth, we should be honest human beings. Some people claim to have faith in their religion but act counter to its ethical injunctions. They pray for the success of their dishonest and corrupt actions, asking God, Buddha, and so forth for help in covering up their wrongdoings! People like that should give up saying they are religious.

Our world now faces an ethical crisis related to lack of respect for spiritual principles and ethical values. These cannot be forced on society by legislation or by science, and ethical conduct due to fear does not work. Rather, we must think and have conviction in the worth of ethical principles so that we want to live ethically.

The United States and India, for example, both have good governmental structures, but many of the people involved in them lack ethical principles. Self-discipline and ethical self-restraint on the part of political leaders, financial executives, those in the medical field, industrialists, teachers, lawyers, and all other citizens are needed to create a good society. But we cannot impose self-discipline and ethical principles from the outside. We need inner cultivation. That is why spirituality and religion are relevant in the modern world.

India, where I now live, has been home to the ideas of secularism, inclusiveness, and diversity for three thousand years. One philosophical tradition—in ancient times they were known as *Cārvāka*—asserts that only what we know through our five senses exists. Other Indian philosophical schools criticize this nihilistic view but still regard the people who hold it as *rishis*, or sages. In Indian secularism, they are respected by other traditions despite their different philosophy. In the same way, we must all respect those of other religions as well as nonbelievers. I promote this type of secularism, the essence of which is to be a kind person who does not harm others whether you are religious or not.

In previous centuries, Tibetans knew little about the rest of the world. We lived on a high and broad plateau surrounded by the world's highest mountains. Almost everyone, except for a small community of Muslims, was Buddhist, and very few foreigners came to our land. Since we went into exile in 1959, Tibetans have been in contact with the rest of the world;

we relate with diverse religions, ethnic groups, and cultures with a broad spectrum of views. We also live in a world where modern scientific views are prominent. In addition, Tibetan youth now receive a modern education in which they are exposed to views not traditionally found in the Tibetan community. Therefore it is imperative that Tibetan Buddhists be able to clearly explain their tenets and beliefs to others using reason. Simply quoting from Buddhist scriptures does not convince people who did not grow up as Buddhists of the validity of the Buddha's doctrine. If we try to prove points only by quoting scripture, these people may respond, "Why should I believe that scripture? Everyone has a book they can quote from!"

Religion in general faces three principal challenges today: communism, modern science, and the combination of consumerism and materialism. Regarding communism, although the Cold War ended many years ago, communist beliefs and governments still strongly affect life in Buddhist countries. For example, in Tibet the communist government controls who can ordain as a monk or nun and regulates life in the monasteries and nunneries. It also controls the educational system, teaching children that Buddhism is old-fashioned.

Modern science, up until now, has confined itself to studying phenomena that are material in nature. Because scientists by and large examine only things that can be measured with scientific instruments, this limits the scope of their investigations and consequently their understanding of the universe. Phenomena such as rebirth and the existence of mind as a phenomenon separate from the brain are beyond the scope of scientific investigation. Although they have no proof that these things do not exist, some scientists assume that they do not exist and consider these topics as unworthy of consideration. However, in the last two or three decades, I have met with many open-minded scientists, and we have had mutually beneficial discussions that have highlighted our common points as well as our diverging views. These discussions have been carried out with mutual respect, so that both scientists and Buddhists are expanding their worldviews.

The third challenge is the combination of materialism and consumerism. Religion values ethical conduct, which may involve delayed gratification, whereas consumerism directs us toward immediate happiness. Religion stresses inner satisfaction, saying that happiness results from a peaceful mind, while materialism tells us that happiness comes from external objects.

Religious values such as kindness, generosity, and honesty get lost in the rush to make more money and have more and better possessions. As a result, many people's minds are confused about what happiness is and how to create the causes for happiness.

As you begin to learn the Buddha's teachings, you may find that some of them are in harmony with your views on societal values, science, and consumerism, and some of them are not. That is fine. Continue to investigate and reflect on what you learn. In this way, whatever conclusion you reach will be based on reasons, not simply on tradition, peer pressure, or blind faith.

A Broad Perspective

Dharma practice is not comprised of simply one meditation technique. Our minds are far too complex for one meditation technique or one Dharma topic to transform every aspect of our minds. Although some newcomers to the Dharma may want one simple technique to practice and may see progress by sticking to it, they should not think that in the long term this is sufficient to generate all the realizations of the path.

The Dharma encompasses an entire worldview, and practice necessitates examining all aspects of your life. Some of the Buddha's ideas will be new to you and may challenge some of your deeply held beliefs. Be open-minded and curious, investigate these ideas, and observe your mind. Check the teachings using reasoning and apply them to your life to see if they describe your experience. Do not accept them simply because the Buddha taught them, and don't reject them simply because they are foreign to your existing ideas.

If you cultivate a broad outlook and a deeper view about the meaning of life, you will understand not only this life but also the existence of many lives to come. In addition, you will understand your own happiness and suffering as well as that of the countless sentient beings who are similar to you in wanting to be happy and to avoid suffering. This broad view that considers many lives and many sentient beings will contribute to peace and happiness in this life.

If we are chiefly engrossed with our own personal happiness and problems and do not bother much about the happiness and suffering of others, our vision is quite narrow. When we encounter difficulties, such a limited view will make us think that all the problems of the world have landed on us and we are the most unfortunate person alive. This pessimistic way of looking at our own life will make it difficult for us to be happy here and now, and we will drag ourselves through life day and night.

On the other hand, if we have a wider view and are aware of the experiences of other sentient beings, then when we encounter difficulties, we will understand that unsatisfactory experiences are not isolated cases happening to us alone but are the nature of cyclic existence; they happen to everyone. This mental attitude will help us to maintain stability in life and to face the situations we encounter in a productive way. To take it a step further, if we do not think solely about the betterment of this life and allow for the possibility of many subsequent lives, then when we encounter difficulties in the present, we will be better able to weather them and remain positive about the future. Thinking only about the pleasures of this life and putting all our hopes in this life alone, we feel let down when things inevitably do not turn out the way we wanted. Therefore a broad perspective of life and an understanding of the nature of duḥkha—suffering and dissatisfaction—helps us to improve our life now and in many lives to come.

In the first two of his four truths, the Buddha describes duḥkha and its causes. We may wonder, "Why should I think about this? It will only make me more depressed and unhappy!" Although reflecting on duḥkha and its causes may initially bring some uneasiness, suffering is still there even if we do not think about it in this systematic and purposeful way. If we simply let things take their course, suffering will strike when we are unaware and overwhelm us. We will be confounded regarding the nature of duḥkha, its causes, and how to eliminate it, and feelings of hopelessness and desperation may further complicate our situation and make us even more miserable.

Say we undergo a certain illness or injury for which we are not prepared. We have the suffering of the ailment, and on top of that, we also suffer feelings of shock and vulnerability. But if we know about a physical condition and calmly accept it, we go to a doctor for treatment. Because we have accepted the existence of that ailment and are ready to deal with it, even if the doctor prescribes surgery, we will accept it with happiness because we know that we are following a method to remove the suffering.

Similarly, if we know and accept the unsatisfactory nature of cyclic existence, we will be in a much better position to deal with it when it occurs. We should not simply wait until a tragedy strikes us but reflect on cyclic existence, learn about it, and have a method to face it.

As we now go on to investigate other topics, it's important that you know that I am nothing special. I am a human being, just like you. We all have the same potential, and that is what makes one person's experience relevant and expressible to others. If you have the idea that the Dalai Lama is some extraordinary, special kind of being, then you may also think that you cannot relate to or benefit from what I say. That is foolish.

Some people think I have healing powers. If I did, I would have used them to avoid gall bladder surgery. It is because we are the same that you may be able to derive some benefit from my words and experiences.

2 | The Buddhist View of Life

O UR MIND DETERMINES our state of existence. Someone with a mind stained by afflictions is a being in saṃsāra. Someone who has eradicated all *afflictive obscurations*—mental afflictions and the karma causing rebirth in saṃsāra—is a liberated being, an arhat. Someone whose mind has eliminated even the subtlest *cognitive obscurations* is a buddha. This is determined by the extent to which that person's mind has been purified. In this regard, the *Sublime Continuum* (*Ratnagotravibhāga*) speaks of three types of beings: polluted beings, who revolve in cyclic existence; unpolluted beings, who do not revolve in cyclic existence; and completely unpolluted beings, who are buddhas. A person's level of spiritual attainment does not depend on external features but on his or her state of mind.

Although we can practice Buddhist meditation and apply its psychology to our lives without becoming Buddhists, understanding the Buddhist worldview is essential to glean the full impact of the Buddha's teachings. In this chapter, we will investigate some of the most important aspects of the Buddhist worldview: the nature of the mind, the self, the four truths of the āryas, dependent arising and emptiness, and the possibility of ending suffering.

What Is Mind?

Modern science focuses principally on gaining knowledge about the external world of matter. Scientists have developed sophisticated tools to manipulate even subatomic particles and have created instruments to measure minute changes in the chemical and electrical states of neurons. We now know about stars light years away from Earth and tiny organisms that our eyes cannot see.

While science has made great strides in understanding the external world, matter, and its subatomic components, it has not given as much attention to the inner world of mind, consciousness, and experience. Science lacks a cohesive concept of mind, its nature, causes, and potential, and while there are many books about the anatomy and physiology of the brain, the mind is rarely mentioned.

Nowadays, many people who think about the mind explain it in terms of material phenomena. Neurologists portray it in terms of the actions of neurons, especially those in the brain. Behavioral psychologists describe it by referring to a person's deeds and speech. Cognitive scientists study perception, thinking, and mental processes in terms of external measurable behavior and brain activity. The difficulties with these models is that they do not give us any means to accurately or deeply understand experience. Scientists may tell us about the neural events in the brain, the hormonal reaction that accompanies compassion or anger, and people's behavior when they are angry, but this does not convey what these emotions feel like, what the experience of them is.

Other people speak of the mind as an immaterial, permanent self or spirit. But they, too, are not able to suggest tools to observe consciousness. The Buddha's teachings may be considered a "science of mind" in that they provide a complete study of the mind, setting forth specific means for observing it, delineating the various types of consciousness and mental factors, making known the mind's potential, and describing ways to transform the mind.

The nature of the mind is not material; it lacks the tangible quality of physical objects. While mind and brain are related and affect each other when a person is alive, the mind is distinct from the physical organ of the brain, which is matter and can be investigated with scientific instruments that measure physical events. The mind is what experiences; it is what makes an organism sentient. Those of us who have sat with the body of a deceased loved one know that while his or her brain is still there, something else is missing. What is no longer present is the mind, the agent that experiences what life presents and is the essential differentiating factor between a corpse and a living being.

Buddhism has a 2,600-year history of investigating the mind. Many treatises about the mind were written in ancient India, where the Buddha lived, as well as in the countries to which Buddhism has spread throughout the centuries. In recent years, fruitful dialogue between Buddhists and scientists has begun, and I have great interest in seeing how this dialogue develops and the positive contributions to the well-being of sentient beings that it will produce.

Every topic in this series relates to the mind. We will look at the mind from many perspectives: its nature, causes, potential, functions, levels, and so on. We will investigate what obscures its potential and how to cultivate the antidotes to these obscurations so as to reveal the potential of the mind in its wondrous glory that we call full awakening or buddhahood.

The Sanskrit word translated as "mind" may also be translated as "heart." From a Buddhist perspective, expressions like "He has a kind heart" or "Her mind is very intelligent" both refer to the same entity, the conscious, experiential part of a living being. Although our mind is right here with us and we use it all the time, we don't understand it very well. In the Buddha-dharma, the mind is defined as "clarity and cognizance." *Clarity* indicates that unlike the body, the mind is not material. Clarity also indicates that when the mind meets with certain conditions it is able to reflect objects, like a clear mirror. Due to its quality of *cognizance*, it can engage with or cognize that object.

From our own experience, we know that our mind changes from moment to moment. That quality of changeability indicates that it is under the influence of causes and conditions. Each moment of mind arises due to its own unique cause—the previous moment of mind. The mind is a continuum, a series of "mind moments" that we call a mindstream. Each being has his or her own mindstream; mindstreams or parts of individual mindstreams do not merge. Because the mind is influenced by other factors and changes in each moment, when the appropriate conditions are present, mental transformation occurs. A mind that is flooded with disturbing emotions can become one that is peaceful and joyful.

The mind has two natures: its conventional nature (how it functions and relates to other things) and its ultimate nature (its actual mode of existence). *The conventional nature*—its clarity and cognizance—may be compared to pure water that is free from contaminants. When dirt is mixed into this water, its pure nature is obscured, although it is still there. Sometimes the dirt is stirred up and the water is more obscured than at other times. But no matter how much dirt is in the water, it is not the nature of the water; the water can be purified and the dirt removed. Similarly, the mind is pure even when it is obscured by afflictions. Sometimes our mind is comparatively calm, and other times it is agitated by anger or attachment. These afflictions are temporary; someone may be upset in the morning but relaxed in the afternoon. While the mindstream endures, anger is not always present in it. This is because anger and other afflictions have not entered the nature of the mind.

The mind may be colored by different emotions at different times. Anger and lovingkindness are opposite; they cannot be manifest in our mind at the same time, although they may arise at different times. Even people such as Hitler or Stalin, who had great hatred, felt love for their family members and children. The fact that the mind can be dominated by anger at one time and by an opposite emotion such as love at another indicates that the emotions are not in the nature of the mind. The mind itself is pure; it is like colorless water that can be colored by a variety of hues or by none at all.

Our body is like a house, and the mind is its inhabitant. As long as the body remains, the mind is a long-term resident. However, various mental factors—which include emotions and attitudes—are like visitors. One day resentment comes, another day compassion comes, but neither remains long. While both are visitors, one visitor is respectful, useful, and pleasant—like someone reliable whom we can trust and want to make a member of the family. We invite that visitor to remain in the house all the time and cultivate the conditions so that she will. Meanwhile, the other visitor is rude and disturbs our own and others' peace. We don't want him to visit let alone move in, so we do not invite him in and evict him if he sneaks in. Similarly, it is possible to banish anger and cultivate compassion limitlessly, making it our constant companion.

The *ultimate nature of the mind* is its emptiness of independent or inherent existence. Inherent existence is a false mode of existence that we superimpose on all phenomena; we believe that they have their own findable essence that makes them what they are, that they exist independently of all other factors such as their causes and parts. In fact, they are empty of all such fabricated ways of existing because they exist dependent on other factors. In the *Eight-Thousand-Line Perfection of Wisdom Sūtra* (*Aṣṭasāhasrikā Prajñāpāramitā Sūtra*), the Buddha says:

> The mind is devoid of mind, for the nature of mind is clear light.

"The mind is devoid of mind." This leads us to investigate what the mind actually is, its ultimate mode of existence, how it really exists. "The mind" refers to the clear and cognizant conventional nature of mind. When we search that clear and cognizant nature, we cannot find something that is the mind. Within the clarity and cognizance, there is nothing we can pinpoint that is inherently the mind. If we were able to find a real mind, then the mind would inherently exist with its own independent essence. However, when we search to find the mind, we do not find the mind in the mind; we do not find an inherently existent mind. That is why it says here that the mind "is devoid of mind." The final nature of the mind, its ultimate mode of existence, is its emptiness of inherent existence.

Since the mind is devoid of mind, we might think that the mind does not exist at all. But this is not the case. The words "the mind" indicates that the mind exists; it is the basis of our analysis. That the mind exists is shown by the fact that I can explain these statements due to the workings of my mind and you can understand them due to the workings of your mind. Saying that the mind does not abide in the mind means that an inherently existent mind is not the final mode of existence of the mind. It does not mean that the mind does not exist at all.

The mind exists, but it is empty of inherent existence. This is the meaning of "the nature of mind is clear light." This ultimate nature of the mind is pure in that it is free from inherent existence. But the fact that the mind is empty of inherent existence alone does not mean the afflictions such as ignorance, anger, and attachment can be eliminated from it. These afflictions also lack inherent existence, but we cannot say they are pure by nature.

Ignorance is a mental factor that grasps phenomena as inherently existent, with their own independent essences. It is the source of all other disturbing emotions, such as anger, craving, jealousy, and conceit. The fact that the mind, as well as all other phenomena, do not inherently exist means that the ignorance that grasps the mind as inherently existent contradicts reality. If the mind did inherently exist, ignorance would be a correct mind that sees reality. In that case, it could not be eliminated. However, since ignorance perceives the opposite of reality, it can be eliminated by the wisdom that sees reality correctly, the wisdom that realizes the emptiness of inherent existence.

Because ignorance and other afflictions are erroneous mental factors that lack an inherently existent foundation, they are not embedded in the nature of the mind and can be eliminated forever. Just as clouds temporarily obscure the open sky although they are not the nature of the sky, ignorance and other afflictions temporarily obscure the pure nature of the mind. But unlike clouds, which once gone can reappear, ignorance and afflictions, once they have been eliminated from their root by wisdom, can no longer obscure the mind. Meanwhile, other mental factors, such as love, compassion, and fortitude, do not depend on ignorance to exist and therefore remain as part of our mindstream forever.

REFLECTION

1. The conventional nature of the mind is clarity and cognizance, meaning the mind can reflect and cognize objects.

2. The conventional nature of the mind is pure: the afflictions have not entered into its nature, although they may temporarily color or obscure the mind.

3. The body is material in nature; it is like a house, and the mind is its immaterial inhabitant.

4. The ultimate nature of the mind is empty of inherent existence; it lacks any essence that is findable when we search for how the mind ultimately exists.

Body, Mind, Rebirth, and Self

Our body and mind influence each other while we are alive, although they have different natures and different continua. The body is material and depends on physical causes, such as the sperm and egg of our parents, to come into existence. The food we eat—also material in nature—is the condition that allows our body to survive and grow. The mind, however, is not matter and cannot be known or measured by scientific instruments designed to measure matter.

According to those who advocate scientific reductionism, the mind is nothing more than the brain. Other scientists, however, assert that the mind is a function of brain processes, and that mental processes and emotional experiences either correlate with or are due to biochemical processes in the brain. However, many aspects of our mind cannot be accounted for by this neuroscientific view. For example, by simply looking at chemical processes in the brain, we cannot determine if a thought is valid—if it is an instance of knowledge or affliction. By examining brain processes we cannot discern whether a mental event is a direct perceiver of a sense object or a conception (a memory or a thought about something).

At the experiential level, there is great difference between the pain we experience due to our own situation and the pain that comes from compassion for others' suffering. The experience of our own pain arises involuntarily and forcefully, and we usually respond to it with fear and anger. The pain that is attendant upon compassion for another's suffering has an element of deliberate sharing and embracing of that pain, and we react to it with courage. However, in terms of the biochemical processes in the brain, these two types of pain are indistinguishable.

Tears can well up in our eyes when we are very joyful or very sad. On the physical level, our eyes do not distinguish the two. But on the mental level, there is a big difference in the cause of the tears and how we experience them. For all these reasons, it is difficult to claim that all aspects of our experiential consciousness can be explained simply through the biological processes of the brain.

All functioning things—things that produce effects—come about due to causes and conditions. To trace back the causes and conditions of our present body, we follow a sequence of material causes and effects that goes to our parents and generations of previous ancestors. Scientists posit the theory of evolution when tracing back the origin of the human body. Before life existed on Earth, the continua of the physical elements that later became our bodies were present, and their continua are traced back to the Big Bang. Since matter—be it gross or subtle—was present at the time of the Big Bang and even before it, its causes must also have been matter or energy that can transform into matter. Although our body wasn't present when this universe began to form, its previous continuity in the form of material causes and physical elements was.

According to the *Kālacakra Tantra*, the ultimate source of the body is space particles that exist between the disappearance of the previous universe and the production of the subsequent one. They provide the continuum of potential for material during that time. Containing a trace of each of the grosser elemental particles, they are the basic stuff from which all other forms arise when a new universe develops.

It is difficult to identify the essential characteristics of mind. On a daily level, we experience sensory perceptions and the thoughts that chase after objects of the senses. Sense perceivers—our visual, auditory, olfactory, gustatory, and tactile consciousnesses—focus on the external world and assume the aspect of the objects they perceive.[1] The conceptual mind that thinks about these objects also assumes the aspect of these external objects, and even when our mind is directed inward to our own feelings, it assumes the aspect of the feelings. It is difficult for us to separate out the clarity and cognizance of the mind and be aware of the mind alone without also being aware of its objects. However, with meditation it is possible to experience the nature of the mind.

Results are produced from concordant causes—causes that have the ability to produce them; they cannot arise from discordant causes. Since the mind is immaterial, its substantial cause—the principal thing that transforms into a particular moment of mind—must also be immaterial. This is the preceding moment of mind. One moment of mind arises due to the previous moment of mind, which arose due to the moment of mind that preceded it. This can be traced back to the time of conception. The moment of mind at the time of conception arose due to a cause, a previous moment of mind, and in this way the continuum of mind prior to this life is established.

Conception is the coming together of the sperm, egg, and subtle mind. This creates a new life. The material aspect of this new life, the sperm and egg, come from the parents. The immaterial, conscious aspect—the mind—does not come from the parents. It must come from a previous moment of mind, which, at the moment of conception, is the mind of a being in the previous life.

At the time of death, the body and mind separate. Here, too, they have different continua. The body becomes a corpse and is recycled in nature. The mind continues on, one moment of mind producing the next. In the case of ordinary beings, the mind usually takes a new body and another life begins.

Buddhist scriptures describe different levels and types of mind. In terms of levels of mind, there are coarse consciousnesses, such as our five sense consciousnesses; subtler consciousness, such as our mental consciousness that thinks and dreams; and the subtlest mind that becomes manifest in ordinary beings at the time of death. This subtlest mind, which goes from one life to the next, can persist without depending on the coarse physical body, including the brain and nervous system. The subtlest mind is a continuity of ever-changing moments of mind; it is not a permanent self or soul. The terms "subtlest mind" and "fundamental, innate mind of clear light" are merely designated in dependence on a continuum of extremely subtle, transitory moments of clarity and cognizance.

The Buddha explained the continuity of life and rebirth principally on the basis of the continuity of mind. The continuity of mind across lifetimes is not the gross level of mind that is dependent on the physical body. It is the subtlest mind—the fundamental, innate mind of clear light that is the final basis of designation of the person—that connects one life with the next. The detailed explanation of this mind is found only in texts from the highest-yoga class of Buddhist tantras.

Rebirth can also be validated by personal experience. I heard about a Tibetan boy who could read without being taught. Some people may say this is due to his genetic makeup, but to me it makes more sense to say it is due to the continuity of his consciousness from a previous life. I also heard about an Indian girl who had many memories of her previous life. Her parents from her previous life and this life met and confirmed the details. Both now accept her as their daughter, so she has four parents!

Generally speaking, once a mind conjoins with a fertilized egg, a new life has begun. In dependence on that body and mind, we designate "person," "living being," "I," or "self." Our outlook on life, perceptions, feelings, and emotions are all based on the notion of a self. We say, "I did this. I think that. I feel sad or happy." Although this is our experience, seldom have we stopped to ask ourselves, "Who is this I upon which everything is predicated?" The question regarding the identity of the self is important because it is the self, the I, that wants to be happy and to avoid suffering. If the self existed independently from other phenomena, we should be able to isolate and identify it.

The Buddha taught that a person is composed of five psychophysical aggregates—form, feelings, discrimination, miscellaneous factors, and consciousness. The form aggregate is our body, and the other four aggregates constitute our mind. If we search among these five aggregates, we cannot pinpoint a person who is totally separate from them; nor can we identify a person who is identical to his or her body and mind. The collection of the two also is not a person. A person exists in dependence on his mind and body, but is neither totally one with them nor completely separate from them.

The self depends on the body: when our body is ill, we say, "I'm sick." If the self were a separate entity from the body, we could not say this. The self also depends on the mind. When the mind is happy, we say, "I'm happy." If the self were separate from the mind, we couldn't say this. On the basis of the mind seeing a flower, we say that the person possessing that mind sees the flower. Other than this, we cannot find a person who sees something.

In short, "I" is designated in dependence on our body and mind, yet when we search for a findable thing that is "me," we can't find it within the body, the mind, the collection of the two, or separate from them. This indicates that the person exists dependently; we lack an inherent, findable, unchanging essence. Since we lack an independent self, we can change, grow, and progress from confusion to awakening.

The person or self creates the causes for happiness and suffering. The person also experiences the pleasurable and painful results of these actions. Although we cannot pinpoint anything that is the self, the existence of a person who creates causes and experiences effects is undeniable.

Countless sentient beings have this feeling of self, although it is difficult to identify what that self is. However, the fact that each and every sentient being wants happiness and not suffering is indisputable; no reason is needed to prove this. Being born, enjoying life, enduring suffering, and dying are conditioned phenomena that are products of previous causes. If there were no person who experiences them, none of these would be tenable. Similarly, we distinguish afflictive saṃsāric existence from the awakened state of nirvāṇa based on whether the person has gained realizations. This distinction between saṃsāra and nirvāṇa would be irrelevant if no person existed.

The self exists, but from the perspective of the deeper nature of reality, our view of it is mistaken. This incongruity between how the self actually exists and how we apprehend it is the source of all our confusion and suffering. As we cultivate correct views, our mental strength increases; this leads to mental peace, which, in turn, brings joy and a sense of fulfillment. A mental state that sees the world as it is is free from fear and anxiety.

REFLECTION

1. The body is material in nature; the mind is immaterial. While the brain and the mind influence each other, they are not the same.

2. Our body and its substantial cause—the sperm and egg of our parents—are both material. Our mind and its substantial cause—the previous moment of mind—are immaterial; they are mere clarity and cognizance. At the time of conception they meet, forming a new life.

3. At the time of death, the continuity of the body is a corpse that decomposes to become material elements. The continuity of mind in the form of the very subtle mind continues to the next life.

The Four Truths of the Āryas

The topics of the first discourse the Buddha gave after attaining awakening, the four truths of the āryas, well known as the "four noble truths," form the foundation and structure of the Buddhist path. He taught these at the beginning for a specific purpose. Each sentient being has the innate wish for stable peace, happiness, and freedom from suffering. The longing for these motivates us to engage in many activities in an attempt to gain them. However, until now everything we have done has not brought about stable peace and joy because we live in cyclic existence (saṃsāra)—the state of having a body and mind under the influence of mental afflictions and karma. Within cyclic existence we encounter only duḥkha—unsatisfactory conditions and suffering.[2] Without choice, we take a body that gets old, sick, and dies and have a mind that becomes anxious, fearful, and angry. The I—the person that is merely designated in dependence upon the body and mind—revolves in cyclic existence. Our five aggregates of body and mind are unsatisfactory by nature and constitute the first truth of the āryas, *the truth of duḥkha.* The causes of the five aggregates are mental afflictions—skewed attitudes and disturbing emotions, the chief of which is ignorance—and polluted actions.[3] These constitute the second truth, *the true origins of duḥkha.*

The final *true cessation*—the third truth—is liberation and nirvāṇa, the state of peace, joy, and fulfillment that we seek. Here ignorance, afflictions, and polluted actions and the unsatisfactory experiences they cause have been extinguished from the root so that they can no longer arise.

True cessations are attained by depending on a method that eradicates ignorance. This is *true paths*, the fourth truth, which consist primarily of the wisdom realizing the ultimate nature—the emptiness of inherent existence of all persons and phenomena—and the virtuous consciousnesses supported by that wisdom. These paths require time and diligent effort to develop; we cannot hire someone else to accomplish them for us, like employing a mechanic to fix our car. How to cultivate these paths and actualize nirvāṇa is the subject of this series.

The process of attaining nirvāṇa begins with understanding the first truth, the nature of duḥkha and the various types of unsatisfactory circumstances and suffering that afflict sentient beings in cyclic existence. When some people hear this, they fear that reflecting on their suffering may only make it worse, and therefore believe that no benefit would come from learning the Buddha's teachings. This would be true if it were impossible to free ourselves from the causes of duḥkha. However, since the root cause of duḥkha, ignorance—a mental factor that misapprehends reality and grasps phenomena as inherently existent—is erroneous, it can be eliminated by the wisdom that sees things as they really are—as empty of inherent existence. By gradually eradicating ignorance and other afflictions, we can bring greater satisfaction and freedom into our lives. After all its causes have been accumulated, we attain the final true cessation of duḥkha and its causes, nirvāṇa. While nirvāṇa may sound like a far-off goal, we can easily see steps going in that direction: the more we cease anger, the greater harmony we experience, and the more our greed diminishes, the greater contentment we have. As we gradually reduce ignorance and afflictions through the application of wisdom, tranquility and fulfillment correspondingly increase, culminating in nirvāṇa.

Hence recognizing and reflecting on our suffering has a special, beneficial purpose: it activates us to discover its root and subsidiary causes and to eradicate them by practicing the path to peace that leads to the true freedom of nirvāṇa.

The Buddha spoke of three types of duḥkha. The first is the duḥkha of pain. This is the physical and mental suffering that all beings see as undesirable. All world religions agree that destructive actions, such as killing, stealing, and lying, bring physical and/or mental pain. To counter this pain and the actions that cause it, all religions teach some form of ethical conduct. Scientists also seek to remedy physical and mental pain; they do this by developing the means to change its external causes that are in our environment or due to the malfunction of our body, our brain and nervous system, or our genes.

The second type of duḥkha is the duḥkha of change, which refers to worldly happiness. Why did the Buddha call what is conventionally considered happiness—such as pleasant sensations—duḥkha? Worldly happiness is unsatisfactory because the activities, people, and things that initially give us pleasure do not continue to do so. Although eating, being with friends, receiving praise, and hearing good music may initially relieve pain or boredom and bring pleasure, if we continue to do them, they will eventually bring discomfort or fatigue.

Most people do not recognize worldly happiness as being unsatisfactory by nature, although many religions do. Some Hindus see the unsatisfactory nature of worldly pleasures and seek deep states of single-pointed concentration that are far more enjoyable. Some Christians abandon worldly pleasures in favor of a state of rapture or grace.

The third type of duḥkha—the pervasive duḥkha of conditioning—is the fact that we have a body and mind that are not under our control. Without choice, we take a body that is born, falls ill, ages, and dies. Between birth and death, we encounter problems even though we try to avoid them. We cannot obtain everything we want even though we try hard to get it, and even when our desires are fulfilled, that happiness is not stable: we become disillusioned or separated from what we crave.

The description of the third type of duḥkha—the pervasive duḥkha of conditioning—is unique to Buddhadharma. Neither other religions nor science identify our taking a body and mind under the control of ignorance, afflictions, and polluted karma as problematic. They don't look for the causes of the pervasive duḥkha of conditioning, let alone work to eliminate them. Instead, they try to make the situation better by focusing their efforts on eliminating the duḥkha of pain.

Having identified the pervasive duḥkha of conditioning as the basic unsatisfactory condition we sentient beings suffer from, the Buddha sought out its root cause. He identified it as the ignorance grasping inherent existence and saw that this ignorance can be eliminated completely only by cultivating its opposite, the wisdom perceiving the emptiness of inherent existence. Here the Buddha's teachings on selflessness (anātman)[4] become important. He explained that when we search for what ignorance apprehends—the inherent or independent existence of persons and phenomena—we cannot find it. The wisdom that realizes this—the true path—has the ability to gradually eradicate all ignorance from the mind, resulting in nirvana, the final true cessation. Here we see that the Buddha's explanation of the origin of duḥkha, the ultimate nature of reality, the wisdom realizing it, and the attainment of nirvāṇa are also unique.

In this way, the Dharma—true cessations and true paths—is a unique refuge. The Buddha who taught this Dharma is a unique teacher, and the Saṅgha—those followers who have realized directly the lack of inherent existence—are unique companions on the path. These three objects of refuge as described in Buddhism are unequaled and are not found elsewhere.

The situations described in the four truths were not created by the Buddha. He simply described things as they are. If duḥkha, its origin and cessation, and the path did not exist, there would be no need to practice Dharma. Of course it is up to each of us to test the veracity of the four truths for ourselves. By observing our own experience, we will come to know that duḥkha and its origins exist. Although we may not directly know true cessations and true paths at this time, they, too, also exist. Through understanding that duḥkha and its origins can be eliminated, we understand that true cessation can be attained. This brings conviction that true paths are the means to bring about peace in our minds.

REFLECTION

1. The first two of the four truths of the āryas describe our present experience: we are subject to three main types of unsatisfactory circumstances: pain, change, and pervasive conditioning. These are rooted in ignorance of the ultimate nature of reality.

2. The last two of the four truths describe possibilities: a state of freedom from ignorance and duḥkha exists, and a path to that state also exists.

3. It is up to us to learn and reflect on these to gain conviction in them and to cultivate wisdom in order to free ourselves.

Dependent Arising and Emptiness

In the above explanations of the four truths, several topics repeatedly arose: ignorance, which grasps inherent existence; the emptiness of inherent existence, which is the ultimate nature of all persons and phenomena; the wisdom realizing emptiness that counteracts ignorance; and nirvāṇa, which is the state of peace attained from doing so. Another essential topic—dependent arising—ties all of these together.

The Madhyamaka tenet system as explained by the Indian sage Nāgārjuna speaks of three levels of dependent arising. The first, which is common to all Buddhist tenet systems, is *causal dependence*—the fact that products (conditioned things) depend on causes. A table depends on the wood, which is its substantial cause—what actually turns into the result—and the people who make it, who are the cooperative condition that helps to bring about the result. Similarly, our body, mind, and present rebirth depend on their respective causes and conditions. Such dependency rules out the possibility of things arising haphazardly without any cause. It also precludes things arising due to discordant causes—things that do not have the ability to cause them. Barley cannot grow from rice seeds, and happiness does not come from destructive actions.

In addition to chemical, biological, and physical causality, karma and its effects is another system of causal dependence. Karma is volitional actions done physically, verbally, or mentally. These causes bring their effects: the rebirths we take, our experiences in our lives, and the environment in which we are born.

The second type of dependency is *dependent designation,* which has two branches: mutual dependence and mere designation by term and concept. *Mutual dependence* refers to things existing in relation to each other: long and short, parent and child, whole and parts, and agent, object, and action. Our body—which is a "whole"—depends on its parts—arms, legs, skin, and internal organs. The organs and limbs only become "parts" in dependence upon the body as a whole.

A hard, spherical object the size of a small apple becomes a baseball only because there is the game of baseball, a pitcher, a batter, and a bat. Apart from this context, this round object would neither be called a baseball nor function as a baseball. A parent is identified only in relation to a child, and someone becomes a child only in relation to a parent. Neither the parent nor the child exists independently of each other.

On a daily basis we use conventions and terms and engage in actions based on language. Doing this does not require there to be a direct, one-to-one objective referent for each term. Rather terms are defined relationally and derive meaning only in the context of mutually dependent relations.

The second type of dependent designation is *mere designation by term and concept.* In dependence on the collection of arms, legs, a torso, head, and so on, the mind conceives and designates "body." In dependence on the collection of body and mind, the mind conceives and imputes "person." In this way, all phenomena exist in dependence upon mind. Whatever identity an object has is contingent upon the interaction between a basis of designation and a mind that conceives and designates an object in dependence on that basis.

This interdependent nature is built into phenomena. If phenomena had an independent identity unrelated to others, we should be able to find the true referent of a term when we search for it. However, we do not find an independent essence in any phenomenon. This shows that all existent objects exist by being merely designated by term and concept. Being dependent, all phenomena are empty of independent existence. This is the subtlest meaning of dependent arising.

Dependent Arising and the Three Jewels

Indicating the importance of realizing dependent arising, the Buddha says in the *Rice Seedling Sūtra* (*Śālistamba Sūtra*):

> Monastics, whoever sees dependent arising sees the Dharma. Whoever sees the Dharma sees the Tathāgata [the Buddha].

How does seeing dependent arising lead to seeing the Dharma, which leads to seeing the Buddha? A process of progressive understanding is needed. When we realize causal dependence—that everything we perceive and experience arises as a result of its own causes and conditions—our perspective on the world and on our inner experiences shifts. Due to understanding that these exist only because their causes and conditions exist, our world, our experience, and even ourselves no longer seem so fixed and solid. Being dependent, they have no essence of their own.

As our understanding of mutual dependence and mere designation by name and concept deepens, we will appreciate that a disparity exists between the way things appear and the way they exist. While things appear to be autonomous, objective, independent realities "out there," they do not in fact exist in this way. If we focus repeatedly on branches, trunk, twigs, and leaves arranged in a certain manner and question, "What makes this collection of things a tree?" we will begin to understand that neither the individual parts nor the collection of those parts is a tree and that the tree exists by being merely designated in dependence on its parts. Dependent on the collection of parts of a tree (the basis of designation of a tree) and on the mind that conceives and designates "tree," a tree exists. Because it is dependent on all these factors, the tree is empty of objective, independent, or inherent existence. It does not exist in isolation—from its own side or under its own power—because it depends on causes, conditions, parts, and the conceiving and designating mind.

While an inherently existent tree cannot be found under analysis, a tree still exists. How does it exist? It exists dependently. Thus, we see that emptiness and dependent arising are not contradictory and, in fact, are mutually complementary. Everything is empty of inherent existence, and simultaneously everything exists, but not in the independent fashion that it appears to. It exists in dependence on other factors.

Underlying strong emotions such as clinging attachment, anger, and jealousy is an assumption that we are inherently existent, independent persons, that exist in and of ourselves. Similarly, there appears to be an independent reality of objectively existent people and things in the world. By recognizing the disparity between appearance and reality, we come to understand that our perceptions and ideas of things are exaggerated. Investigating how our mind perceives and interprets the things we encounter, we develop insight into the functions of the mind and the different types and levels of consciousness operating within us. We also come to appreciate that although some of our emotional states seem so strong and their objects appear so vividly, they are in fact similar to illusions in that they do not exist in the way they appear to us.

Dependent arising is the foundation for all Dharma practices. The two levels of dependent arising—causal dependence and dependent designation—are the main factors through which spiritual practitioners accomplish their aspirations. By developing a deep understanding of the nature of reality in terms of causal dependence, we come to appreciate the workings of karma and its results: our actions bring results. Pain and suffering arise due to destructive actions, and happiness and desirable experiences are the results of constructive actions. Understanding this, we choose to live with good ethical conduct, which enables us to have a higher rebirth in the future.

Through deep contemplation of dependent designation, we come to realize emptiness, the ultimate mode of existence. This wisdom tackles the fundamental ignorance keeping us bound in cyclic existence, allowing us to fulfill our spiritual goals of liberation and full awakening.

Dependent arising also underlies the four truths. Through such reflection and analysis, we understand that the self-grasping ignorance that misapprehends reality gives rise to our mental afflictions (true origins), and that these, in turn, bring about the suffering we experience (true duḥkha). Understanding dependent arising also enables us to realize the lack of independent existence of persons and phenomena—their emptiness.

This wisdom realizing emptiness (true path) has the power to overcome all ignorance, wrong views, and afflictions because they lack a valid basis, while emptiness and dependent arising can be proven by reasoning as well as directly experienced. Through this, we will appreciate that a state exists in which all ignorance and afflictions have been removed. This is nirvāṇa, true cessations, the third truth. Thus the Dharma Jewel—true cessation and true paths—exists.

If such a state as nirvāṇa exists, individuals must be able to actualize it. This leads us to understand the existence of the ārya Saṅgha—those beings who perceive emptiness directly. It also demonstrates the existence of the buddhas—omniscient beings who have perfected this state of cessation. In this way, the understanding of dependent arising leads us to establish the existence of the Three Jewels of refuge: the Buddhas, Dharma, and Saṅgha. For this reason, the Buddha said that those who see dependent arising see the Dharma and those who see the Dharma see the Tathāgata.

I believe this statement of the Buddha could also mean that by seeing dependent arising on the level of conventional appearance, we see causal relationships and understand karma, compassion, bodhicitta, and the method aspect of the path. Through accomplishing the method aspect of the path, we come to "see"—that is, actualize—the form body (*rūpakāya*) of a buddha. By understanding dependent arising in relation to the ultimate mode of existence, we experience the meaning of emptiness—the *suchness* (*tathatā*) of all phenomena—and by that, we "see" (actualize) the truth body (*dharmakāya*) of a buddha, a buddha's mind, specifically an awakened one's wisdom of ultimate reality. In this way, both the body and mind of a buddha are actualized.

REFLECTION

1. All persons and phenomena exist in dependence on other factors. There are three types of dependence: causal dependence (for impermanent things only), mutual dependence, and mere designation by terms and concept.

2. Dependent arising contradicts the possibility of independent or inherent existence. Understanding this can eradicate grasping inherent existence, the root of our duḥkha in cyclic existence.

3. The wisdom that eradicates ignorance (the true paths) and the freedom from duḥkha that comes about due to it (true cessations) are the Dharma Jewel.

4. People who have actualized the Dharma Jewel in their minds are the Saṅgha Jewel and the Buddha Jewel. Thus the Three Jewels of refuge exist.

The Possibility of Ending Duḥkha

If the possibility to end suffering exists, then pursuing that aim is worthwhile. But if duḥkha is a given, trying to eliminate it is a waste of effort. From the Buddhist viewpoint, two factors make liberation possible: the clear-light nature of the mind and the adventitious nature of the defilements. The *clear-light nature of the mind* refers to the basic capacity of the mind to cognize objects, its clear and cognizant nature.[5] The mind's failure to know objects must then be due to obstructing factors. In some cases, obstructing factors may be physical; if we put our hand over our eyes, we cannot see. But in a deeper sense, our seeing is hindered by two types of obstructions: afflictive obscurations that prevent liberation from cyclic existence and cognitive obscurations that prevent omniscience.

Each Buddhist tenet system has a different way of identifying what constitutes these two obstructions. The description here is based on the writings of Nāgārjuna, the great second-century Indian sage. In *Seventy Stanzas on Emptiness* (*Śūnyatāsaptati*), he notes that the conception that things that arise from causes and conditions exist in their own right is ignorance. The clear-light nature of mind has the ability to cognize all objects, but ignorance and its latencies obstruct this. All faulty states of mind are based on and depend on ignorance, and the twelve links of dependent arising—the process through which cyclic existence arises lifetime after lifetime—follow from ignorance. Āryadeva, Nāgārjuna's chief disciple, states (CŚ 350):

> The consciousness that is the seed of existence has objects as its
> sphere of activity.

When selflessness is seen in objects, the seed of existence is destroyed.

What is the consciousness that is the seed of cyclic existence? If consciousness in general were the root of cyclic existence, there would be no way to
overcome cyclic existence because consciousness has a clear and cognizant
nature, and nothing can counteract its nature or sever its continuity. Here
Āryadeva is referring not to consciousness in general but to a specific type
of consciousness—ignorance. His point is that cyclic existence does not
arise without a cause, from a discordant cause, or from a permanent creator.
Cyclic existence arises from an undisciplined, ignorant mind.

By saying that consciousness has objects as its sphere of activity, Āryadeva
indicates the mind's potential to realize objects. Then he stresses that by
realizing selflessness, self-grasping ignorance can be eliminated. Since ignorance grasps inherent existence (self), it can be overcome by the wisdom
realizing the opposite—the selflessness or emptiness of inherent existence.
By removing the ignorance that obscures our knowledge of phenomena, the
ability to perceive all objects is possible.

In *Treatise on the Middle Way* (*Mūlamadhyamakakārikā*, 24.18) Nāgārjuna says, "That which is dependent arising is explained to be empty." But
when objects appear to us, they do not appear to be dependent or related to
other factors. They appear as independent, discrete objects that exist under
their own power—with their own inherent essence, from their own side.
This appearance of objects as existing in their own right is false, and the idea
that objects exist in that way is erroneous and can be refuted by reasoning.
Using investigation and analysis, we can establish the emptiness of inherent
existence for ourselves. Inherent existence—also called existence from its
own side—is called the *object of negation*; it is what is refuted or negated
by analysis and reasoning. Once the analysis is complete, the consciousness
realizing that persons and phenomena do not exist from their own side is
generated in our mindstream. This wisdom consciousness damages and
eventually completely overcomes the conception and grasping that objects
exist inherently.

In his *Commentary on the "Compendium of Reliable Cognition"* (*Pramā-
ṇavārttika*),[6] Dharmakīrti says that mental states influenced by ignorance,
like any other wrong conception or erroneous consciousness, lack a valid

foundation, and mental states influenced by wisdom, like any other accurate consciousness, have a valid foundation. Thus the more we become accustomed to correct consciousnesses, the more the faulty ones will diminish. Wisdom's mode of apprehension directly contradicts that of ignorance, so by familiarizing ourselves with wisdom, ignorance decreases and is finally extinguished.

Here we see a unique quality of the Buddhist approach: erroneous mental states can be eradicated by cultivating their opposite—accurate states of mind. They are not removed simply through prayer, requesting blessings from the Buddha or deities, or gaining single-pointed concentration (*samādhi*).

Because ignorance has an antidote, it can be removed. This is the meaning of ignorance being adventitious. Thus because of the two factors mentioned earlier—the mind being the nature of clear light and defilements being adventitious—liberation is an attainable possibility. The *Sublime Continuum* (1.62) says:

> This clear and luminous nature of mind is as changeless as space.
> It is not afflicted by desire and so on, the adventitious stains that
> spring from false conceptions.

Each of the various Buddhist tenet systems has its own slightly different explanation of nirvāṇa or liberation, but they all agree that it is a quality of the mind, the quality of the mind having separated forever from the defilements that cause cyclic existence through the application of antidotes to those defilements.

When we examine that separation from defilements, we discover it is the ultimate nature of the mind that is free from defilements. This ultimate nature of mind exists from beginningless time; it exists as long as there is mind. In the continua of sentient beings, the ultimate nature of the mind is called *buddha nature* or *buddha potential*. When it becomes endowed with the quality of having separated from defilements, it is called *nirvāṇa*. Therefore, the very basis for nirvāṇa, the emptiness of the mind, is always with us. It's not something that is newly created or gained from outside.

3 | Mind and Emotions

WE ARE EMOTIONAL BEINGS. Our feelings of pleasure or pain provoke different emotions, and our emotions motivate us to act. Some of our emotions are afflictive and unrealistic; others are more realistic and beneficial. As a result, some of our actions bring more pain, while others bring happiness. Learning to differentiate destructive from constructive emotions so we can subdue the former and nourish the latter is a worthy endeavor on a personal as well as societal level.

Buddhas have eliminated all afflictive emotions, but that does not mean that they are emotionally flat, apathetic, and unreceptive to human contact. In fact, it is the opposite: by going through the gradual process of overcoming destructive emotions such as greed and anger, buddhas have built up and expanded constructive emotions such as love and compassion. Due to this inner transformation, their work in the world is wiser and more effective. In this chapter, you'll be introduced to the Buddhist view of emotions, comparing and contrasting that view with Western paradigms. We'll also examine how specific emotions affect our daily life and how to work with difficult emotions and cultivate positive ones.

Buddhism, Science, and Emotions

Buddhists and scientists have some similar and some very different ideas about emotions. In general, scientists describe an emotion as having three components: a physiological component, an experiential component, and a behavioral component. The physiological component includes the chemical and electrical changes in the brain as well as galvanic skin response, heart rate, and other changes in the body. The experiential component is the subjective experience—the psychological mood or feeling aspect of an emotion. The behavioral aspect includes the words and actions of a person motivated by that emotion.

From the Buddhist perspective, emotions are mental states and subjective experiences. They may be accompanied by changes in the body's physiology, but the brain's activities are not the emotion itself. For example, if we could put some live brain cells in a petri dish in front of us, we would not say their chemical and electrical interactions were anger or affection, because anger and affection are internal mental experiences of a living being. This experience may be correlated with activity in a certain area of the brain, but that neurological activity is not the experience of anger. Similarly, an emotion may lead to an action, but that action is an effect of the emotion, not the emotion itself. Consequently, of the three components mentioned above, Buddhists speak of emotions only in terms of the second—what we experience, feel, and think.

Buddhism does not deny that the mind and body affect and influence each other. When our knee hits the table, our mind experiences pain, and we may become irritated. When our mind is calm, our physical health improves. In *Commentary on Reliable Cognition*, Dharmakīrti says that when the body is healthy, attachment to sexual pleasure increases in the mind, whereas when the body is weak, anger arises more easily.

On a subtler level, certain emotions correlate with specific chemical and electrical changes in the brain. Does this correlation indicate a cause-and-effect relationship? Science has made fascinating discoveries correlating certain cognitive and emotional states with specific areas in the brain and particular neuron activity, but we must be careful not to attribute causality when there is merely correlation. Whereas some scientists believe that physiological events in the brain cause the emotions, Buddhists think that in general, the mental states precede the physiological changes. This is an important area open for research, and in recent years many scientists have begun to explore it. But regardless of whether the subtle changes in the brain cause, are caused by, or simply correlate with emotions, Buddhism emphasizes that emotions and feelings are mental states in living beings. Without mind, there is no experience: a corpse certainly doesn't have love or hatred, and a group of neurons or a cluster of genes does not feel pleasure or pain. Living beings do. Feelings, emotions, thoughts, views, attitudes, and so forth occur in the mind—they are mental states experienced by living beings.

These mental states motivate our physical and verbal actions. It is unreasonable and even dangerous to say, "My biological makeup makes me harm others." Such an attitude leads us down the slippery slope of abdicating responsibility for our actions by attributing their causes to physical elements over which we have no control. In addition to creating a sense of powerlessness in us, it could be used to justify eliminating individuals with certain genetic or neurological makeups.

The vast majority of our physical and verbal actions are prompted by intentions in our minds, and these intentions are influenced by our feelings, emotions, and views. Although many of our intentions are very subtle and some seem more like primal urges than conceived plans, they are present nonetheless. The fact that our intentions and emotions are the forces behind what we say and do means that by changing them, we can transform our actions and our lives. We are not doomed to a life circumscribed by the limitations of our genes, neural pathways, and biological processes over which we have very little choice or control. While we still have to deal with the effects of genetic and physiological processes, we need not develop a defeatist attitude regarding them. We have human intelligence and the seeds of love, compassion, wisdom, and other magnificent qualities inside us. These can be consciously developed, and many great sages in a variety of cultures and spiritual traditions have done this.

Many years ago I challenged one of the scientists in our Mind and Life dialogues to research the effects of cultivating well-being and positive emotions on the brain. After investigating for some years, he reported that due to a combination of the brain's neuroplasticity and people's meditation practice, there were changes in the brain circuits of people who cultivated four selected qualities: resilience, positive outlook, attention, and generosity. Each of these has corresponding Buddhist practices to develop them. *Resilience* is the speed with which we recover from adversity; a *positive outlook* is seeing the basic goodness in others and letting that influence all that we do; *attention* is the ability to focus on an object and enables us to complete what we begin; and *generosity* is an attitude of giving and sharing. All of these activate brain circuits that are correlated with a sense of well-being.

The researchers' conclusion was that well-being can be learned, so they've been developing programs that teach meditation and mindfulness and using them in schools, hospitals, and so forth with great success.

Happiness and Unhappiness, Virtue and Nonvirtue

While both Buddhism and psychology seek to help people have more happiness and fulfillment and decrease their unhappiness and misery, they differ somewhat in what they consider positive and negative emotions. Some psychologists and scientists I have spoken with say that a negative emotion is one that feels bad and makes the person unhappy at the time it is manifest in the mind. A positive emotion makes the person feel happy at the time it is manifest.

In Buddhism, what differentiates positive and negative emotions is not our immediate feeling of happiness or discomfort but the happiness or suffering that is the long-term result of those emotions. That is because the long-term effects of our actions are considered more important than their short-term effects, which tend to be fleeting in comparison. If, in the long term, an emotion produces unpleasant experiences, it is considered negative; if it brings happiness in the long term, it is positive. Buddhism explains that virtuous (positive, constructive, wholesome) emotions lead to happiness in the long term, while nonvirtuous (negative, destructive, unwholesome) emotions lead to suffering.

The Buddha presented four scenarios in which present happiness/pain and virtue/nonvirtue are at play (MN 70.7):

> Here, when someone feels a certain kind of pleasant feeling, nonvirtuous states increase in him and virtuous states diminish; but when someone feels another kind of pleasant feeling, nonvirtuous states diminish in him and virtuous states increase. Here, when someone feels a certain kind of painful feeling, nonvirtuous states increase in him and virtuous states diminish; but when someone feels another kind of painful feeling, nonvirtuous states diminish in him and virtuous states increase.

This thought-provoking citation is worthy of some illustrations. As it says, there are four possible permutations of feelings and ethical value. In the first, a pleasant feeling accompanies the increase of nonvirtue and the decrease of virtue. An example is feeling happy when we successfully deceive others about a vile action we have committed. Even though it may be accompanied by a pleasant feeling, our action is not virtuous, since it is the cause of future suffering.

In the second, there is a pleasant feeling when a nonvirtuous state decreases and a virtuous one increases. An example is taking delight in making a generous offering to a charity that helps refugees or the poor and hungry. This kind of happiness is win-win: we feel joyful now, and our action creates the cause for future happiness for self and others.

The third occurs when an unpleasant feeling accompanies an increase in nonvirtue and a decrease in virtue. An example is the pain of someone who angrily rejects being sentenced to prison after being convicted of embezzlement. Not taking responsibility for his nonvirtuous action, he angrily blames others, creating more nonvirtue. If he accepted responsibility for his action and regretted it, his virtue would increase, and his pain would lead him to change his ways.

In the fourth situation, we have a painful feeling, but our nonvirtue diminishes and our virtue increases. An example is taking a lower-paying job to avoid having to lie to clients or customers. In this case, creating virtue that will bring happiness in the future and peace of mind right now also brings some unhappiness of a loss in income. But it is undoubtedly worthwhile in the long term.

Making some examples of these from your own experience is useful. Such an exercise helps us to value our ethical integrity more than the fleeting happiness of getting what we want at the moment. Since our self-esteem and feelings of self-worth depend more on our ethical integrity than on sensual pleasure, it is worthwhile to take the time to remind ourselves of these values before an impulse arises, so that when the time comes we will make wise decisions.

REFLECTION

1. When you act against your ethical values, how do you feel at the moment of doing the action? How do you feel later, when reflecting on your action?

2. When you give up an immediate pleasure due to your sense of personal integrity or for the sake of long-term happiness, how do you feel at the time? How do you feel later, when reflecting on your action?

3. How integral is ethical conduct to your happiness? Based on what you conclude here, make some determinations about how you want to live.

Emotions and Kleśas

Before going deeper with the discussion of emotions, we need to clarify terms. Although everyone in the West understands the meaning of the word *emotion*, there is not a parallel word in Tibetan. When I, Chodron, was reviewing this chapter with His Holiness, he and his translators engaged in a lengthy discussion about the meaning of *emotion* and how it could be translated into Tibetan. Some Tibetans suggest the Tibetan word *myong 'tshor* as a translation, although this word is not widely used. Etymologically, *myong* means "experience" and *'tshor* means "feeling." Both of these qualities pertain to other mental states that are not emotions. Other Tibetans have proposed the word *gyer bag*, found in Gyaltsab Rinpoche's commentary to Dharmakīrti's *Commentary on Reliable Cognition.* However, it is an archaic word and does not include what in English we consider positive emotions.

Our discussion led to the conclusion that at present there is no widely used Tibetan word that directly translates the meaning of the English word *emotion*. However, the Tibetan language contains words for the various emotions spoken of in Western languages. The lack of a term and concept for emotion piqued my interest because those of us in the West continually talk about our emotions. I imagined what it would be like to grow up in a culture that wasn't focused on "my emotions."

An English dictionary defines *emotion* as "a strong feeling about somebody or something." The word *feeling* (*vedanā*) is also vague and is already used in Buddhist translations to indicate the aggregate of pleasant (happy), unpleasant (unhappy, painful), or neutral experiences. This aggregate does not include what we would call *feelings* in English, such as anger or love.

The Sanskrit word *kleśa* is a commonly used word in Buddhist texts that refers to mental factors that afflict the mind and do not allow it to abide peacefully. These disturbing emotions and views enslave the mind, confining it to a narrow perspective and motivate actions that hinder the happiness of both ourselves and others. As such, kleśa are obscurations on the path to liberation, and Buddhist texts speak of their disadvantages and the antidotes to them. However, there is no English equivalent to the word *kleśa* that encompasses mental factors as diverse as emotions, attitudes, philosophical views, and innate, unquestioned assumptions about ourselves and the world. For the sake of simplicity in this series, we translate *kleśa* as "afflictions" and sometimes expand it and say "disturbing emotions and wrong views." Some afflictions, such as the view of a personal identity, are called *views* in English, while others—for example, anger and jealousy—are called *emotions*. Mental states such as not believing that awakening is possible are called *views*.

All people have the same types of emotion and similar attitudes and views about the way they and the world exist—some of which are conducive for long-term happiness and peace, others of which are hindrances. However, the words we use to speak of them and the concepts that influence how we relate to them vary. Similarly, the behaviors motivated by certain emotions will be socially acceptable in some cultures but not to others. For example, sticking out our tongue, which is a sign of friendliness and respect in Tibetan culture, is discouraged in Western cultures, while clapping our hands—a sign of being pleased in Western cultures—indicates aversion in Tibetan culture.

The words used to label emotions have many nuances. In addition, there may not always be an exact correspondence in meaning between the Sanskrit or Tibetan word and the English term used to translate it. When reading Buddhist works in English, we must take care not to impute the ordinary meaning of a word onto a term that has a specific meaning in the Buddhist context.

Constructive and Destructive Emotions

When speaking of positive and negative emotions, Buddhists differentiate multiple meanings of the words for some emotions. For example, attachment, fear, anger, and disillusionment have multiple meanings depending on the circumstance, and it is important to distinguish the different forms of these emotions in order to avoid confusion.

ATTACHMENT

Among the multiple meanings of the word *attachment*, one form of attachment is necessary for our physical and psychological well-being; another is one of what are called the *three poisons*—three afflictions that poison our own and others' well-being.

The first form of attachment is spoken of in psychology and refers to a feeling of closeness or connection among people. For example, psychologists speak of the attachment a baby has for his or her mother. Such attachment or bonding with the mother or mother figure is necessary for the psychological well-being of the child.

This feeling of closeness or attachment is present in families and enables them to function together as a unit for the benefit of each member. Healthy attachment in a harmonious family has a realistic understanding of the other family members' capabilities and fosters mutual respect. Similarly, attachment unifies the citizens of a country, facilitating their cooperation for the benefit of their society. This form of attachment produces good results.

Buddhists have a positive use of the term as well. Bodhisattvas are said to be "attached" to sentient beings because they feel a tremendous sense of closeness and responsibility for the welfare of each and every sentient being that spurs them to practice. Their love for sentient beings invigorates them to do whatever they can to alleviate suffering and bring happiness. They do this with greater energy and joy than we ordinary people work to benefit ourselves.

More commonly in Buddhism, however, *attachment* (*tṛṣṇā* and *rāga*) refers to one of the three poisons and one of the six root afflictions. This attachment is a mental factor that, based on exaggeration or projection of good qualities, clings onto its desired object. With attachment, we hunger after, crave, cling to, and become obsessed with an object, person, idea, place, and so forth. When we succeed in procuring the object of our attachment, we are happy; but when that desire is frustrated, we become angry, resentful, and jealous. These emotions, in turn, motivate destructive actions to procure or protect the cherished object. We can clearly see that the greed of a CEO for money or the craving of a sports or movie star for fame leads to harmful actions and suffering for himself and others.

When attachment is moderate, society in general considers it to be a positive emotion. There is a feeling of happiness or excitement at meeting someone wonderful, receiving a desired possession, or being praised by the people we value. However, from a Buddhist viewpoint, such attachment is based on exaggeration, and while it may be captivating at the beginning of a new relationship, it will hinder the relationship from being harmonious and mutually beneficial in the long term. This is because attachment leads to unrealistic expectations. Difficulties and disappointments naturally follow when we discover that the object of our attachment doesn't possess all the wonderful qualities we thought it did.

This attachment is sneaky. For example, when family members' affection becomes neediness and possessiveness and generates demands based on unrealistic expectations, it turns into unhealthy attachment. If someone's appreciation for his country makes him suspicious of foreigners on the basis of nationality or ethnicity alone, attachment has set in. This emotion can cause prejudice and discrimination, and the person may go so far as to deny others their human rights.

Once I met a Chilean scientist who spoke of scientists being attached to their field of study. He said that any exaggerated clinging onto one's field of study, political beliefs, or religion is harmful. This man was not a Buddhist, but he understood that it is the mental state of clinging, not the object clung to, that causes problems. In the case of a scientist, such attachment could lead to ignoring contrary evidence or even rigging the result of experiments or misreporting data collected from them. Similar disadvantages accrue to a person attached to their own religion or political views.

Some people ask whether it is possible to be attached to nirvāṇa or to the Buddha. Aspiring for nirvāṇa or to have the Buddha's qualities is not attachment. The mind is clear, and although it is attracted to its object, there is no exaggeration present because the Buddha and nirvāṇa possess magnificent qualities. Still, according to the Prāsaṅgika viewpoint, as long as there is subtle self-grasping—in this case, grasping nirvāṇa or the Buddha to exist inherently—there is the potential for subtle attachment to arise. If someone then clings to nirvāṇa and desperately wants to attain it as if it were an external object, exaggeration is present in the mind. When this person studies and practices the Dharma, eventually the distorted aspect will be dispelled, and she will have a genuine aspiration for nirvāṇa that is free from attachment.

REFLECTION

1. What are some of the common meanings of the English word *attachment*?

2. What are the disadvantages of the afflictive type of attachment?

3. Is it easy to tell when attachment in the sense of affection and respect slips into exaggeration and expectations?

FEAR

Fear is another emotion that can be spoken of in two ways. In common parlance, fear is usually associated with panic, anxiety, worry, and distress; it is considered a negative emotion because it feels so unpleasant and is often based on unrealistic thinking. From a Buddhist viewpoint, this kind of fear is afflictive because it is based on exaggeration and self-preoccupation, and it leads a person to engage in actions or make decisions that are unwise.

Another kind of fear has an element of wisdom; it is an awareness of possible danger that causes us to exercise caution. While this fear may sometimes feel unpleasant, it is useful and is free from the emotional torment of ordinary fear. For example, awareness that you live in an area that is prone to earthquakes encourages people to make and heed building codes to protect buildings from collapsing. People lay careful plans and take precautions without being immersed in uncontrollable panic. This wisdom-fear is also at work when we merge onto a highway. Aware of the danger of other vehicles driving at high speeds, we drive carefully. Parents instill in young children a respectful fear of matches. In the above examples, fear is useful and is not afflictive. The difference between afflictive fear and wisdom-fear is the presence or absence of exaggeration. When we are attuned to facts of the situation, fear is not distorted, but when we exaggerate some aspect of the situation, fear is unrealistic and leads to suffering.

Certain meditations in the stages of the path are designed to arouse wisdom-fear in us. When we meditate on the disadvantages of cyclic existence, wisdom-fear motivates us to practice the path to liberate ourselves from saṃsāric suffering. The meditation on death is meant to provoke not an emotional, panicky fear of death, which is of no benefit at all, but a wise awareness of our mortality that leads us to set good priorities in life, abandon harmful actions, and live ethically and kindly.

In Thailand, some monks from the forest tradition meditate in fearful places such as cemeteries, jungles, and forests with ferocious animals. Before 1959, meditators in Tibet did the same. If panicky fear arose in their minds, motivated by the suffering that such fear produces, they would make a strong effort to generate samādhi or the wisdom realizing emptiness in order to overcome it. Ajahn Mun, a famous ascetic Thai monk who lived in the late nineteenth and early twentieth century, and his disciples practiced in this way, and there are many stories of them entering deep states of samādhi when encountering a tiger in the jungle. The great Tibetan yogi Milarepa practiced similarly, and meditators in the Chod lineage deliberately invoke spirits and ghosts to spur them to generate deep bodhicitta and wisdom.

If someone meditates on the sufferings of the lower realms, and panicky fear, instead of wisdom-fear arises, what should she do? First she should remind herself that panic is not the desired outcome of the meditation. Then, realizing that she has the ability to avoid the causes for such a rebirth, she should turn her mind to the Three Jewels and take refuge in them. Instead of allowing herself to be overwhelmed by this unrealistic fear, a well-trained practitioner will use it to reaffirm her connection to the Three Jewels.

Some scriptures speak of using the presence or absence of panicky fear as a way to examine whether or not a person is an arhat. When that person is meditating or sitting casually, someone makes a sudden, sharp, loud sound. If the person does not jump or gasp with fear, it is said that he has attained high levels of the path. According to this example, it seems that some level of self-grasping is present when an ordinary person experiences fear but is absent when they are liberated from cyclic existence.

Sometimes it is said that bodhisattvas fear saṃsāra as well as the personal peace of an arhat's nirvāṇa. While the word "fear" is used to indicate their unwillingness to stay in either of these states, it is not the fear that we ordinary people experience. Our fear is usually based on self-grasping and self-centeredness, while bodhisattvas' fear is underlain with compassion and wisdom that wants to attain buddhahood in order to benefit others as soon as they can.

ANGER

Most of us would agree that in general anger is a destructive emotion. Under its influence, we speak in ways that break the trust in relationships with people we care deeply about. Overwhelmed by anger, we act in ways that are dangerous and destructive to our own and others' well-being. While we often believe that our anger is justified—"any sane person would be angry in this situation"—that doesn't alleviate the downside of anger. When we later calm down, we can see that our mind was exaggerating the negative qualities of a person or situation, or even projecting negative qualities that aren't there.

Some people argue that some forms of anger are constructive. For example, if a student is wasting her time and not actualizing her potential, her teacher may become angry. This anger stems from the teacher's wish that the student succeed and, from that perspective, could be considered a positive form of anger, some people say. Nevertheless, we need to examine each individual situation and check our motivation carefully. It is easy to justify abusive behavior by saying, "I'm doing it for your own good."

Moral outrage at injustice in the world is another form of anger that some people say is beneficial because it leads to constructive change in society. But here, too, we need to examine if exaggeration is present. Years ago when I, Chodron, was at an anti-war protest, I saw another protester pick up a brick and throw it at the police. His action shocked me into realizing that his mental state had become like the mental state of those who were responsible for the war. There was bias for his own side and animosity toward the other. He was protective of those who agreed with him but sought to harm those who didn't. It is all too easy in a situation of conflict to forget that people on the "other side" are human beings who want happiness and freedom from suffering just as we do. Painting them as thoroughly evil and never to be trusted is definitely an exaggeration.

Anger is not the only emotion that can motivate us to tackle social injustice. Compassion can be a strong motivating factor as well. Because a compassionate mind is concerned with the well-being of all parties in a conflict, there is a greater chance of reaching an outcome that benefits everyone. We are able to think more clearly when we are free from anger. Ārya bodhisattvas who are liberated from cyclic existence have no anger whatsoever. If they see one person harming another, they have compassion for both people and intercede to avert the harm. Compassion does not mean being passive and ineffective. Rather, it impels us to act assertively when appropriate, but without anger or hatred.

It is difficult to experience the emotions associated with anger—hatred, resentment, vengeance, and so on—without some degree of hostility toward others. When we closely examine such emotions, we find that they are based on self-centeredness. As such, from a Buddhist perspective, emotions falling under the umbrella of anger are distorted and harmful mental states to be abandoned. Having said that, we must be careful not to confuse anger with assertiveness. A person can speak or act firmly and forcefully without being angry, just as an angry person can be passive and withdrawn.

Sūtrayāna—the path based on the sūtras—sees all instances of anger as based on distortion and hence damaging. Tantrayāna—the path based on the tantras—speaks of using anger in the path. In our discussions, His Holiness speculated that when a bodhisattva practicing tantra speaks harshly to someone, the causal motivation—the initial thought to do the action—is compassion, but the immediate motivation at the time of the act is anger. One difference between this anger and ordinary anger is that ordinary anger wants to harm or punish the person, while anger that has been transformed into the path aims to stop the person's harmful actions. A bodhisattva has tremendous concern and compassion for the person and uses fierce actions to stop him from harming others and from creating destructive karma that will later ripen in his own suffering. In addition, the bodhisattva has deep wisdom that realizes the agent, the action, and the object all lack inherent existence.

In speaking of the possibility of using anger in the path, a guideline is warranted. Since we beginners lack the requisite compassion, wisdom, and skill to transform a destructive emotion into the path, it is better for us to apply the antidotes as taught in the Sūtrayāna path and to practice restraint.

DISILLUSIONMENT

We commonly speak of disillusionment as a negative emotion because it brings unhappiness. When we feel disillusioned because a person does not turn out to be all we thought he was, we feel uncomfortable, and it may lead to despondency, depression, and in some cases, cynicism. This happens because we previously constructed an unrealistic expectation of the other person, clung to it as true, and now we see the falsehood of it.

But not all disillusionment is bad. When we contemplate the defects of cyclic existence, the shortcomings of saṃsāric rebirth, and the deceptive nature of temporary pleasures, we feel disillusioned with chasing after a type of happiness that we can never secure. From a Buddhist viewpoint, this disillusionment is positive because it will lead us to aspire for liberation and create the causes to attain it. Being disillusioned with cyclic existence, practitioners are happy to relinquish their attachment to it. Although disillusionment makes our mind sober, we need not be despondent or demoralized, because there exists a remedy to the misery of saṃsāra. Such disillusionment makes the mind peaceful and is conducive for cultivating deep states of concentration because it frees our minds from needless worry about the concerns of only this life.

Emotions and Survival

Science tells us that there is a biological basis for our emotions—both afflicted emotions and beneficial ones. We have instincts to draw closer to whatever supports staying alive and to drive away whatever harms us. The need for food, shelter, and companionship motivates us to seek and procure these requirements for human life. According to this theory, certain emotions are conducive to our survival and arise due to biological factors. For example, jealousy and arrogance both encourage competition, which leads to better performance and a greater likelihood of our genes being passed down to offspring. Anger and fear can be useful to avoid or destroy what threatens our life and well-being. Scientists say that from an evolutionary perspective, those emotions would not be present in us if they didn't serve a useful purpose. When we are angry, blood goes to our arm muscles in case we need to fight, but when fear comes, the blood goes to our legs so we can flee. On a purely biological level, emotions such as attachment, anger, and fear may assist animals and human beings to stay alive, and from that perspective, they may be considered beneficial.

Why, then, does the Buddha call emotions such as attachment, anger, jealousy, arrogance, and fear "afflictions"? Why does he say they cause suffering and recommend counteracting them? The difficulty with these emotions, again, is that they are fueled by exaggeration and grasping and thus do not perform their functions in a reasonable way. They may exaggerate the potential danger of the situation, the primacy of one's own self-interest, or the potential benefit to be gained. When afflictions are manifest, our minds are clouded and we don't think clearly. Instead of responding to a situation intelligently, we react impulsively, following an urge without sufficiently contemplating the likely effects of doing so. The results are often disastrous. In some conflicts, anger exposes us to far greater danger by making us act irrationally, which incites the other party to counter with more violent means. Fear also can endanger our survival, for when we exaggerate danger, we may lash out when the threat is nonexistent or minor. We may freeze when it would be wiser to act, or we may act heedlessly in our panic. It is especially tragic when a government or its citizens collectively fall into these distorted emotions.

Some psychologists say that disturbing emotions are 90 percent exaggeration and projection. While there may be a biological component, exaggeration and projection come from the mind, and we are not generally aware when they step in. A sense of danger that is reasonable in one instance can be later exaggerated and projected onto many other situations, making a person unnecessarily anxious. The anger that produces the rush of adrenalin that helps us to protect ourselves becomes a habit, and we create drama and conflict in our lives because the resulting adrenalin makes us feel alive.

Applying our human intelligence to our emotional lives enables us to discern which emotions lead to well-being and which lead to difficulties. Here we see—and psychological and sociological studies verify this—that children who grow up with kindness are generally more secure and emotionally balanced, while those who live in families with a lot of anger and physical or verbal violence are more anxious. Angry, resentful, and vindictive thoughts also make us unhappy and tense. These emotions impact our physical health and harm our immune system, while compassion is conducive to better health.

There is a world of difference between constructive and destructive emotions. In ordinary beings, afflictive emotions arise easily; they are impulsive and reactive. Genuinely constructive emotions like compassion and generosity come through investigation and effort. While destructive emotions distort our view of a situation, constructive emotions are conducive to accurate assessment. Destructive emotions cause us to regret our actions, while constructive emotions do not.

By examining the disadvantages and unrealistic perspectives of the afflictions, we will come to a point where we will make a determination to stop letting them run our lives. Seeing the benefits of realistic and beneficial emotions, we will consciously cultivate them. In his teachings, the Buddha described the ways to think and meditate that make positive emotions arise. By familiarizing ourselves with these and with the antidotes to the afflictions again and again, our habitual emotions will change, and in situations where anger once mushroomed, compassion will radiate.

For example, when harmed by another, we can think, "While this person's action is harmful and I must act to stop it, he has the same wish to be happy as I do." In this way, we develop a sense of concern for the other person. This will not only alleviate tension and anxiety in our own minds, but will also help us reach out to improve his situation. This, in turn, will result in that person responding to our kindness. This type of kindness and compassion is developed only through reasoning and training; it does not arise instinctively. When we truly care about others' welfare, we do not want to engage in harmful actions.

While biased compassion and kindness—the kind we might have for our child or parent—may have a biological basis, we must consciously purify them of attachment and greed. Instead of mindlessly following anger, we must assess if it is to our benefit. In many situations, responding with tolerance and kindness protects our own interests and well-being more effectively than hostility. Anger may destroy an aggressor or opponent, but that can have devastating repercussions. Compassion cares for both the perpetrator and victim of harm and thus allows us to intervene in abusive situations in a balanced, thoughtful way that enables us to remedy the situation with minimal harm to self and others.

There is a progressive development in our reasons for not harming others. People who have not considered the benefits of kindness and the disadvantages of anger and greed may restrain themselves from killing, stealing, unwise sexual behavior, and lying in order to avoid punishment. While such restraint is beneficial, there is not a great deal of virtue in the intention behind it. However, it helps people get along better with others, and that's important.

A step up from this is thinking, "Killing, stealing, and such are nonvirtuous. If I do them, I will have to face the consequences after death, and these results could be dire." While this restraint is self-referenced, there is virtue in the person's motivation, because she is considering the ethical dimension of her action.

The third step is thinking, "This sentient being wants to be happy. His or her life is as sacred as mine." As a consequence, we avoid harming this person. Or we think, "This person will suffer if she loses her possessions. Therefore I will respect and protect her possessions," and in this way we refrain from stealing. The outward action is the same as in the two preceding cases, but our internal motivation is different and is very virtuous because it considers the effects of our actions on the other person.

An even more advanced motivation is restraining ourselves from harming others because it not only causes them pain but also interferes with our ability to attain full awakening and be of the greatest benefit to sentient beings. Here we see the effect of having bodhicitta—the altruistic intention aspiring for full awakening in order to benefit sentient beings. Refraining from nonvirtue with this precious motivation is extremely virtuous and beneficial.

Working with Afflictions

While disturbing emotions may arise naturally in us ordinary beings, they can be eliminated. They are not an intrinsic part of the mind; they haven't penetrated its clear and cognizant nature. Afflictions are rooted in ignorance and other distorted conceptions, and as such they are fragile and can't stand up to the powerful states of mind that understand reality. The stronger our wisdom grows, the weaker the afflictions become, until eventually they are completely eradicated.

In contrast, constructive states of mind can be developed limitlessly. The fundamental nature of the mind is pure and stable. The innate, subtle mind of clear light, which is the basis of the cultivation of positive states of mind, is stable in that it continues eternally without interruption. While afflictions have powerful antidotes that can destroy them, no such counteracting forces exist that can eliminate constructive emotions and attitudes forever. They are based on accurate perception and thus can be continually enhanced. Furthermore, the nature of the mind is such that once we become thoroughly habituated to these virtuous states, we don't need to make repeated effort to cultivate them. They will continue on limitlessly.

People commonly regard emotions as raw feelings distinct from thought or other cognitive processes; they seem to arise spontaneously, not through conscious effort. We believe that emotions happen to us and that any reasonable person would feel the way we do in the same situation.

However, learning how destructive emotions arise and observing this process with mindfulness enables us to see that they are not givens. We can learn to detect harmful emotions while they are still small and swiftly apply their antidotes. When we ruminate on the harms others have caused us, for example, our resentment increases; when we contemplate the kindness of others, gratitude wells up.

Furthermore, deliberately cultivating accurate perspectives increases the strength of constructive emotions. Due to the force of habituation, these new perspectives gradually become natural, as do the beneficial emotions.

Awareness of our body and physical sensations is especially helpful in becoming aware of disturbing emotions when they begin to arise. Changes in our breathing, heart rate, body temperature, and muscle tension are some of the physical signals that accompany the emergence of a disturbing emotion. Making it a habit to check in with our body regularly can be very helpful.

For some people, observing the mood or texture of their mind enables them to detect a disturbing emotion while it is still small. Regardless of how we do it, the more aware we become of our thoughts and emotions, the quicker we will be able to evaluate them and decide whether to cultivate or counteract them. Engaging in regular meditation practice helps us to consciously practice cultivating constructive emotions and counteracting destructive ones. Through such training, we can establish new emotional habits, and with time, they will naturally manifest in our daily life.

Intelligence—the ability to precisely discriminate or analyze the characteristics of an object—is another mental factor that can increase or decrease the force of an emotion. When corrupted, intelligence incorrectly understands how things exist and creates more problems for us. When used correctly, our human intelligence and analytical capacity help us to overcome our destructive emotions. This intelligence may be a thought—such as a clear understanding of the disadvantages of anger—or it may directly perceive a deeper characteristic of things, such as their constantly changing nature.

Some afflictions are "corrupted intelligence" (Tib. *shes rab nyon mong chen*). They are called "intelligence" because they involve an analytic process, but because that process is deeply flawed, the conclusion reached is wrong. Consider the two extreme philosophical views: absolutism (grasping at persons and phenomena as inherently existent) and nihilism (believing conventionally existent phenomena are nonexistent). Simply saying to ourselves "This is a wrong view" will not make either of these disappear; nor are prayers and virtuous aspirations sufficient to vanquish them. We have to counteract them directly by developing the wisdom or intelligence (*prajñā*) that understands reality. Absolutism and nihilism arise through thought processes, so they need to be counteracted through correct reasoning that shatters our previous certainty. As our understanding deepens, our wisdom will become the direct, nonconceptual perception of the nature of reality.

It's helpful to be aware of the mental processes that lie behind emotions. We may have habitual ways of interpreting events that make them appear threatening or desirable when they are not. If so, we can consciously begin to change our interpretations and thus change the emotions that result from them. This is the theory behind the thought-training teachings, such as those describing how to transform adversity into the path to awakening.

For example, a colleague offers to help us with a project, and we think, "Why, all of a sudden, does he want to join in? Does he want some of the credit for himself? Or maybe he wants to slow my work down so that our boss will be upset with me." Although we are not trained psychologists, we may even attribute a mental disorder, "This guy is passive-aggressive, and he's manipulating me because he wants my job." We are "mind reading"—projecting a motivation to someone's action with little evidence. Becoming suspicious and hostile, we respond with a snide remark, and a conflict takes off. Unfortunately, many misunderstandings and arguments among people, groups, and nations occur in this way.

In addition to developing our human intelligence and learning to use our logical abilities correctly, we need to make our mind receptive so that the seeds of constructive emotions and attitudes can grow in it. We do this by engaging in spiritual practices that diminish and purify the seeds of harmful deeds in our mindstream. In addition, practices that accumulate merit—seeds of constructive karma—increase the force of our wholesome tendencies. These practices include being generous, living ethically, and cultivating lovingkindness.

Learning how to consciously direct our thoughts in a more positive way is essential for counteracting afflictive mental states. Repeating, "Anger is awful; may it disappear. Compassion is so wonderful; I wish I had it" isn't sufficient to transform our minds. Praying, "Buddha, please inspire me to be compassionate" or "Buddha, please get rid of my afflictions" without our cultivating the causes won't work either. To be free of our anger, we must contemplate the kindness of others and train our mind in forgiveness and love by practicing the meditations that evoke these virtuous emotions. While thinking about the value of compassion and requesting inspiration to develop it are useful, the real work is to contemplate the benefits of compassion and then practice the series of meditations to generate it. In our daily lives, too, we must repeatedly bring compassion to mind when we interact with others so that it becomes habitual.

Compassion broadens the scope of our mind and makes it more accepting and inclusive of others. Destructive emotions such as attachment and anger usually focus on one person or one class of people, whereas compassion can be extended to all living beings. The object of our compassion doesn't need to be someone we have met because we already know that everyone wants to be free from suffering and seeks happiness.

When our mind is unhappy, compassion and love uplift us. The best offering to make to all the buddhas is to abandon harming others physically, verbally, or mentally. Unlike afflictive emotions, virtuous mental states do not have self-grasping ignorance as a support, so cultivating the wisdom that overcomes ignorance won't harm our virtuous emotions. If anything, it will eliminate obstacles to generating them. If we really care about ourselves, we'll generate an altruistic intention because it gives us encouragement, enthusiasm, resilience, and a good heart. So a wisely selfish person is altruistic!

Habituating ourselves to constructive perspectives is one of the purposes of the *gāthas*, or short phrases used in the mind-training practice. For example, while cleaning the dishes or washing the car, we think, "I am cleansing away my defilements and those of all other sentient beings." When going upstairs, "I will lead all sentient beings to awakening," and when going downstairs, "I am willing to go to suffering abodes to benefit sentient beings." In this way, neutral everyday actions are transformed into the path to awakening.

Some afflictions are destructive emotions that are counteracted by generating opposing emotions. For example, to counteract anger and hatred, we meditate on love. Other afflictions are distorted attitudes and wrong views that are counteracted by seeing that the object they apprehend is false. For example, the ignorance that grasps true existence is counteracted by the wisdom realizing the emptiness of true existence.

Imagination may be used as a skillful means to counteract harmful emotions. For example, as an antidote to lust, the Abhidharma prescribes meditating on the universe being filled with bones. Although the universe isn't actually brimming with bones, by having us contemplate the inside of the body, this technique works to eliminate obsession with sex. In cultivating lovingkindness as an antidote to anger, we may imagine others being happy, and when cultivating compassion, we may reflect on their suffering. Scientists have noticed that when we imagine a situation, the same area of the brain is activated as when we actually experience that situation. This supports the Buddhist view of the usefulness of imagination in developing wholesome and balanced mental states.

Applying an antidote may initially make us feel deflated, but this is not detrimental. For example, when we are arrogant, making the mind more sober is beneficial. However, if we are depressed, deflating our mood is not useful. We must evaluate our mental states, first determining if a destructive emotion is present or not, and if so, then choosing an appropriate antidote.

In short, we learn to become doctors to our own mind, diagnosing our mental ailments, selecting the correct Dharma medicine, and then skillfully applying that medicine.

Working with afflictive emotions requires a two-pronged approach. Managing unwholesome emotions and stopping actions motivated by them are important components, but they don't resolve all problems. We also need to cultivate wholesome emotions. Although we may not initially be able to call upon these positive emotions in the heat of the moment, gradually and diligently cultivating them in our meditation practice affects our temperament and influences our emotional patterns. The more familiar we are with these beneficial emotions, the less susceptible we are to harmful emotions. Developing constructive emotions is similar to bolstering our immune system. Cultivating love strengthens our emotional immunity to anger. Developing compassion prevents cruelty, joy opposes jealousy, and equanimity averts bias due to attachment, anger, and apathy.

Reflecting on the benefits of having a particular wholesome emotion invigorates our efforts to develop it. For instance, if we contemplate the benefits of seeing sentient beings as loveable and imagine the good feeling that will derive from that, we will happily meditate on their kindness. This will cause feelings of gratitude and appreciation for others to arise naturally in our mind. To see the advantages of certain practices, we can ask ourselves, "What is disrupting my inner contentment?" We then see the negative emotions as the culprits and want to oppose them. With this determination, we will seek the methods to counteract those disturbing emotions and diligently practice these methods.

REFLECTION

1. How can you differentiate a destructive emotion from a constructive one?

2. What are the benefits of subduing disturbing emotions and cultivating wholesome ones?

3. Review the methods to subdue each disturbing emotion and cultivate each wholesome one.

Cultivating Love and Compassion

To generate beneficial emotions such as lovingkindness and compassion for all sentient beings, we must first have a correct understanding of those emotions. The love and compassion we cultivate in our spiritual practice should not be confused with the ordinary love and compassion we feel for our dear ones, which is usually grounded in self-referential considerations, "This person is my friend, my spouse, my child, my parent," and so on. While such love may be very strong, it is tainted with attachment because it is partial toward those who please us and biased against those who displease us. As we have seen, once we are attached to someone, the stage is set to later be angry at them when they fail to meet our expectations, fulfill our needs, or do what we want. The love and compassion we seek to cultivate in Dharma practice is based on having an equal-hearted sense of concern for all beings simply because they exist and they want happiness and not suffering, just as we do.

Even if we understand the meaning of genuine constructive emotions, we may doubt that it is possible to develop them. We must remember that the seeds of constructive emotions are naturally in our mindstream and, when cultivated, they will increase. Everything becomes easier with familiarity, and positive emotions are no exception.

When we have the confidence that it is possible to develop positive emotions, we make the effort to do so. At this point we engage in the meditations to cultivate equanimity and to see others as kind that precede the actual cultivation of love and compassion. Meditation on equanimity enables us to go beyond the limitations of our judgmental attitude that classifies people as friends, enemies, and strangers and elicits the emotions of attachment, animosity, and apathy toward them. By seeing that everyone is just like us in wanting happiness and not suffering, equanimity sets the stage for cultivating love and compassion for all beings, no matter what they believe or how they treat us.

We then cultivate the sense that others are loveable, which is done by remembering their kindness to us. Here we reflect not just on the kindness of friends and family, but the kindness of all those who do their various jobs in society that enable us to have what we need. We also reflect on the kindness of those whose disruptive actions challenge us to develop forgiveness, patience, and fortitude.

We now turn our attention to the expansive love we seek to develop in our spiritual practice. This love is the simple wish for others to have happiness and its causes. Visualizing a variety of people, extend this wish to them and imagine them having happiness and its causes. Having done this, cultivate compassion wishing them to be free of suffering and its causes. Do this with a few individuals to begin with, and then generalize it to groups of people and finally to all living beings.

Initially the feelings of impartial love or compassion that arise in the depth of our hearts will last only a short while. At this level, they are still contrived in that we have to make effort to experience them. However, through habituation, the time will come when, as soon as we see even a small insect, feelings of love and compassion for it will arise spontaneously and effortlessly. This new experience manifests as a result of having made an effort over a long period of time. Such mental transformation brings about an enduring change in our moods and emotions.

Scientists and Buddhists agree that habituation is necessary for long-lasting change in our thoughts, emotions, and behaviors to occur. When we practice something repeatedly, it becomes part of our temperament. Buddhists describe this as a process of habituating ourselves with new emotional responses. Scientists explain this as building up new neural pathways in the brain. When a certain pathway associated with an emotion is well lubricated, that emotion arises more easily.

Although Buddhism emphasizes cultivating love and compassion for others, we must not neglect ourselves. The happiness of others is one of our goals, so we must take care of ourselves so that we will have the physical energy and the mental clarity to benefit them. If we ignore our own welfare, not only will we be unable to benefit others, they will have to take care of us!

REFLECTION

1. Follow the steps for cultivating love and compassion explained above. Make your contemplation personal.

2. Enjoy the expansive feeling in your heart as you release anger and judgment and allow unbiased affection to arise.

A Good State of Mind

The calmer our mind, the easier it will be to deal with problems. Rather than wait for a crisis and then search for a way to handle it, we should practice open-mindedness and kindness on a daily basis. Then when problems or even traumatic events occur, their impact will be less severe, and we'll be able to return to a balanced state of mind more quickly. On the other hand, if we indulge our bad moods, we'll feel overwhelmed when even small, unpleasant events occur.

Tibetans have a motto, "Hope for the best and prepare for the worst." The main preparation is to let go of the self-centered attitude that magnifies our own problems and to cultivate compassion for ourselves and others. When difficulties arise, looking at them from a broad perspective is useful. Concentrating on *my* problems brings more frustration and unhappiness, while recollecting that everyone faces difficulties puts mine in perspective. In addition, if we see difficult circumstances as a challenge to rise to our potential and as an opportunity to call forth our compassion, we'll be more effective in managing a stressful situation and contributing something useful to it. In this way, our life will be worthwhile, and our mind will be relaxed and open.

In the next few sections, we will discuss some mental states and situations that people frequently see as troublesome—fear, depression, acceptance, comparing ourselves with others, and disagreement and conflict—and ways to train our minds to address them effectively.

Working with Fear, Developing Courage

Above we briefly considered the two types of fear, one based on wisdom and the other that succumbs to panic. The first type of fear stems from reason and is healthy. When we light a fire, we are aware of the danger and take care to avoid it. That fear protects us. Similarly, when we correctly analyze the causes of cyclic existence, we have a wise fear of them and that makes us conscientious about our moods and actions. This wisdom-based fear is important in daily life and on the path.

Panicked fear is problematic because it prevents us from seeing the situation clearly. For example, when I was a child and passed through some dark rooms in the Potala, I feared someone was hiding there. If just a small mouse ran by, I jumped with fright. This kind of fear is due to our imagination; it is mentally created. Getting accurate information and changing our view of the situation can counteract it. For example, when we feel insecure, fearful, and lonely, we can meditate on the kindness we have received from others so that a sense of connection and gratitude arises in our hearts and we know we have support. If we are skeptical and suspicious of someone, it is helpful to consider him as another human being, just like us. In that way, our attitude will be more receptive, and we will be able to assess the situation with greater clarity and wisdom.

Another unrealistic fear may occur when we are threatened with losing our job. Our minds imagine that we will immediately be homeless, sitting on the street with our hungry children. Applying our intelligence, we should investigate whether we are viewing the situation accurately or exaggerating certain aspects. We may find that the situation is unlikely to occur as we imagined it, and even if it did, we have skills to manage it. There are resources in society and in our network of friends and relatives to help us, so we need not paint a dire picture of circumstances that don't exist at this moment.

Some people look at the political, economic, social, and environmental situation of the world and develop a wisdom-fear that inspires them to work to prevent harm to the planet and its living beings. Looking at the same situation, other people develop a despondent fear. Such a discouraged mental state immobilizes them, and their wish to help gets lost amid waves of despair. To counter this, we must constantly maintain our compassion and keep our hearts open, so that no matter what others' responses are, we remain earnest.

Courage comes from the way we regard situations. For example, from one viewpoint the current situation in Tibet is dire; from another there is hope. Focusing on the positive, while being aware of but not discouraged by the negative, enables us to make every effort to improve conditions.

One single practice or method alone cannot develop courage; it requires contemplation of several topics over a period of time. These topics include the preciousness of our human life; the potential of ourselves and all others to become fully awakened buddhas; the compassionate, awakening activities of the buddhas and bodhisattvas; the life stories of great masters; the kindness we have received from all sentient beings; and love, compassion, and taking others' suffering and giving them our happiness. These will uplift and balance the mind so that we then view situations from a broad perspective.

In addition to courage, we need confidence. To develop this, I keep in mind some basic beliefs: Human nature is gentle and compassionate. Each and every one of us does not want suffering, and we have a right to try to overcome it. All beings have the potential to become wise, altruistic buddhas. Reflecting on these gives me inner strength and determination. A compassionate motivation and a clear, beneficial goal give me self-confidence and destroy doubts. In other words, confidence arises not from being successful in our projects but from engaging in them with a wise and kind motivation.

Human beings have remarkable intelligence, which if applied correctly, can solve problems and conflicts. Fatalistic attitudes are useless. We have the capacity to prevent hardships and improve what is good; we must do our best to use our abilities in constructive ways. If we make every effort and still fail, we need not have regrets. We can accept what happens. However, if due to lack of care or hope, negative things happen, that is extremely sad.

Hope, Desire, and Acceptance

Just as fear has two aspects—one to abandon and one to cultivate—so do hope, desire, and acceptance. For example, when we hope for good things for ourselves—a new house, a good job, a wonderful family, money, and material possessions—we become distracted from our spiritual concerns and entrenched in attachment. Dharma texts that speak of abandoning all hopes are referring to these hopes concerning worldly gain that inevitably let us down.

On the other hand, we must have hope for a better future so that we will work to create the causes for it. Here the future we hope for is not a self-centered one based on worldly desires but one that takes others into consideration and wants happiness for many. This latter type of hope will motivate us to practice the Dharma and to engage in projects that directly benefit others.

No matter what situation we are in, we should not lose hope. Losing hope and sinking into a defeatist attitude are the real causes of failure. They are also distorted mental states. We have human lives with our unique human intelligence, and these give us the capacity to overcome problems. Therefore we should be calm and wisely investigate various alternatives rather than throwing up our hands in despair, which often makes the problem worse.

The negative desire is related to attachment and keeps us bound in cyclic existence. In contrast, desire can also refer to a positive aspiration, such as the desire to meditate on equanimity or the desire to become a buddha. Such desires are not based on self-grasping or self-preoccupation. They have positive goals and increase our joyous effort to attain what is worthwhile.

Acceptance, too, has two sides. The disempowering kind of acceptance is acquiescence—accepting something unpleasant with a disconsolate heart. Such acceptance leads us to despondency and destroys our enthusiasm for life and for Dharma practice.

The good kind of acceptance acknowledges and accepts our own and others' faults and failures and at the same time wants to improve in the future. There is no use in fighting the reality of the present moment, but we know we can change and improve in the future. We accept the present suffering, for the causes for it have been created and are already ripening. Future suffering, however, can still be prevented, so our mind remains optimistic. By accepting the present situation, our time and energy is not consumed in anger or grief, and we can direct ourselves instead to purifying the causes for future suffering, avoiding the creation of more such causes, and creating the causes for future happiness.

Comparing Ourselves with Others and Self-Worth

Although all sentient beings are equal in wanting happiness and not wanting suffering, each of us has different talents and weaknesses. We can acknowledge that others are better than us in terms of education, health, physical appearance, social standing, wealth, and so on, but that need not lead to jealousy. It is a simple acknowledgement of what is.

Problems begin if we begin to think, "Since I am less than, I am hopeless," and feel inferior. Comparing ourselves with others and feeling hopeless is the result of a narrow outlook, for we see only our weaknesses and ignore our potential. Here, we should remember that although that person is more successful than we are, she is also a human being, just as we are, and that we have the same potential to succeed.

It is also important to remember that each of us has our own unique good qualities and talents. Comparing ourselves to others is like comparing apples and cars. They may both be red, but they are useful in different situations, so it's good to appreciate both. Similarly, it's good that people have different interests, talents, and abilities. By pooling these together, all of us benefit. We can rejoice in the good qualities of others and rejoice in our own, too, even though they may be different.

Some people often make black-and-white distinctions, with no middle ground. If something good happens, they become too happy and excited, and if something bad happens, they become discouraged and depressed. Life is complex: suffering is bound to happen and good things come as well. When good things occur, some people still do not feel content and push themselves to have more and better until they collapse. With this kind of attitude, if they see their neighbor is more successful, they succumb to jealousy and hopelessness. All this is avoidable with a wider perspective on life.

Counteracting Depression

Some types of severe, clinical depression appear to have a chemical component in the brain, but here we will examine the psychological aspect of depression. The psychologists I have spoken with tell me that in large part depression is due to a lack of affection, love, and compassion in the family and the community. I believe that we human beings are by nature social animals. Our basic nature is such that we appreciate the affection of others, and when we receive insufficient affection or are deprived of it altogether, we become unhappy and listless.

The techniques to counter depression depend very much on the individual, whether he or she follows a spiritual tradition and, if so, which tradition. A nonbeliever can reflect that human nature is gentle. We have experienced some form of love and compassion from many people since we were born. We have received much kindness from others throughout our life. Sometimes we are blind to the kindness around us; other times we are dissatisfied with it and wish it were more or better. Here it is good to cultivate contentment with the affection and kindness we have received and to rejoice in it. See its positive effects on our life. From the time we were born until now, all our happiness in one way or another has depended on the kindness of others. Just the fact that we are alive is due to the kindness we've received from so many other beings.

To counteract depression, Buddhists can think in two ways. First we develop a sense of our own potential by reflecting on buddha nature. No matter how confused or weak we may sometimes be on a superficial level, deep down our buddha nature is there. On the most basic level of having a mind, no difference exists between the Buddha and us. Each person has the *natural buddha nature* (the emptiness of inherent existence of the mind) as well as the *evolving buddha nature* (those factors that can be increased and whose continuity will continue to awakening). Thus everyone has the potential to become fully awakened.

Second, consider the nature of cyclic existence. At present we are under the control of afflictions and karma. As long as that situation exists, some kind of problem will be present. For example, when our body is ill, we experience pain. We must expect that and accept it. Worrying about the pain is useless. If we do not want the pain, we must remove its cause. If it is possible to remove the cause, we should try to do that. If it is not possible, no benefit comes from worrying.

We can think in a similar way about the nature of cyclic existence. As long as we have a body and mind that are under the influence of ignorance, problems will arise. This is reality. It is to be expected in cyclic existence, and we must accept it. If we do not like these problems, we should try to eliminate their causes—afflictions and polluted karma—and attain liberation. This gives us enthusiasm to practice the Dharma and seek nirvāṇa.

Depression also arises by focusing too much on our own situation and problems. Look around at others and see that everyone suffers in one way or another. Reflecting deeply on this, our hearts will open, and the strength of our love and compassion for others will increase.

Disagreement and Conflict

Disagreements always arise among sentient beings. Differences in views and opinions are potentially positive and can be a source of progress. However, when we are attached to our ideas, possessions, and status, these disagreements may lead to violence or oppression. For this reason, it is important to remember that we are all part of the human community. We need each other; we depend on each other.

Every day I have disagreements within myself as an individual. In the morning I believe one thing is right, and after further investigation, by the evening I have discovered that another course of action is better. This does not cause confusion, and I can manage this disagreement within myself. Similarly, if we see ourselves as one human community, one organism, then we can tolerate differing opinions and learn together. We should listen to others' ideas and investigate their reasons as well as share our experience and knowledge.

Some disagreements arise over economic issues because one group is disadvantaged. This group tries to change the situation using reason and negotiation, but when these fail, they feel frustrated and may become violent. If we look at the situation through a narrow lens, that violence may seem useful. But when looking from a wider perspective, we see that violence may solve one problem while creating another. For example, each party in ethnic conflicts has reasons to support their actions, but in the eyes of the rest of the world, their fighting is madness, for it creates more suffering than was there before. Therefore we must avoid any form of violence. Just as ignorance is decreased through education, our human tendency toward violence can be reduced through education in nonviolence, mediation, and conflict resolution. Learning to listen with an open mind and heart is helpful too; often people's anger dies down when they feel that someone hears their concerns and understands them.

Sometimes we may think that a situation is unjust and want to strike out or rebel. But looking from a wider angle, we note that aggression will bring many complications and that other ways to deal with the difficulties exist. These other methods may take longer, but seeing that in the end they are more beneficial, we adopt them and are patient. I consider such patience and tolerance a sign of strength, not weakness. This is the strategy I have adopted in dealing with the unjust occupation of Tibet.

Violence not only creates new problems, it also goes against human nature. One of my fundamental beliefs is that human nature is gentle. From the time we are born, we are unhappy when we see the harsh treatment of one person by another. But when we see expressions of compassion and love, we naturally feel joy. This is the case even with infants. The educational system should teach the value of human life and the disadvantages of violence. We must instruct children in methods to control anger and manage conflict, and most importantly as adults, we must model tolerance, empathy, and good listening. At present, the educational systems in most countries emphasize the transmission of information and neglect the creation of good human beings with a sense of responsibility for each other. We need to change this.

The Buddha lays out the root of disputes (AN 6.36):

> There are, O monastics, these six roots of disputes. What six? Here a monastic is (1) angry and vengeful, or (2) contemptuous and domineering, or (3) envious and miserly, or (4) deceitful and hypocritical, or (5) he has evil desires and wrong views, or (6) he adheres to his own views, holding to them tenaciously and relinquishing them with difficulty.

Because the Buddha was addressing a group of monastics, he used a monastic as an example. But the same could be said about a person in any group, be it a work situation, club, family, sports team, or a group of social or environmental activists. It just takes one person's uncontrolled mind to throw a group into disarray, preventing it from accomplishing its purpose.

In the passage above, the Buddha outlines ways in which our mind may be uncontrolled. First, we are angry and vengeful. We speak badly about other people behind their backs, retaliate for any and all perceived insults, and make distorted and unjust accusations about others. We can surely think of many examples when we have been around such people, but the point here is not what others have or have not done; it is about our own behavior and emotions. We must examine our angry outbursts and vengeful actions and seek their causes within ourselves. How were we viewing the situation? What are our emotional and behavioral patterns? In short, before thinking about what to say or do, it is best to calm our minds and return them to a more balanced state.

Here's a helpful exercise incorporating the above account of the causes of dispute. Contemplate when you have acted in these ways and consider other ways to look at the situation and methods to adjust your motivation so that it benefits, not harms, yourself and others.

The second root of disputes is being contemptuous and domineering. A person seeks to lead a group whether or not she has the skills or has been given the authority. If others lead, she is disdainful and uncooperative, only participating if things go her way. Leaders and followers must cooperate. Both have specific duties and require different talents and abilities, and neither can function well without the other.

The third root is envy and miserliness. Insecure, a person is jealous and does not like when others are more successful than he is. He is stingy with information, time, and effort and doesn't help others on the team.

The fourth is being deceitful and hypocritical. People who lie and are dishonest are difficult to trust and therefore difficult to work or live with. They say one thing but mean another; their speech is for their own benefit, without consideration of the situations or feelings of others.

The fifth root of discord is having evil desires and wrong views. Holding bad intentions and wrong views, a person propounds a fallacious doctrine and leads others astray. This is especially pernicious because it can inhibit one's own and others' ability to encounter the Buddha's teachings for many lives to come.

Lastly, someone adheres to his own views, holding on to them tenaciously and relinquishing them with difficulty. Such a person is stubborn and argumentative. He jumps to conclusions and stubbornly defends his ideas. Even if he has thought about an issue, once he forms an opinion, his mind is closed to any new information or other perspectives.

What are the results of possessing a root of dispute? The Buddha continues:

> Such a monk dwells without respect and deference toward the Teacher, the Dhamma, and the Saṅgha, and he does not fulfill the training. Such a monastic creates a dispute in the Saṅgha that leads to the harm and unhappiness of the multitude, to the ruin, harm, and suffering of devas and humans.

This person lacks respect for the Three Jewels and is unable to practice sincerely or attain the benefits of practice. She generates disharmony in the family, workplace, factory, school, club, or group. This disharmony harms not only herself but disrupts others' relationships, thwarts their activities, diverts energy, and upsets many others. When we notice a root of dispute within ourselves, it is important to reflect on its disadvantages so that we are motivated to change that mental habit or behavior. How can we deal with situations when we find any or all of these roots of dispute within ourselves? The Buddha continues:

> If, monks, you perceive any such root of dispute either in yourselves or in others, you should strive to abandon this evil root of dispute. And if you do not see any such root of dispute either in yourselves or others, you should practice so that this evil root of dispute does not emerge in the future.

When we notice a root of dispute within ourselves, we should first restrain our body and speech from acting it out. Then we should work with our mind, applying the antidote to that afflictive emotion. When we notice a root of dispute in another person, we can remind ourselves, "That is what I am like when afflictions overpower my mind. That is the kind of behavior that my afflictions lead me to impose on others. Since these are not emotions and behaviors that I respect or find beneficial, I must take great care not to let them arise." In other words, we take the other person's actions as a warning and make a strong determination not to act in that way.

Once the emotional affliction has decreased and we can again assess the situation in a more balanced way, we can approach the other person and discuss the various points to resolve in a balanced way.[7]

If we do not see any of these roots of discord in ourselves or others, then let's make sure to treat others well and to be mindful ourselves so that they do not erupt. Expressing our gratitude to our colleagues, family members, friends, associates, or others in the group, telling them how much we appreciate their kind actions and reasonable behavior, is good to do as well. So often people express their feelings and thoughts only when they are unhappy. This is a good opportunity to train ourselves in cultivating and expressing appreciation for others. Praising others for their good qualities gladdens their minds, further strengthens the harmony in the group, and makes us feel good as well.

Survival of the Most Cooperative

"Survival of the fittest" is cited to support and promote competitiveness across many fields of endeavor. Instead, we may want to consider "survival of the most cooperative" as the axiom for human progress and prosperity. The way bees and ants cooperate and support each other enables the entire hive or hill to stay alive and flourish. Imagine what would happen if the worker ants packed up and left, saying, "We've had enough of serving the queen ant!" Imagine the consequence if the queen ant quit, "I'm so tired of these pesky worker ants. They never leave me alone!" These tiny insects instinctively know that their entire community will survive and prosper when they work together harmoniously for a common aim. They know that by following their own individual needs and wants, they will perish as individuals and the entire colony will also suffer.

Historically, the world's great civilizations have thrived when people helped each other and worked for the common good. Degeneration has occurred when competitive leaders battled for power and fame, selfishly ignored others, and looked out for only their own welfare. We human beings are dependent on each other just to stay alive; this is true now more than any other time in human history. Most of us do not know how to grow our food, make our clothes, build our homes, or make the medicine that cures our illnesses. We depend on others, and each of us contributes to the common good in his or her own way. The global economy means that we influence each other dramatically. If we human beings use the model of survival of the fittest and try to procure more and better resources for ourselves individually or for just our own group, we will sabotage our personal happiness and endanger the existence of human beings on this planet.

Self-centered concern not only harms others but also harms ourselves. We are dependent beings: we exist in dependence on a multiplicity of other factors, most of which we have due to the efforts of others. The exaggerated sense of self-sufficiency is illusory, and it can and should be replaced by the wise acceptance of mutual interdependence.

Love and compassion are based on an understanding of interdependence. Bodhisattvas, who aspire for full awakening, meditate on interdependence to increase their understanding of the nature of reality as well as their altruism. In this way, they cultivate vibrant self-confidence that they can make a positive contribution to the welfare of others. The more genuine self-confidence we have, the less fear and anger will torment our minds. Especially when we pass through difficulties, compassion and altruism will sustain us.

In a world where the actions of one individual can have far-reaching effects on many people, self-centeredness and ignorance can lead to great damage, while altruism spreads great good. When we cultivate care and concern for others coupled with wisdom that can clearly analyze situations, we are more peaceful inside, and our actions to benefit others are more effective. If we human beings adhere to the self-preoccupied philosophy of survival of the fittest, it may result in the survival of no one. Having the attitude of survival of the most cooperative brings more individual well-being as well as the survival of our species.

REFLECTION

1. Imagine understanding the perspective of someone who has harmed or threatened you or whom you consider an enemy.

2. Imagine having compassion—not pity—for the mental and physical difficulties that person has undergone and will undergo in life.

3. Look at the situation with the eyes of wanting that person to be free from their suffering and to have happiness. After all, if they were happy, they wouldn't be doing the things you find distressful.

4. Imagine speaking to that person with kindness, clarity, and balance.

4 | The Spread of the Buddhadharma and Buddhist Canons

N OT ALL PEOPLE THINK ALIKE. They have different needs, interests, and dispositions in almost every area of their lives, including religion. In this light, the Buddha, a skillful teacher, gave multiple teachings to correspond to the variety of sentient beings. As the Buddhadharma spread across the Indian subcontinent and into other lands, people had access to different sūtras and found certain teachings more suitable for their minds than teachings in other sūtras.

In this way, multiple Buddhist traditions came about. The development of these traditions and their presentation of the teachings were also influenced by the economic and political situations in each land, as well as the climate, social structure, language, and culture of each place. While all Buddhist teachings share the four truths, their selection of texts, imagery, rituals, textual interpretations, points of emphasis, and religious institutions were influenced by the society in which they were produced.

Knowing the history of the Buddhadharma is important to avoid absorbing sectarian biases that have been passed down for centuries. It also aids us in understanding why Buddhism developed the way it did in different places. This, in turn, stimulates us to discern the actual Buddhadharma from cultural overlays, so that we can practice the true Dharma without confusing it with cultural traditions.

Learning about the history of Buddhism helps us to see Buddhism as a living tradition that influences various societies and is influenced by them. We come to differentiate the Three Jewels that are perfect objects of refuge from religious institutions established by limited human beings. While the

Dharma Jewel goes beyond space and time, Buddhist institutions are not refuge objects, although they do their best to serve the Dharma.

All Buddhist traditions have their own accounts of Buddhism's history, the place of their own tradition within that, and the authenticity of their own and others' scriptures. These are generally based on oral tradition that was written down in later centuries. Modern academics, employing tools and methods of historical research that are not used in the traditional presentations of Buddhist history, also have their views. While traditional accounts do not change with time, the views of academics change as new discoveries are made.

Speaking of the various Buddhist traditions and teachings can only be done in a general way. As we know, people don't always fit into neat categories with well-defined borders. As in *Buddhism: One Teacher, Many Traditions*, we will speak of two principal Buddhist traditions according to the language they came to be written in—the Pāli and Sanskrit traditions. The Buddha himself taught in some form of Prakrit, a group of languages spoken in India by the common people of his time. After his parinirvāṇa, the discourses were collated into groups and passed on orally for several centuries. The earliest written texts we have date from around the first century BCE, and both Pāli and Sanskrit emerged as primary languages for transmitting the words of the Buddha. The Sanskrit tradition as we describe it here also includes texts in ancient Central Asian languages such as Gāndhārī.

But before exploring the historical development of these traditions, it is helpful to be acquainted with the spiritual vehicles that they teach.

Vehicles and Paths

Vehicle and *path* are synonyms. While these terms are frequently used to refer to a progressive set of spiritual practices, they technically refer to exalted "knowers"—wisdom consciousnesses—that are conjoined with the uncontrived determination to be free from saṃsāra. When our Teacher, Śākyamuni Buddha, lived in India, he turned the Dharma wheel (that is, he taught the Dharma) by giving teachings for beings of the three vehicles: the Śrāvaka, Solitary Realizer (Pratyekabuddha), and Bodhisattva vehicles. These are called *vehicles* (*yāna*) because they convey their respective practitioners to distinct spiritual attainments.

According to the Sanskrit tradition, the three vehicles are differentiated in terms of the motivation to attain a specific goal, their principal meditation object, and the accumulation of merit and length of time necessary to attain their goals. Each vehicle leads to its own awakening. Both the Pāli and Sanskrit traditions contain teachings on all three vehicles, although the Pāli tradition places more emphasis on the Śrāvaka Vehicle and the Sanskrit tradition on the Bodhisattva Vehicle.

Sometimes the Śrāvaka and Solitary Realizer vehicles are subsumed under the name Fundamental Vehicle. While both the Pāli and Sanskrit traditions explain the Bodhisattva Vehicle, in the Sanskrit tradition it is called the Universal Vehicle and relies on sūtras that were widely disseminated later.

The Bodhisattva Vehicle is further divided into two according to method: the Perfection Vehicle and the Tantric Vehicle. These are both practiced on the basis of the Fundamental Vehicle, and the Tantric Vehicle is also practiced on the basis of the Perfection Vehicle. The Tantric Vehicle can also be divided in different ways. One way is described in an explanatory tantra, the *Vajra Tent Tantra* (*Vajrapañjara Tantra*), which speaks of four tantric classes: action, performance, yoga, and highest yoga tantra.

BUDDHIST TRADITIONS

Pāli Tradition

- Śrāvaka Vehicle (P. Sāvakayāna)
- Solitary Realizer Vehicle (P. Paccekabuddhayāna)
- Bodhisattva Vehicle (P. Bodhisattayāna)

Sanskrit Tradition

- Śrāvaka Vehicle (Śrāvakayāna)
- Solitary Realizer Vehicle (Pratyekabuddhayāna)
- Bodhisattva Vehicle (Bodhisattvayāna) or Universal Vehicle (Mahāyāna)
  - Perfection Vehicle (Pāramitāyāna)
  - Tantric Vehicle (Tantrayāna, Vajrayāna, Mantrayāna)

Nowadays the vehicles of the śrāvakas and bodhisattvas are prominent. In their last lives, solitary realizers appear in a time and place where no Buddha has turned the Dharma wheel. Since this is the case, when we speak of śrāvakas it will include solitary realizers, unless there is a specific reason to delineate their practice separately. While the teachings on the Bodhisattva Vehicle in the Pāli and Sanskrit traditions overlap in several ways, the name "Mahāyāna" refers to the bodhisattva teachings and scriptures in the Sanskrit tradition.

The Buddha's Life

Buddhism in our world began with Śākyamuni Buddha, who in the view common to all Buddhists, was born Siddhārtha Gautama, a prince from the Śākya clan, most likely in the fifth century BCE near what is today the India-Nepal border.[8] His kind heart and great intelligence were evident from childhood. Despite a sheltered life in the palace, he ventured into the town, where for the first time he saw a sick person, an old person, and a corpse. This prompted him to reflect on the suffering living beings experience, and after seeing a wandering mendicant, he aspired to be free from the cycle of constantly recurring problems called saṃsāra. Disillusioned with the pleasures of palace life and seeking liberation, at the age of twenty-nine he left his family and royal position, shed his elegant clothing, and adopted the lifestyle of a wandering mendicant.

He studied and mastered the meditation techniques of the great teachers of his time, but he saw that they did not bring freedom from cyclic existence. For six years he practiced severe asceticism, but realizing that torturing the body doesn't tame the mind, he relinquished this for the middle path of keeping the body healthy without indulging in sensual pleasure.

Sitting under the bodhi tree in what is present-day Bodhgaya, India, he determined to arise only after attaining full awakening. On the full moon of the fourth lunar month—the Buddhist holiday of Vesak—he completed the process of cleansing his mind of all obscurations and developing all good qualities and became a buddha, a fully awakened one. Thirty-five years old at that time, he spent the next forty-five years teaching what he had discovered through his own experience to whomever came to hear.

The Buddha taught men and women of all ages, races, and social classes— royalty, beggars, merchants, officials, thieves, farmers, musicians, and prostitutes. Many of his students chose to relinquish the householder's life and adopt the monastic life, and thus the saṅgha community of ordained beings was born. As his followers attained realizations and became skilled in teaching the Dharma, he asked them to share with others what they had realized "for the welfare of the multitude, for the happiness of the multitude, out of compassion for the world; for the benefit, welfare, and happiness of gods and humans" (AN 1.170). Thus the Buddha's teachings spread throughout the Indian subcontinent, and in subsequent centuries to present-day Sri Lanka, Southeast Asia, Indonesia, China, Korea, Japan, Central Asia, Tibet, Mongolia, Pakistan, and Afghanistan. In recent years, Dharma centers have opened in locations all around the world.

Personally speaking, I feel a deep connection to Śākyamuni Buddha as well as profound gratitude for his teachings and the example of how he lived his life—abiding in the pure ethical conduct of a monastic and sharing the teachings impartially. The Buddha had insights into the workings of the mind that were previously unknown on the Earth. He taught that our experiences of suffering and happiness are intricately related to our minds and emotions. Suffering is not thrust upon us by other people; it is a product of our ignorant views and beliefs. Happiness is not a gift from the gods; it is a result of our cultivation of wisdom and compassion.

The Buddha's life is a teaching in itself: he questioned the meaning of worldly life and reached the decision to practice the Dharma while facing pressure from his family and society to inherit the kingship. Despite the hardships he encountered, he practiced diligently and did not give up until he had attained full awakening. He dealt compassionately with the people who berated him or criticized his teachings. Sometimes his followers were uncooperative and belligerent, but he did not give up on them, although he sometimes had to address them sternly. The sūtras show that he engaged with many different kinds of people with great skill and compassion, and he was completely uninterested in fame or praise. Reflecting on the kindness of the Buddha for providing teachings that suit the various dispositions and interests of the variety of sentient beings, I feel deep reverence. I hope that you, too, by learning and practicing the Buddha's teachings, will develop this sense of personal connection with our Teacher, the Buddha.

Early Buddhist Schools

The historical evolution of Buddhism is a fluid and dynamic process that brought forth various schools, traditions, and tenet systems. We may speak of one school or another as if they were distinct entities with clear boundaries. However, Buddhism "on the ground" was not so clear. We see this even today with Theravāda monastics who take the bodhisattva precepts, practitioners of Tibetan Buddhism who are ordained in the Dharmaguptaka vinaya lineage followed in Taiwan, Chinese monastics practicing insight meditation as taught in the Pāli tradition, and so on.

It is important to keep in mind when discussing Buddhist history that we can't say for sure what happened in the past. In our present lives, our memory of a specific event differs from that of the person standing next to us. History appears differently according to our perspective; each person selects certain details to focus on, and the interpretation of those details varies from person to person. Despite the subjectivity of history, it is nevertheless useful to have a general knowledge of the historical background of the Dharma we study.

After the Buddha's passing (*parinirvāṇa*), the arhat Mahākāśyapa gathered five hundred arhats together at Rājagṛha to recite the Buddha's discourses at what came to be called the first council. In the early centuries, these sūtras were passed down orally principally by *bhāṇakas*,[9] monastics whose duty it was to memorize and recite the scriptures. Each group of bhāṇakas was assigned a group of scriptures, and for many centuries every successive generation of bhāṇakas memorized the texts and taught them to others. Although the Buddha did not repeat verbatim every talk he gave on a particular topic, passages on certain important themes were standardized for ease in memorization. Thus there are stock phrases and passages—and some almost identical sūtras—in the *nikāyas* of the Pāli canon and in the *āgamas* of the Chinese canon. A famine in the first century BCE threatened the continued existence of the scriptures in present-day Sri Lanka, propelling the monks to preserve them in written form. During this time, other groups of bhāṇakas continued to orally disseminate the Buddha's discourses in many other parts of India.

In the centuries following the second council in 383 BCE,[10] a variety of different Buddhist sects appeared—it is said eighteen in all. There is more than one list of the eighteen, and each list classifies the major schools and their branches differently, but in any case, there was clearly a great profusion of Buddhist lineages in the Indian subcontinent and nearby areas as well. Many factors influenced the development of these different śrāvaka schools—location, climate, language, culture, and the availability of sūtras and teachings, to mention a few. Since the sūtras were passed down orally and the groups were separated by great distances, each school developed slightly different versions of the Tripiṭaka—the three baskets of Vinaya, Sūtra, and Abhidharma texts—although the majority of the material was shared in common.

Aside from some basic information, little is known about many of these eighteen-plus schools. While they surely debated each other, Buddhist sects and schools by and large maintained friendly relations. The names of some of these eighteen schools are today preserved in the three extant lineages of monastic precepts: the Theravāda (descended from the Sthavira sect and Mahāvihāra Monastery), the Mūlasarvāstivāda (a branch descended from the Sarvāstivāda),[11] and the Dharmaguptaka. In ancient times, the Theravāda flourished in South and Southeast Asia, the Sarvāstivāda was located primarily in northern India and Kashmir, and the Dharmaguptaka was prominent in Gandhāra and Central Asia, from where it was transmitted to China.

Indian and Sri Lankan sages began composing commentaries, unpacking the meaning of what the Buddha said in the suttas. Thus began a commentarial tradition. Some of the differences among the eighteen schools were doctrinal; others were due to people living in different climates and cultures. While the Theravāda, as recorded in ancient Sri Lankan manuscripts, sees the separation into various schools as schisms within the Buddhist community, other Buddhist traditions do not.

Academic scholars previously accepted the material in the Pāli canon as older than that of the schools in northern India. However, they are now revising their view due to recent discoveries of heretofore unknown scriptures in Afghanistan, Pakistan, and China. Fragments of scriptures of some of the early schools have been found and are now being studied by scholars such as Richard Salomon and Collette Cox in the Early Buddhist Manuscripts Project at the University of Washington. Some of these scriptures go back to the first and second centuries CE. Considering the fragile materials used for writing in those days, it is astounding that these manuscripts have survived. Other scholars, such as Bhikkhu K. L. Dhammajoti at the University of Hong Kong, have determined that there are Sarvāstivāda texts that date within two or three centuries of the Buddha's life. The results of continuing research will give us a clearer idea of the early schools and their scriptures.

Looking back on their forebears, Buddhists in northern India in the medieval period said there were four main śrāvaka schools that subsumed all eighteen: (1) the Sarvāstivāda school, which used Sanskrit, (2) the Mahāsāṃghika, which used a Prakrit dialect, (3) the Saṃmitīya, which used Apabhraṃśa, another Prakrit dialect, and (4) the Sthavira, which used Paiśācī.[12] Interestingly, most of the early scriptures do not self-identify as being from one or another of the eighteen schools, so modern scholars must make intelligent guesses about which school newly found manuscripts are from.

We don't know exactly how long each of the ancient schools existed and why they ceased. The schools in some areas—such as present-day Iran, Afghanistan, Pakistan, and Central Asian republics—became extinct first. They may have died out due to economic, political, and social changes, invasions, or natural disasters in their locales. The remnants of some schools may have merged with others. Because Buddhism was heavily concentrated in monasteries and not in village homes, once the monasteries were destroyed in India during the Turkic invasions in the thirteenth century, Buddhism all but vanished in India.

While some Indian masters such as Bhāvaviveka, and most Tibetans, saw the eighteen schools as branches of the Vaibhāṣika philosophical system,[13] there is little agreement about this elsewhere. The Vaibhāṣika school is unknown in South and Southeast Asia, and the Theravāda does not consider itself a branch of Vaibhāṣika.

Early Buddhism in Sri Lanka

Buddhism was transmitted to Sri Lanka by the son and daughter of the Indian king Aśoka in the third century BCE. Some of the Indian commentaries came, too; they were preserved and augmented in the old Sinhala language by Sinhalese monks. In the fifth century CE, the Indian monk Buddhaghosa traveled to Sri Lanka, where he compiled and edited the contents of these ancient commentaries when writing his own numerous commentaries in Pāli. While Buddhaghosa's works have been widely studied up to the present, the ancient sages' scriptures in Sinhala unfortunately no longer exist. Due to Buddhaghosa's translation work, Pāli became the scriptural language of all Theravāda Buddhists.

Buddhism flourished in Sri Lanka, and three major sects—the Mahāvihāra, Abhayagiri, and Jetavana—evolved, each with its own monastery. Chinese pilgrims recorded that Abhayagiri, the largest and wealthiest monastery, followed both the early scriptures and the Mahāyāna scriptures; some of the Mahāyāna sūtras in the Chinese Tripiṭaka were obtained in Sri Lanka. There were also many bodhisattva statues and Mahāyāna art on the island, and there is evidence that some tantric teachings were present there as well.

When a dispute arose between the Abhayagiri and Jetavana monasteries—both of which had some Mahāyāna elements—and the Mahāvihāra, who said the Mahāyāna sūtras were inauthentic, King Mahāsena (271–301) supported Abhayagiri and Jetavana. After he died, however, the Mahāvihāra sect gained royal support. As the collection of written scriptures grew, the Mahāvihāra gained more legitimacy as the holder of "pure" Buddhism, free from the heterodox ideas and scriptures found in the Abhayagiri and Jetavana.

The *Dīpavaṃsa* (*Island Chronicle*) and *Mahāvaṃsa* (*Great Chronicle*) presented Buddhist history according to the narrative of the Mahāvihāra. The *Dīpavaṃsa* was probably authored by Mahāvihāra monks in the third or fourth century and the *Mahāvaṃsa* in the second half of the fifth century. Their authors claimed to be the true Theravādins, the spiritual descendants of arhats of the first council. The historical chronicles also spoke of the lineage of Sri Lankan kings and events occurring during their reigns, mythology, and legend. They portrayed Sri Lanka as the island where the Buddha prophesized that his teachings would be purely preserved, thus encouraging a nationalist spirit. Claiming that other monasteries followed sūtras that were not from the original transmission of sūtras to Sri Lanka, and thus were not the Buddha's word, the Mahāvihārans emphasized that they held the one true canon with the complete *Buddhavacana* (Buddha's word), free from the degenerations of the Mahāyāna present in the Abhayagiri and Jetavana monasteries.

The Dharma developed in Sri Lanka over several centuries with the appearance of written sūtras and commentaries, the formation of a closed canon of scriptures, the establishment of authoritative commentaries, and the creation of official histories in the two chronicles. While helping to preserve the Dharma in Sri Lanka, these factors also served to legitimize and reinforce the authority of the Mahāvihāra sect as the one that preserved the true Dharma with authentic scriptures.[14]

While the Mahāvihāra gained momentum, it did not become dominant until the tenth century. By the twelfth century, King Parakkamabāhu "unified" all the monks by suppressing the Abhayagiri and Jetavana monasteries and their texts and called for their monks to either disrobe or join the Mahāvihāra.

It is not clear what the term Theravāda referred to historically or when it came into common use. While it is often presented nowadays as referring to "original Buddhism," in fact the term Theravāda is rarely found in Pāli literature, and for the first millennium of the Buddha's dispensation it was used infrequently in inscriptions, historical chronicles, or other ancient texts in Southeast Asia. Interestingly, it seems the term Theravāda first appeared in Nāgārjunakoṇḍa, in southeastern India, where proto-Mahāyāna views were promulgated. Chinese pilgrims called the Sri Lankan monks living there Mahāyāna Theravādins.[15] The term Theravāda does not seem to have indicated a school in India prior to Buddhism having gone to Sri Lanka but a school originating in Sri Lanka.

Historically, Theravāda has not been a monolithic religious or institutional entity in South and Southeast Asia. While people in that area initially received their monastic ordinations from Sri Lanka, the saṅghas that grew up in these locales functioned independently. When the ordination lineage was extinguished in Sri Lanka during the Chola invasion in the early eleventh century, Sri Lankan kings requested monks from Burma to come and restore it. This began a trend in South and Southeast Asia that continues to this day. Whenever a group of monastics is deemed corrupt, the king invites monastics from another Theravāda country who practice well to come and give the ordination again. Still, the Sri Lankan ordination lineage commands great respect, and monks from other countries traveled to Sri Lanka to ordain in later centuries.

In recent years academics have revised their idea that the Theravāda tradition contains the oldest and most authentic scriptures of the eighteen schools. Some say Theravāda is a modern term and a recent school derived from the Sthaviras but not identical to it. Others say Theravāda is descendant from the Mahāvihāra[16] or was derived from the Indian school, Vibhajyavāda.

Much of the Pāli literature consists of the commentaries and subcommentaries that were compiled or written beginning in the fifth century. The Pāli scriptures were transmitted in different scripts according to the country; the words were pronounced and recited differently, and this is true even today. Different lineages and *nikāyas* (traditions) developed in each country. The monks also were not a unified whole: those who dwelled in the cities and in the forests lived very differently. Nevertheless, most Buddhists in South and Southeast Asia saw themselves as related in many ways, even though a unifying and common identity as Theravādins may not have developed until the twentieth century. For example, previously in Thailand the Buddhism in Sri Lanka was called *Sinhala-śāsana*, the doctrine in Sinhala. Skilling says, "The centering of 'Theravāda' in the Pāli canon, above all in the 'four main *nikāyas*,' is a child of the late nineteenth and twentieth centuries. It has grown up to become what we might call a 'new Theravāda,' largely Anglophonic but increasingly international in influence and outreach."[17]

Some scholars[18] state that the standard account of Sri Lankan Buddhist history was made not by Sri Lankans but by British scholars of the early to mid-nineteenth century who misread the historical chronicles and lacked the knowledge of Buddhist and Sri Lankan history that is now available. Reading the commentaries and chronicles, these scholars assumed that they were objective narratives of the facts, not understanding that Mahāvihāran accounts of Buddhist history were disputed by their contemporaries in the Abhayagiri and Jetavana monasteries.

While Sinhalese historical documents have portrayed the Pāli canon as equivalent to early Buddhism and Theravāda Buddhism as the unique upholder of early Buddhism, scholars now question this.[19] The Pāli canon is usually presented by Theravāda Buddhists as a closed collection of texts that present the Buddha's own words. However, the words *pāli*, *tripiṭaka*, and *buddhavacana* did not originally refer to a closed canon.

Apart from some specific texts mentioned in Aśoka's inscriptions, we don't have a clear idea of what texts were recited—and thus affirmed as existing by that group of monastic reciters—during various councils and communal recitations. The Pāli canon wasn't closed and fixed until the fifth century CE, so for about a millennium after the Buddha, the collection of scriptures was open. While the bhāṇakas had strict standards for what they considered to be the Buddha's teachings, there was some fluidity in the contents of this collection if for no other reason than differences in geographical locale.

In short, some academic scholars now question three "facts" presented in the Mahāvihāra literature: the Theravāda originated at the first council, Sri Lankan Theravāda is and has always been a descendant of only this early Buddhism, and the Mahāvihāra was the original and true upholder of these teachings.[20] Whatever the historical truth may be, the Theravāda is a noble Buddhist tradition that has inspired faith in millions of people, led to their individual betterment and the improvement of society, and produced many highly realized holy beings.

Growth of the Mahāyāna

Mahāyāna sūtras, which emphasized the bodhisattva path, began to appear publicly in India in the first century BCE. Some were transmitted to Central Asia—Buddhism began to spread to Central Asia in the third century BCE and later flourished there for many centuries—and from there to China where they were translated into Chinese by the second half of the second century CE. The Āgamas preserved in the Chinese canon are very early sūtras that are remarkably similar to those in the Pāli Nikāyas. With newly discovered Vinaya texts and other scriptures that date from early on, the Pāli canon is no longer seen as the only literature of early Buddhism, although it is the only canon preserved in an Indic language.

Academic scholars, as well as practitioners of the Pāli tradition, have questioned the authenticity of the Mahāyāna sūtras, asserting that they were not spoken by the Buddha but were written later over a span of several centuries. One of the chief reasons for this claim is that the Pāli suttas were more publicly known and widespread in the early centuries than the Mahāyāna sūtras. The discovery in Pakistan and Afghanistan over the last few decades of many Buddhist manuscripts that date from the end of the first century BCE has changed academic scholars' view of the Mahāyāna. The newly found manuscripts written in Gāndhārī Prakrit are older than any previously discovered. Many of them are from the Dharmaguptaka school, and some are Mahāyāna sūtras.[21] Although some of these texts are called "early Mahāyāna," their ideas and presentation of the bodhisattva path are mature. With the revision in the dates of the Buddha's life to later than previously thought and the discovery of older Mahāyāna texts, modern scholars are reconsidering their ideas concerning the Mahāyāna sūtras.

When previously unknown bodhisattva sūtras first appeared publicly and for several centuries afterward, Mahāyāna was not identified as a separate tradition within Buddhism. Initially the term Mahāyāna referred to the goal of the path—buddhahood—rather than the attainment of arhatship that was prominent in the early sūtras. As time went on, Mahāyāna began to refer to a body of literature, and in the fourth century Asaṅga[22] used it to indicate scriptures explaining the path of a bodhisattva. By the sixth century, people were calling themselves Mahāyānists, indicating that they saw themselves as a distinct Buddhist group. However, due to the great number of Mahāyāna scriptures and the broad distance over which they spread, it seems that their followers did not become a single unified group in India, nor was any Mahāyāna canon ever compiled in India to our knowledge.

Mahāyāna was not a religion and did not have distinct institutions. It had no specific geographical location where its hierarchy was predominant. Monastics following the Śrāvaka Vehicle and Bodhisattva Vehicle lived together and probably recited the *prātimokṣa*, the monastic precepts, together. In the fifth to twelfth centuries, the great Buddhist universities such as Nālandā, Vikramaśīla, and Odantapurī, where Buddhism flourished, were inhabited by monastics and lay practitioners from many different branches, sects, and schools of Buddhism. They studied and debated the Buddha's teachings, learning from each other.

Mahāyāna scriptures contain many philosophical positions and practices; it has never been a monolithic doctrine, although those who self-identify as Mahāyānist have shared beliefs, such as the bodhisattva path and practices. The early Mahāyāna scriptures were not limited to one language, appearing in Buddhist Hybrid Sanskrit, Buddhist Sanskrit, classical Sanskrit, and Gāndhārī. While many Mahāyāna scriptures were in Sanskrit, not all Sanskrit scriptures are Mahāyāna; some teach the Śrāvaka Vehicle.

Mahāyāna did not dismiss the Śrāvaka Vehicle texts or teachings; in fact, it taught that the bodhisattva practice is based on a thorough understanding of the four truths of the āryas, the thirty-seven aids to awakening, the three higher trainings, the four immeasurables, serenity, and insight. Many ideas are held in common between the Śrāvaka Vehicle and the Mahāyāna, and all Buddhists, no matter what tradition they belong to, take refuge in the Three Jewels.

While most Mahāyāna sūtras publicly appeared after the Pāli suttas, some appeared before some scriptures in the Pāli canon. The Pāli canon contains texts from many time periods, ranging from the Buddha's time until it became a closed canon ten centuries later. The commentaries in the Pāli canon were written later than some Mahāyāna treatises and commentaries, such as those by Nāgārjuna, Vasubandhu, and Buddhapālita. The earliest scriptures recently discovered in Pakistan and Afghanistan were from both the Śrāvaka Vehicle and the Mahāyāna. In short, many Buddhist schools developed over a long period of time. They had both overlapping and distinct tenets and scriptures. Buddhadharma was, and still is, a living, dynamic tradition.

Mahāyāna is not an ordination order or lineage. There is no such thing as "Mahāyāna Vinaya" or a "Mahāyāna monastic ordination." From early times until the present, Mahāyāna practitioners have ordained in the Vinaya traditions of the eighteen schools: Asaṅga in the Sarvāstivādin, Vimuktisena in the Saṃmitīya, Atiśa in the Mahāsāṃghika, and so forth. The Chinese pilgrims spoke of some of the monasteries of their time as Mahāyāna-Sthavira. While we aren't sure about the meaning of that term, it could refer to monastics who ordained in the Sthavira Vinaya—the lineage of today's Theravāda—and practiced Mahāyāna. Mahāyāna monastics live in monasteries, follow the ethical conduct prescribed in the Vinaya, and conduct monastic rites in accordance with the Vinaya. Practicing the Bodhisattva Vehicle does not make one ethically lax; in fact, in addition to the various sets of prātimokṣa precepts such as the five lay precepts and monastic precepts, Mahāyāna practitioners also take bodhisattva precepts.

Calling Theravāda "mainstream Buddhism" is incorrect and confusing. In each location and at each time period, one or another school may be more well established. There were at least eighteen schools that all saw themselves as mainstream Buddhism in their own locales. Mahāyāna was well received and flourished all over India and Central Asia, and spread to

East Asia, Sri Lanka, Southeast Asia, and Indonesia. Contrary to being a minority movement, it was mainstream.

The Mahāyāna and Śrāvaka Vehicle both include rituals, chanting, mantras, and *dhāraṇis*.[23] Both show reverence in the presence of stūpas, statues, paintings, and relics. While many Mahāyāna sūtras emphasize the importance of copying those sūtras, practitioners of both vehicles engaged in the activity of copying sūtras.

In India and sometimes in Sri Lanka prior to the twelfth century, the Śrāvaka Vehicle and Mahāyāna flourished together. Practitioners of both vehicles often lived in the same monastery, received monastic ordination in the same lineage, and performed the Vinaya rituals together. They shared many common texts and tenets and debated their unique ones. Both developed commentarial traditions, although the interpretations sometimes differed. The two vehicles had some differences as well, in areas such as the principal sūtras they studied, the intention for practice, the view of the ultimate nature, the path, and the result. Most of the Śrāvaka Vehicle lineages in India disappeared over time due to a variety of conditions such as the political rise of the brahmins, changes in governmental structure, the popularity of Hinduism, and the monastics' lack of involvement in the lives of the lay people. Later on, many of these same factors also affected Mahāyāna groups. While Buddhism largely disappeared in India by the early thirteenth century, both the Sanskrit and Pāli traditions have spread widely throughout Asia and beyond.

The Development of Tantra

The teachings of Buddhist Tantrayāna were practiced and passed down in a circumspect and private way until the sixth century, when they became more widespread. By the ninth century, tantric studies were recognized as a scholarly discipline. At Nālandā Monastic University, the Prajñāpāramitā teachings were conjoined with tantric practice, indicating that tantra has a firm basis in the Perfection Vehicle and is not a separate teaching unrelated to other teachings the Buddha gave.

Buddhist tantra flourished in northern India and spread to Sri Lanka, Southeast Asia, and Indonesia, where many tantric artifacts have been found. It later faded in these areas as Sri Lankan and Thai kings made Theravāda the dominant tradition and Muslims occupied and converted much of the Malay Peninsula and Indonesia.

Tantra later spread to China and Tibet, and Kukai introduced it in the ninth century into Japan, where it became known as the Shingon school. Since tantra's public dissemination coincided with the time that many Buddhist scriptures were being brought to Tibet, tantra became very popular there. However, Buddhism was already well established in China at that time, so the Chinese tantric school did not become widespread.

Hinduism and Jainism also have tantric adepts, although their tantric systems differ considerably from Buddhist tantra, which is rooted in the four truths, refuge in the Three Jewels, renunciation of saṃsāra, bodhicitta, and the wisdom realizing emptiness.

Unfortunately, misconceptions about tantra exist due to lack of proper information. These misunderstandings will be clarified in a future volume on tantra in this series.

Buddhist Canons

Considering the vast array of Buddhist sūtras and the complexity of establishing their authenticity, we can understand the reasons to form canons and the difficulties involved in doing so. At present three Buddhist canons are extant: Pāli, Chinese, and Tibetan. Each of these has been translated into other languages or written in various scripts throughout the centuries. For example, the Tibetan canon has been translated into Mongolian,[24] the Pāli canon into English, and the Chinese into Japanese and Vietnamese. Each of the canons is divided into three "baskets" (*piṭaka*), or categories of teachings, which are said to correspond to the three higher trainings. The Vinaya Basket deals chiefly with monastic discipline (*śīla*), the Sūtra Basket emphasizes meditative concentration (*samādhi*), and the Abhidharma Basket is concerned with wisdom (*prajñā*).

THE PĀLI CANON

The Pāli canon was codified first, but as we saw above, it was not a closed canon until the fifth century. Its Vinaya Piṭaka has three books that contain not only the monastic code but also stories of the Buddha's disciples.

These are (1) the *Suttavibhaṅga,* which contains the pāṭimokkha precepts, (2) the *Khandhaka,* which consists of two parts, the Mahāvagga and Cūla-vagga, and (3) the *Parivāra,* which is an appendix. The Sutta Piṭaka has five Nikāyas, or collections of suttas, described below, and the Abhidhamma Piṭaka consists of seven scholastic works that are unique to the Pāli tradition. The Sutta Piṭaka's five collections are:

1. Dīgha Nikāya (Long Discourses) with thirty-four of the most extensive suttas
2. Majjhima Nikāya (Middle-Length Discourses) with 152 diverse suttas of moderate length
3. Saṃyutta Nikāya (Connected Discourses) with fifty-six thematically connected sections of brief suttas
4. Aṅguttara Nikāya (Numerical Discourses) with eleven sections, each collecting suttas with items of the same number
5. Khuddaka Nikāya (Collection of Little Texts), fifteen distinct works. In addition to containing sutta collections like the *Suttanipāta,* the Khuddaka Nikāya also includes the famous collected sayings such as the *Dhammapada* and the *Udāna,* collections of stories of the Buddha's previous lives such as the *Jātaka* tales, verses (*gāthā*) of early monks and nuns, early commentarial works, and histories of previous buddhas like the *Buddhavaṃsa.*[25]

THE CHINESE CANON

Buddhism came to China in the first century CE, about seven centuries before it entered Tibet. It entered first from Central Asia via the Silk Road and later by sea from India and Sri Lanka. As noted above, Buddhist texts began to be translated into Chinese by the second century. Many of the early translations employed Taoist terminology, leading to some misunderstanding of Buddhist thought. By the fifth century, translation terms were more standardized, especially with the literary translations of Kumārajīva. The early fifth century also marked the translation of many more Vinaya texts, which furthered the development of the saṅgha.

In 983 the first Chinese canon was published, with other renditions following. Currently, the *Taisho Shinshu Daizokyo,* published in Tokyo in the 1920s, is the canon commonly used in China, Taiwan, Korea, Japan, and parts of Vietnam. It consists of four sections: the first three—sūtras, vinaya, and śāstras (treatises)—were translated from Sanskrit and Central Asian languages into Chinese. The fourth, miscellaneous texts, were originally written in Chinese.

The Chinese canon is very inclusive and extensive, containing a vast array of scriptures, including the Āgamas, which correspond to the first four of the five Nikāyas of the Pāli canon. The Āgamas were translated not from Pāli but from Sanskrit sūtras, mainly from the Sarvāstivāda school, although some came from other Indian Buddhist schools. The Chinese canon contains many Fundamental Vehicle sūtras that were popular during this early period and are not found in the Tibetan canon. It also contains a plethora of Mahāyāna sūtras and Indian commentaries as well as some tantras. Many of these are found in the Tibetan canon as well. Initially, most of the Indian sūtras were translated into Mandarin from Gāndhārī, until the fifth and sixth century, when more Sanskrit texts arrived in China. The monk Xuanzang famously traveled to India and Nālandā Monastery by way of Gandhāra in the seventh century and returned home seventeen years later with hundreds of texts, especially from the Yogācāra school. His translations from Sanskrit are now part of the Chinese canon as well.

While the majority of translation into Mandarin occurred in these earlier centuries, there continued to be an active interest in and translation of valuable Buddhist texts into the Song (960–1279) and Ming (1368–1644) dynasties. In the early twentieth century, translations were made of Buddhist scriptures from other countries, including Tibet.

The Tibetan Canon

Tibetans had been collecting Buddhist scriptures from the inception of Buddhism in Tibet in the seventh century, and the Tibetan canon as we know it today took shape in the early fourteenth century through the editorial efforts of Buton Rinpoche (1290–1364) and other scholars. The first full rendition was printed in Beijing in 1411. Later editions were printed in Tibet itself, notably in Narthang in 1731–32 and in Derge in 1733. Although today there are multiple versions of the canon, the contents overall are very similar.

The Tibetan Buddhist canon is composed of the Kangyur—108 volumes of the Buddha's word—and the Tengyur—225 volumes of Indian commentaries. The canon of the Nyingma tradition differs somewhat from that of the other Tibetan traditions in that it contains tantras from the first transmission of Buddhism into Tibet. The Tibetan system for translation customarily involved an Indian translator and a Tibetan translator working in tandem, which greatly improved the quality of the translations. A number of modern scholars working on these texts have observed that translations from Indian sources into Tibetan are, in general, very accurate.

About twenty-four sūtras in the Tibetan canon correspond to the suttas of the Pāli Nikāyas, and a few Śrāvaka Vehicle sūtras absent in the Pāli and Chinese canons are found in the Tibetan canon. About one hundred sūtras in the Tibetan canon do not have the word Mahāyāna in their titles and are probably Śrāvaka Vehicle sūtras, principally of the Sarvāstivāda school.

About ten or twenty sūtras in the Tibetan canon were translated from Chinese.[26] Among these are the *Sūtra of the Golden Light* (*Suvarṇaprabhāsottama Sūtra*), the *Mahāparinirvāṇa Sūtra*, and the *Descent into Lanka Sūtra* (*Laṅkāvatāra Sūtra*), and several sūtras from the Heap of Jewels (Ratnakūṭa) collection, all of which are seminal Mahāyāna sūtras. Some commentaries in the Tibetan canon—notably Kuiji's commentary on the *Lotus Sūtra* and Wonchuk's commentary on the *Sūtra Unraveling the Thought* (*Saṃdhinirmocana Sūtra*)—were also translated from Chinese.

More Prajñāpāramitā sūtras were translated into Chinese than into Tibetan, and many early sūtras in the Pāli canon are not found in Tibetan. To enrich the understanding of Tibetan practitioners, it is important to translate these scriptures into Tibetan.

Texts on the stages of the path authored by Tibetan masters contain much material that is also found in the Pāli suttas and Chinese Āgamas. Considering that not a huge number of these early sūtras were translated into Tibetan, how did this material find its way into treatises authored by Tibetans? Vasubandhu's *Principles of Exegesis* (*Vyākhyāyukti*), his autocommentary on the *Treasury of Knowledge* (*Abhidharmakośabhāṣya*), and his *One Hundred Extracts from the Sūtras on Principles of Exegesis* (*Vyākhyāyuktisūtrakhaṇḍaśata*) contain quotations from over one hundred early sūtras from different schools, including the Sthavira and Sarvāstivāda. In addition, Śamathadeva's commentary on the *Treasury of Abhidharma* contains many passages from a variety of early sūtras.[27] One of the biggest sources of sūtra quotations in the stages of the path literature is Śāntideva's *Compendium of Training* (*Śikṣāsamuccaya*). The *Compendium of Sūtras* (*Sūtrasamuccaya*) attributed to Nāgārjuna also has many.

Furthermore, some Mahāyāna sūtras cover the same material as do the early sūtras. For example, the *Sūtra on the Ten Grounds* (*Daśabhūmika Sūtra*) explains the thirty-seven aids to awakening, and commentaries and treatises by great Indian scholars—Asaṅga, Śāntideva, and others—contain many passages from the early sūtras. Nāgārjuna's *Precious Garland* (*Ratnāvalī*) and *Letter to a Friend* (*Suhṛllekha*) also share much material with Sarvāstivāda sūtras that are similar to Pāli suttas. In this way, many passages shared with Pāli suttas and Chinese āgamas made their way into Tibet through the commentaries and treatises of the great Indian sages.

A Tibetan monarch issued a decree establishing a convention that enables readers to immediately identify which of the Three Baskets a scripture belonged to. Translators composed a verse of homage placed at the beginning of the text. An homage to the omniscient Buddha indicated texts from the Vinaya Basket that dealt with the higher training of ethical conduct; homage to the buddhas and bodhisattvas showed the text belonged to the Sūtra Basket and concerned the higher training of concentration; homage to Mañjuśrī, the embodiment of wisdom, indicated texts from the Abhidharma Basket, which deals with knowledge and wisdom.

Vinaya Basket

The Chinese canon contains the Vinayas of five early schools: Dharmaguptaka, Mahīśāsaka, Mahāsāṃghika, Sarvāstivāda, and Mūlasarvāstivāda. It also contains Buddhaghosa's commentary on the Vinaya, *Entirely Pleasing* (*Samantapāsādikā*). The Tibetan canon contains the Mūlasarvāstivāda Vinaya, and the Pāli canon has the Theravāda Vinaya.

Sūtra Basket

Outside of India, sūtras dealing with the bodhisattva practices were mainly transmitted in the Chinese and Tibetan languages. The Chinese and Tibetan canons contain the Prajñāpāramitā sūtras, the Ratnakūṭa sūtras, the *Flower Ornament Sūtra* (*Avataṃsaka Sūtra*), *Vimalakīrti's Instructions* (*Vimalakīrtinirdeśa*), and many other Mahāyāna sūtras. Both canons have Nāgārjuna's *Treatise on the Middle Way* as well as many of his other texts. Because Buddhism was rooted in China several centuries before its resurgence in Tibet in the eleventh century, which brought the translation of many later Indian texts into Tibetan, the Tibetan canon contains the works of Candrakīrti and later Mādhyamikas, as well as Dignāga and Dharmakīrti's works on logic, while the Chinese canon does not. However, many of these texts were translated from Tibetan into Chinese in the twentieth century by the great Chinese translator Fazun, who also translated many of Tsongkhapa's works.

Both canons contain works from the Cittamātra and Madhyamaka perspectives, although in general the Chinese follow different Cittamātrin and Madhyamaka commentaries than the Tibetans do. Maitreya's *Ornament of Clear Realizations* (*Abhisamayālaṃkāra*), which is widely studied in the Tibetan community, is not found in the Chinese canon,[28] although Fazun also translated it in the twentieth century.

Based on the Chinese canon, the Buddhadharma spread to Japan, Korea, and Vietnam. Relying on the Tibetan canon, Buddhism developed in Mongolia, four areas in Russia—Tuva, Aginsky, Buryatia, and Kalmykia—and in the Himalayan region. Today, the Chinese and Tibetan languages are the richest living languages that transmit all the practices and teachings of the bodhisattva vehicle.

ABHIDHARMA BASKET

The Pāli, Chinese, and Tibetan canons have different perspectives on the origin of the Abhidharma Piṭaka and the texts contained in it. According to one Theravāda account, the Buddha spent a rainy season—about three months—teaching six of the seven Abhidhamma works in the celestial realm of the Thirty-Three (gods) to thousands of *devas* (celestial beings), including his mother Maya, who had passed away a week after his birth. Each day the Buddha would go back to the human realm and repeat to his disciple Sāriputta what he had taught in the celestial realm that day. Sāriputta then organized the Abhidhamma literature, which was recited at the first council and passed down orally until the third council (circa 250 BCE), when it was included in what became the Pāli canon.

According to this traditional Theravāda account, six of its seven Abhidhamma texts are the Buddha's literal word, and the Buddha himself also outlined the *Points of Controversy* (*Kathāvatthu*), the seventh text, which Moggaliputta Tissa would compose in a future century.

Not all contemporary Theravādins agree that the Pāli Abhidhamma originated as described above. Some say that the seven Abhidhamma works were spoken by arhats; others concur with academic scholars that they developed gradually over several centuries and were later incorporated into the Pāli canon. Most other schools[29] see the Abhidharma Piṭakas in their canons as the works of later generations of scholars.

The seven Abhidhamma works in the Pāli canon[30] differ from the seven Abhidharma texts propagated by the Sarvāstivāda school. Almost all of the seven Sarvāstivāda Abhidharma works are included in the Chinese canon,[31] as are the *Abhidharma Treatise of Śāriputra* (*Śāriputrābhidharma Śāstra*),[32] the *Mahāvibhāṣā*, and other early Abhidharma texts, including those by Saṅghabhadra, and the *Path of Freedom* (*Vimuttimagga*).

While Tibetans are aware of the seven Sarvāstivāda Abhidharma works, they do not consider them to be the Buddha's word. Only part of one of the seven is included in the Tengyur section of the Tibetan canon. Passages belonging to the Abhidharma Basket are interspersed in other sūtras in the Kangyur section of the Tibetan canon. The two main Abhidharma texts studied by the Tibetans are: *Treasury of Knowledge*[33] by Vasubandhu, which summarizes the *Mahāvibhāṣā*, and the *Compendium of Knowledge* (*Abhidharmasamuccaya*) by Asaṅga, who writes from the Cittamātra perspective.[34] Some Abhidharma texts by subsequent Indian masters are also present in the Tengyur. The *Treasury of Abhidharma* is found in both the Chinese and Tibetan canons, but the *Mahāvibhāṣā* is absent from the Tibetan canon. Fazun translated it from Chinese into Tibetan in the twentieth century.

The level of importance given to the Abhidhamma differs among Theravādin practitioners. In Sri Lanka and Myanmar, it is considered very important, whereas in Thailand, it is not emphasized as much.

TANTRA

Spoken by the Buddha when he assumed the form of Vajradhara or a tantric deity, tantras describe Vajrayāna practice. The Tibetan canon contains the most comprehensive collection of Buddhist tantras and tantric commentaries by Indian adepts. While the Chinese canon contains some yoga tantras such as the *Vairocana Tantra* and *Vajra Peak Tantra* (*Vajraśekhara Tantra*), it does not have any highest yoga tantras. It seems that tantric texts arrived in China during a period of social turmoil and were not included in the Chinese canon. The Chinese canon contains the sūtras of Amitābha (*Sukhāvatīvyūha Sūtras*), the *Medicine Buddha Sūtra* (*Bhaiṣajyaguru Sūtra*), and scriptures about other bodhisattvas that have been widely read and practiced in the Chinese community for centuries. While these are considered sūtras in China, in Tibet the practices of these same bodhisattvas are included in the Tantrayāna.[35]

From this summary of the three Buddhist canons, it is clear that no one canon contains everything the Buddha taught or all the great commentaries. Nevertheless, there is more than enough in each canon for us to study, contemplate, and meditate. The teachings necessary to gain realizations are there in the three canons. A respected Thai Theravāda master told me (Chodron), "With both Theravāda and Mahāyāna, the Buddha's teachings are complete," and "Mahāyāna is just a name, Theravāda is just a name. When we see emptiness, there's nothing to cling to."

The various Buddhist traditions share many scriptures and practices in common. Although each has its unique qualities, we should not think of them as separate and unrelated. All three canons contain the Buddha's teachings and must be respected as such. They all contain teachings to be practiced.

Philosophical Systems

In the initial centuries after the Buddha's parinirvāṇa, the Abhidharmikas rose to prominence as they developed intricate taxonomies of phenomena and explored the relationships among phenomena. This included material and cosmological phenomena, but even more so the facets of the mind, such as afflicted mental states and the states of meditation and insight. Their focus was on identifying the building blocks of sentient beings' experience rather than on constructing cohesive interpretations of Buddhist doctrine.

Philosophical systems came about in later centuries, when questions arose about topics that were not clarified in the scriptures themselves, and sages began to explain the meanings of teachings that were not evident to most people. These commentators did not see their writings as new interpretations of the Buddha's teachings but as in-depth explanations of what the

Buddha actually meant. They saw themselves as clarifying in an expanded form what the Buddha had expressed in an abbreviated form.

Another factor bringing about different philosophical tenet systems was the challenge presented by non-Buddhist logicians and scholars. Debate was a widespread Indian custom, and the loser was expected to convert to the winner's school. Buddhist sages had to develop logical arguments to prove the validity of Buddhist doctrine and to deflect philosophical attacks by non-Buddhist scholars. The renowned Buddhist debaters were also great practitioners. Not all Buddhist practitioners were interested in this approach; many preferred to study the sūtras or practice meditation in hermitages.

From the viewpoint of philosophy, Tibetans have categorized Buddhist tenets into four general systems: (1) the Vaibhāṣika (Followers of the *Mahāvibhāṣā*), (2) Sautrāntika (Followers of Sūtra), (3) Yogācāra or Cittamātra (Mind Only), and (4) Madhyamaka (Middle Way). These four schools are mentioned in the *Hevajra Tantra*, indicating that all four schools existed in India before coming to Tibet.[36] Each system has further subdivisions.

Even though not all the Indian texts were translated into Tibetan, many were. Among these, we find texts presenting the philosophical views of all four tenet systems, texts presenting the paths of all three vehicles, and texts presenting the practices of both Sūtrayāna and Tantrayāna.

5 | The Buddha's Teachings Form a Cohesive Whole

As SEEN IN the previous chapter, the Buddha provided a wide variety of teachings, depending on the disposition and interests of various audiences. He taught human beings as well as celestial beings, spirits, and other life forms.

There are many ways to systematize these teachings that reveal how they form a cohesive whole and build on each other, leading us to an ever deeper understanding of the Dharma. One is according to the three capacities of practitioners, which will be discussed in chapter 9. Another is the four tenet systems, briefly mentioned in the previous chapter, which will be elaborated in a future volume. The three turnings of the Dharma wheel are yet another way. The first part of this chapter focuses on the three turnings of the Dharma wheel and then turns to the topic of the authenticity of the Mahāyāna scriptures. In the previous chapter, we examined this from an academic approach. Now we will look at it from the perspective of Buddhist practitioners.

Three Turnings of the Dharma Wheel

"Turning the Dharma wheel" refers to the Buddha giving teachings that lead sentient beings to temporary happiness within cyclic existence and to the highest goodness of liberation and full awakening. From the perspective of the Sanskrit tradition, as described in the *Sūtra Unraveling the Thought*, the Buddha turned the Dharma wheel three times, with each turning primarily addressing the needs of a specific group of disciples.

The teachings of the first turning form the foundation of Buddhist practice for all three vehicles. At the same time, they fulfill the specific needs of śrāvakas, who seek personal liberation. The first turning began with the Buddha's first discourse at Deer Park in Sarnath, India, during which he delineated the main framework for training the mind in the four truths of the āryas. When describing the fourth truth, the truth of the path, he taught the thirty-seven aids to awakening, which establish procedures for putting the four truths into practice. The thirty-seven aids relate to two primary methods of training, the first leading to serenity (single-pointedness of mind), the second bringing forth insight (deep understanding). To put these thirty-seven in the context of the three higher trainings, we begin practicing the higher training in ethical conduct to eliminate coarse negativities of body and speech. On this basis, we cultivate serenity in the higher training in concentration and insight in the higher training of wisdom.

The thirty-seven aids can be divided into seven sets—four establishments of mindfulness, four supreme strivings, four bases of supernormal power, five faculties, five powers, seven awakening factors, and the eightfold noble path—which are the principal practices. Vasubandhu in *Treasury of Knowledge* and Asaṅga in *Compendium of Knowledge* correlate their full-fledged practice with successive levels of the fives paths. In that context, they are set out sequentially. The following is Vasubandhu's presentation.

The first set is the *four establishments of mindfulness*—mindfulness of the body, feelings, mind, and phenomena. As we deepen our practice of these four, we will gain greater enthusiasm and vigor to engage in wholesome activities. This leads us to make effort in the *four supreme strivings*—to abandon nonvirtues already generated, prevent destructive actions in the future, enhance virtues that have already been generated, and generate new virtues in the future.

By engaging in ethical conduct such as avoiding destructive actions and enhancing and engaging in constructive ones, we will develop a certain clarity of mind and single-pointedness. This leads us to practice the third set, the *four bases of spiritual power*—aspiration, effort, intention, and investigation—which are methods to enhance our capability to remain focused single-pointedly on a chosen object of meditation.

When we have single-pointed concentration that can last for prolonged periods of time, all our other virtuous spiritual faculties will be enhanced. We will increase the *five powers*—faith, effort, mindfulness, concentration, and wisdom—and the *five forces*—the strengthening of these same five qualities. When these forces are fully developed, we will progress to practice the *seven awakening factors*—correct mindfulness, discrimination of phenomena, effort, rapture, pliancy, concentration, and equanimity. This leads us to fully follow the core of the Buddhist path, the *eightfold noble path*—right view, intention, speech, action, livelihood, effort, mindfulness, and concentration. Through practicing the thirty-seven aids, our minds will be transformed, and we will attain liberation from cyclic existence.

The second turning of the wheel of Dharma contains the Prajñāpāramitā sūtras, the Buddha's teachings on the perfection of wisdom. Elaborating on the topic of selflessness that the Buddha described briefly in the first turning, here he explains that all phenomena are empty of inherent existence. He also clarifies the meaning of the truth of cessation as the emptiness of a mind from which defilements have been eradicated. Giving an extensive explanation of the six perfections—generosity, ethical conduct, fortitude, joyous effort, meditative stability, and wisdom—the second turning also elaborates on the truth of the path for bodhisattvas. The principal and appropriate audience for the sūtras in the second turning of the Dharma wheel are spiritual aspirants who understand the teachings in the first turning and, in addition, aspire for the full awakening of buddhahood. Although they are not the primary audience, these teachings are also for those who seek personal liberation because a comprehensive explanation of emptiness is indispensable for all practitioners. Many of these sūtras were taught at Vulture's Peak, near Rājagṛha, India.

The third turning of the Dharma wheel contains two categories of sūtras. The first furnishes further explanation of the truth of the path and presents a different interpretation of the Prajñāpāramitā sūtras' statement that all phenomena are empty of inherent existence. These third-turning sūtras were taught primarily to benefit those trainees who, although inclined toward the bodhisattva path, are not yet suitable vessels for the teaching on the absence of inherent existence. If they were to embrace the literal meaning of the Prajñāpāramitā sūtras, they would fall into nihilism by mistakenly thinking that emptiness means the total nonexistence of phenomena. For their benefit, the Buddha spoke of naturelessness (*niḥsvabhāva*) in relation to different natures of phenomena—the dependent, imputed, and consummate natures. Rather than think that all phenomena without exception are empty of inherent existence, the Buddha taught these trainees that different phenomena are empty of different kinds of natures. This category includes sūtras such as the *Sūtra Unraveling the Thought*.

The second category of sūtras comprising the third turning speaks of our potential to become fully awakened beings. These sūtras present and develop the clear-light nature of mind and buddha nature. This category includes sūtras such as the *Tathāgata Essence Sūtra* (*Tathāgatagarbha Sūtra*), which is the basis for Maitreya's *Sublime Continuum* and Nāgārjuna's *Collection of Praises*. The third turning of the wheel of Dharma was taught at Vaiśālī and other places in India; its main audience was both those seeking liberation and those seeking full awakening.

To summarize, the first turning of the wheel of Dharma laid out the basic framework of the Buddhist path to awakening, the four truths of the āryas. The second turning went into greater depth on the third truth, the truth of cessation, which needs to be understood in the context of the ultimate nature of the mind, its emptiness of inherent existence. In addition to having the correct view of the emptiness of the mind as presented in the second turning, a profound subject—a yogic mind that has ceased defilements—is needed. This leads to further discussion in the third turning of the fourth truth, the truth of the path—the mind that realizes the nature of reality and eradicates defilements. By combining our understanding of the wisdom realizing emptiness as presented in the second turning of the Dharma wheel and an understanding of buddha nature and the nature of mind as presented in the third turning of the Dharma wheel, we can gain genuine conviction in the possibility of attaining true cessation.

Some sūtras in the third turning of the wheel of Dharma speak of buddha nature and the subjective experience of emptiness, thus establishing the basis for the Vajrayāna teachings, which emphasize employing the subtlest mind to realize emptiness. In this way, the earlier teachings of the Buddha lay the foundation for topics that are developed more fully in later teachings, and the sūtras of the three turnings of the Dharma wheel complement each other.

The teachings of the first Dharma wheel, which emphasize the practices of the Fundamental Vehicle, form the core of the Pāli tradition. Based on these teachings, the Buddha taught the second and third Dharma wheels, which form the heart of the Sanskrit tradition. The form of Buddhism that flourished in Tibet comprises all of these teachings. For these reasons, we Tibetans believe that it is a comprehensive form of the Buddhadharma because it includes all the essential teachings of the Fundamental Vehicle, Mahāyāna, and Vajrayāna. In the Fundamental Vehicle, selflessness generally refers to the lack of a soul—a self that is permanent, unitary, and independent—or a self-sufficient substantially existent person—a person who is the controller of the body and mind. On the foundation of these teachings, the Mahāyāna describes the development of bodhicitta and the extensive practices of the bodhisattvas. In addition to the selflessness of persons, it teaches the selflessness of phenomena in detail. The special techniques described in the Vajrayāna scriptures enhance these bodhisattva practices.

Without a foundation in the core teachings of the Fundamental Vehicle, proclaiming oneself to be a follower of the Mahāyāna is meaningless. We need a broad, inclusive understanding of the Buddha's teachings to avoid generating mistaken notions. Without doing so, we risk disparaging the teachings of the Buddha by saying either that they are limited in scope or that they are not authentic. It is important to understand that these vehicles and their teachings complement each other. We should embody the essence of all these teachings in our personal practice.

REFLECTION

1. The first turning of the Dharma wheel, which focuses on the four truths of the āryas, forms the foundation for Buddhist practice of all three vehicles. Also, it specifically fulfills the needs of śrāvakas, those seeking personal liberation.

2. The second turning, which includes the Prajñāpāramitā sūtras, elaborates on the meaning of true cessations and true paths and gives an extensive explanation of the six perfections. It is directed mainly toward spiritual aspirants who understand the teachings in the first turning and aspire for full awakening.

3. The third turning contains two types of teachings. The first explains the naturelessness of each of three categories of phenomena; it was taught especially for disciples inclined toward the bodhisattva path who are not

yet ready for the teaching on the emptiness of inherent existence. The second explains buddha nature and the clear-light nature of the mind and leads disciples to Vajrayāna.

Authenticity of the Mahāyāna Scriptures

At the first council, which occurred soon after the Buddha's passing, neither the Mahāyāna sūtras nor the tantras were recited or included in the collection of sūtras. Because the Mahāyāna sūtras and Vajrayāna tantras in the Sanskrit tradition were initially not widely known, doubts were later raised about their authenticity.

Personally speaking, I am fully convinced that the Buddha taught these sūtras. Among the greatest of these sūtras, the Prajñāpāramitā sūtras explicitly teach emptiness and implicitly teach the bodhisattva paths and stages to awakening. According to the traditional account, these sūtras were spoken by the Buddha and then taken for safe custody to the land of the nāgas—dragon-like beings that dwell in lakes or near streams—because the people at that time were not yet suitable vessels to fully understand them. The great Buddhist sage Nāgārjuna then retrieved them from the nāgas and brought them to our world, where they were widely disseminated in India.

According to this account, Nāgārjuna lived over six hundred years. I do not believe that Nāgārjuna lived this long. Being fully awakened, surely Śākyamuni Buddha must have had the ability to extend his lifespan, but he did not do this. Thus it seems strange—not to mention improbable—that Nāgārjuna would live so long. Regarding his going to the nāga land to retrieve the Prajñāpāramitā sūtras, I do not fully believe this, but neither can I deny it. Some people say the Prajñāpāramitā sūtras and other Mahāyāna scriptures were made up later and attributed to the Buddha. To me, both of these explanations are extreme.

Born in South India, Nāgārjuna visited Bodhgaya and lived at a learning center in Magadha, both of which are located in northern India. During his extensive travels, he must have come in contact with the Prajñāpāramitā sūtras and began to gather them together. Nāgārjuna was a Sanskrit scholar as well as an upstanding Buddhist monk. As such, he would never lie. He knew that some people doubted the authenticity of the Mahāyāna teachings. Using reasoning, he investigated whether they were authentic. Since Nāgārjuna lived only a few centuries after the Buddha, it would have been easier for him to research and establish the validity of the Sanskrit sūtras than it is for us nearly twenty-six centuries later. Having done a thorough examination, he was convinced that they were the Buddha's word.

Nāgārjuna's writings contain many quotations from the Prajñāpāramitā sūtras. Knowing that the controversy was due to a lack of awareness, he quoted extensively from these sūtras when he composed the *Compendium of Sūtras* (*Sūtrasamuccaya*), and in *Precious Garland* he made special effort to demonstrate why these scriptures were authentic. If he had doubt about their validity, he never would have done this. Seeing that these remarkable teachings were on the verge of extinction, with great compassion he propagated them because he knew that the people of his own and future generations would benefit tremendously from the wisdom in them.

The Buddha taught the Prajñāpāramitā sūtras to a select group of monastics as well as to bodhisattvas and other beings reported to have been in the audience. These teachings were given at Vulture's Peak, a site that is too small to accommodate the large number of listeners who reportedly attended. Thus we must understand the delivery of those sūtras on a different level, not the ordinary level. While some human disciples were present, many beings who heard those teachings were not visible to the ordinary human eye. Some were great bodhisattvas such as Avalokiteśvara, Mañjuśrī, and Samantabhadra.

Because the contingent of human beings listening to these teachings was comparatively small and these teachings are radical in their presentation of emptiness, they were passed down from teacher to student privately and were not known to the general public for many centuries. While it is generally accepted that the Vinaya and sūtra teachings were passed on orally, I believe the Prajñāpāramitā sūtras may have been written down early on. Although literacy was not widespread, surely some *bhikṣus* (monks) knew how to read and write.[37] Because so few people knew about these teachings, they almost fell into obscurity. Nāgārjuna came in contact with, reproduced, and disseminated the Prajñāpāramitā sūtras.

The later dissemination of previously little-known texts has occurred several times in the history of Buddhism. During the Cultural Revolution, many texts in Tibet were destroyed. But later someone found one copy of a text and from it made many copies. In that way the teaching was preserved. Similarly, texts and Buddhist artifacts dating from the fourth to the twelfth centuries were hidden in the Dunhuang Caves, only to be discovered in the early twentieth century and taken to the British Museum, where others came to know of them. Scriptures written in Gāndhārī that date to the first century were found in pots and discovered only in recent years. It seems to me that something similar could have happened in ancient India; the Prajñāpāramitā sūtras could have been relatively unknown for several centuries and then revived due to Nāgārjuna's interest in them and his compassion for us.

The Buddha did not teach the Prajñāpāramitā sūtras and other Mahāyāna sūtras publicly because it would not have been suitable to teach certain disciples, namely those focused on their own liberation rather than the liberation of all. Additionally, people who were inclined to meditate on the selflessness of a self-sufficient substantially existent person would not have been interested in teachings on the emptiness of all phenomena. The Buddha would never force either the goal of buddhahood or the Madhyamaka view of emptiness on others. He respected people, and according to their present disposition, he set out the view, path, and result suitable for them so that they would practice the thirty-seven aids to awakening, realize the four truths, and progress on the path to arhatship.

Other people had the ability or the karma to see bodhisattvas such as Avalokiteśvara, Maitreya, Tārā, and Mañjuśrī. To them, as well as to some devas, nonhuman beings, and bodhisattvas, the Buddha taught the Mahāyāna teachings. To an exceptional few beings who were suitable spiritual vessels to receive the tantric teachings, the Buddha taught Tantrayāna by appearing as Vajradhara and the maṇḍala (the purified environment and deities in it).

If we accept that Śākyamuni Buddha achieved full awakening as a result of having accumulated merit and wisdom for three countless great eons, then such wonderful things are possible. However, if the Buddha was born as an unenlightened human being who, although he became wiser and more compassionate, was not omniscient and still had a body produced by afflictions and karma—as the Buddha is depicted in the Pāli scriptures—then I don't think it would have been possible for him to deliver such teachings at these high levels. Aside from the Cārvākas, who had a nihilistic or hedonistic view, all the spiritual practitioners and intellectuals in India at that time believed in a soul or self (*ātman*). The two teachers that the Buddha studied with before he attained awakening accepted a self, and the Buddha did not encounter other, wiser teachers than these. Given this situation, it would have been extremely difficult for an ordinary person by himself to discover selflessness.

Furthermore, in the nearly 2,600 years since the Buddha lived, millions of people have benefited from his teachings. Many have realized emptiness and attained arhatship and buddhahood. I don't think someone who began that lifetime as an unenlightened human being could have had this kind of effect on the world. In the same way, I don't think the founders of the world's other great religions were ordinary people. They, too, could have been manifestations of the Buddha. A manifestation of the Buddha doesn't necessarily teach Buddhism; he or she teaches what is most suitable for the audience at that time. What ordinary human beings do with the teachings after the founder's passing is another matter. Most academic scholars see the wisdom in a religion as human knowledge—something that evolves over time, with each generation adding what it learns to the knowledge of the previous generations. My perspective is different. I think the major spiritual traditions that have been able to benefit humanity for centuries were each begun by someone with extraordinary spiritual wisdom and compassion, who taught others through their own spiritual experience.

The view of selflessness and nirvāṇa as presented in the Sanskrit tradition is very sophisticated. In the Pāli scriptures, the Buddha stated that nirvāṇa exists and that it is attained by overcoming the afflictions and polluted karma that causes rebirth in cyclic existence. He did not give an in-depth analysis of the precise meaning of selflessness—especially the selflessness of phenomena—or the subtle characteristics of the self that is negated. Such an analysis facilitates understanding the precise meaning of true cessation and nirvāṇa. To benefit his disciples, he needed to extensively explain the emptiness of inherent existence, and thus he gave the teachings of the second turning. In addition, because the bodhisattva path was only briefly explained in the first turning of the Dharma wheel, the Buddha set forth the teachings in the second and third turnings of the Dharma wheel.

Someone might wonder, "Perhaps the deeper teachings about selflessness and more extensive teachings of the bodhisattva path and resultant buddhahood were not taught by the Buddha but were composed by his followers at a later time." If we say that the Buddha did not teach them, then he must have given a rudimentary teaching, and his followers refined it and deepened its insights. This would mean that his followers were more insightful and wiser than the Buddha himself! For me, this is unacceptable. In my opinion, the Buddha taught all the essential points of the path when he was alive. The Indian and Tibetan commentators in subsequent centuries drew out the meaning and implication of these points, further explicating or systematizing them in order to clarify the meaning for future generations.

If the Mahāyāna sūtras were not the Buddha's word, it would mean that the complete instructions of the bodhisattva path do not exist in our world. Without these teachings, attaining buddhahood would be impossible, and the efforts of millions of people in last 2,600 years to actualize that path would have been wasted.

However, over the centuries people have generated bodhicitta and realized the emptiness of all phenomena. Many people of high spiritual capacity—some Tibetan and Chinese practitioners as well as Ajahn Mun—have experienced credible visions of bodhisattvas and buddhas. These people are ethical and wise individuals and do not lie.[38] Thus these holy beings must exist, and the scriptures explaining how to attain their realizations must be the Buddha's word. To say that the path to full awakening exists but the teachings on how to realize it were fabricated by someone other than the Buddha would be very strange indeed!

The Mahāyāna motivation—the aspiration to attain full awakening for the benefit of all sentient beings—the Mahāyāna path of the six perfections, and the Mahāyāna goal of full buddhahood are wonderful and benefit all beings. What is there to criticize in them? What is the point of saying the Buddha did not teach the Mahāyāna?

I do not accept as literal everything found in Tibetan Buddhist literature about the history of Buddhadharma. Some of it is clearly biased. I appreciate the efforts of Western historians who impartially try to analyze historical events. Nevertheless, I think looking at the history of Buddhism just from the viewpoint of academic scholars—most of whom accept the existence of only this life—is going too far. From their perspective, many things mentioned in Buddhist scriptures would be impossible. However, with a worldview that includes belief in rebirth and the mind's ability to be totally purified and become omniscient, the scope of human experience expands greatly, and our view of history changes as well. Personally, I prefer to consider what seems most reasonable given the view I have of who the Buddha was and what his capabilities were.

In summary, because Śākyamuni Buddha was a fully awakened individual, he knew the spiritual dispositions of different audiences and guided them accordingly, teaching them what was suitable. Because the number of spiritual aspirants receptive to the Mahāyāna teachings was so small at the time of the Buddha, he gave these teachings only to a limited group. These teachings remained in very small pockets of people and almost disappeared. Nāgārjuna made a special effort to collect them and teach them, and for that reason, he is known as a trail blazer.

Personally speaking, I (Chodron) approach the issue of authenticity from a different perspective than those presented above. Having graduated with a degree in history, I'm aware that written histories are partial, both in the sense that the information is not complete and that writers interpret it from their own perspective.

Over the years I have had the fortune to study the Mahāyāna sūtras and commentaries. Even though my knowledge and understanding are limited, these teachings make sense to me when I examine them using reason. They also produce beneficial effects when I apply them in my life. If such profound and effective teachings were not given by a fully awakened being, such as the Buddha, who else would have had the ability to do so? Certainly not limited sentient beings. In short, my experience with these sūtras only confirms my conviction that they are the Buddha's word. While I enjoy learning the different perspectives of the history of Buddhism, my faith is not based on it.

Nāgārjuna on the Authenticity of the Mahāyāna Sūtras

Nāgārjuna gave a reasoned analysis to prove the authenticity of the Mahāyāna scriptures.[39] He argued that if the path to full awakening consisted only of the thirty-seven aids to awakening with no mention of bodhicitta and the bodhisattva practices, there would be little difference between the path leading to arhatship of a śrāvaka or solitary realizer and the path leading to the full awakening of a buddha apart from the amount of time necessary to complete it. A person aspiring for arhatship could accomplish the goal in just a few lifetimes, while following the bodhisattva path to buddhahood would require accumulating merit and wisdom for three countless great eons.

In addition, the early sūtras that comprise the Fundamental Vehicle teachings state that at the time of attaining parinirvāṇa when an arhat dies, that person attains "nirvāṇa without remainder." At that time, the continuum of the polluted mental and physical aggregates are said to cease. However, if we analyze carefully, there is no reason why the continuum of an arhat's mind would totally cease at the time of death. There is no agent or antidote that could bring about the cessation of a continuum of consciousness. According to the natural functioning of things, if a powerful antidote to something exists, that antidote can extinguish that thing, just as water can extinguish fire. Since the afflictions do not abide in the continuity of the innate mind of clear light, when the wisdom realizing selflessness extinguishes the afflictions, the continuity of the innate mind of clear light remains.

If the continuum of an arhat's mind ended at death, then Śākyamuni Buddha, who attained full awakening after having collected merit and wisdom during three countless great eons, would have been able to benefit sentient beings for only a short time. He left the royal life at age twenty-nine, attained full awakening at thirty-five, and passed away at eighty-one. Thus he would have been able to fulfill his vow to work for the benefit of sentient beings for only forty-five years. Considering that he exerted effort on the path for three countless great eons in order to benefit sentient beings, it does not make sense that he had only a few decades to fulfill the purpose for which he attained awakening.

In *Precious Garland* (vv. 386–87), Nāgārjuna explains that the "extinction" mentioned in the Pāli suttas has the same meaning as "nonarising" in the Mahāyāna sūtras. Both are emptiness. *Extinction* refers to the primordial emptiness of inherent existence of duḥkha and the polluted aggregates, and *nonarising* means that phenomena do not arise inherently. The knowledge of extinction and the knowledge of nonarising both refer to the wisdom realizing emptiness, the indispensable cause of liberation for practitioners of all three vehicles. Since this is the case, why would anyone deprecate the scriptures that teach this?

Nāgārjuna wondered why people would doubt the authenticity of the Mahāyāna sūtras (RA 380–82):

The nature of what the Mahāyāna maintains
is generosity, ethical conduct, fortitude, joyous effort,
meditative stability, wisdom, and compassion—
how could it contain a wrong statement?

Others' aims are achieved through generosity and ethical conduct;
one's own through fortitude and joyous effort;
meditative stability and wisdom lead to liberation—
this summarizes the Mahāyāna teachings.

In brief, the teaching of the Buddha includes
what benefits oneself and others, and [the way to attain] liberation.
These topics are contained in the six perfections.
Therefore they are also the Buddha's words.

The six perfections that are central elements of the Mahāyāna path of the bodhisattva are all extensions of practices found in the Fundamental Vehicle, values and practices that benefit the world. Having explained these topics briefly in the early sūtras, the Buddha elaborated on them in the Mahāyāna to give those with the bodhisattva disposition the complete instructions they needed. These people also needed to learn the bodhisattvas' magnificent aspirational prayers, the extensive bodhisattva practices, and the bodhisattvas' dedication of merit. If the Buddha did not teach them, who else could have? Just as an unenlightened being could not possibly have taught the wonderful teachings in the Fundamental Vehicle, neither could such a person fabricate the vast and profound teachings of the Mahāyāna. They must be the Buddha's word.

Nāgārjuna advised people who did not feel comfortable practicing the bodhisattva path due to the long time needed to complete it or who doubted that the Buddha could have the amazing qualities described in the Mahāyāna sūtras to withhold judgment and keep an open mind. Nothing is lost by doing this, and remaining neutral protects one from the negativity that results from disparaging the teachings.

In this way, Nāgārjuna demonstrated the value and authenticity of the Mahāyāna sūtras that show the path to buddhahood. The teachings of the Sanskrit tradition do not contradict the core teachings of the Pāli tradition, and in fact, elaborate on the themes set forth in it. Maitreya in *Ornament of Mahāyāna Sūtras*, Śāntideva in *Engaging in the Bodhisattvas' Deeds* (*Bodhicaryāvatāra*), and Bhāvaviveka in *Heart of the Middle Way* (*Madhyamakahṛdaya*) also affirmed the validity of the Mahāyāna scriptures.

REFLECTION

1. Because the Mahāyāna sūtras found in the Sanskrit tradition appeared publicly at a later date than the suttas that formed the Pāli canon, there has been doubt about their authenticity.

2. Contemplate the reasons His Holiness and Nāgārjuna give for their confidence that these teachings are authentic and will lead to supreme awakening.

3. As you continue learning the Sanskrit tradition, consider that the only person capable of delivering such vast and profound teachings must have been a fully awakened buddha.

Is the Buddha's Word Always Spoken by the Buddha?

Arhats and other ārya disciples of the Buddha delivered some of the suttas in the Pāli canon. In some Sanskrit sūtras, too, the main speaker of the teaching is not the Buddha but another buddha or a bodhisattva. It is said that in the *Heart Sūtra* the Buddha inspired Śāriputra to ask a question and Avalokiteśvara to respond. His reply, a stunning synthesis of the Prajñāpāramitā sūtras, is considered the Buddha's word although it was not spoken directly by the Buddha. The same principle could be used to say that the Mahāyāna sūtras are the words of the Buddha, even though they did not appear publicly until a few centuries after the Buddha lived.

The idea of the Buddha's word being spoken at other times or by other people is also found in the Pāli tradition. In the *Aṭṭhasālinī*, Buddhaghosa said that the *Points of Controversy* (*Kathāvatthu*), one of the seven Abhidhamma texts in the Pāli canon, was the Buddha's word although it was composed by Moggaliputta Tissa around 250 BCE. About it, Buddhaghosa said:

> Now when [the Buddha] laid down the table of contents, he foresaw that, 218 years after his death, Tissa, Moggali's son, seated in the midst of 1,000 bhikkhus, would elaborate the *Kathāvatthu* to the extent of [that is, in accord with] the Dīgha Nikāya, bringing together 500 orthodox and 500 heterodox suttas. So Tissa, Moggali's son, expounded the book not by his own knowledge, but according to the table of contents laid down, as well as by the method given, by the Teacher. Hence, the entire book became the word of the Buddha.[40]

Similarly, in the Numerical Discourses (AN 8:8), Bhikkhu Uttara is said to instruct his fellow monks, "Friends, it is good for a bhikkhu from time to time to review his own failings. It is good for a bhikkhu from time to time to review the failings of others. It is good for a bhikkhu from time to time to review his own achievements. It is good for a bhikkhu from time to time to review the achievements of others."

Overhearing this, the deva king Vessavaṇa asks Sakka, the ruler of the devas, about it. Sakka then approaches Bhikkhu Uttara and asks him whether this was his own discernment or whether it was the word of the Buddha. Uttara replies with a simile, "Suppose not far from a village or town there was a great heap of grain, and a large crowd of people were to take away grain with carrying-poles, baskets, hip-sacks, and their cupped hands. If someone were to approach that large crowd of people and ask them, 'Where did you get this grain?' what should they say?"

Sakka replies that they should say, "We got it from that great heap of grain."

Uttara continues, "So, too, ruler of the devas, whatever is well spoken is all the word of the Blessed One, the Arahant, the Perfectly Awakened One. I myself and others derive our good words from him."

The Buddha's disciples who have understood well the Buddha's thought speak the Buddha's word. From this perspective, the Mahāyāna sūtras spoken by holy beings other than the Buddha can also be considered the Buddha's word. They are certainly in accord with and do not contradict what the Buddha said in the Pāli suttas.

Four Authenticities

The Lamdre (*Path and Result*) teaching of the Sakya tradition speaks of four authentic factors that help us to have confidence in the Buddha's teachings and develop in the Dharma: authentic sūtras of the Buddha, authentic commentaries, authentic teachers, and authentic experience.

In terms of the historical evolution, authentic sūtras taught by the Buddha came into being first. Based on these, many authentic commentaries—treatises written by Nāgārjuna and other great sages who explained the final thought of the Buddha—were composed. Based upon studying these authentic commentaries, authentic teachers who have realized the themes presented in the authentic commentaries have come into being. On the basis of the teachings given by authentic teachers, authentic spiritual realizations or experiences grow in the hearts of practitioners.

In terms of developing a sense of conviction in these four authentic factors, the sequence is reversed. We begin with our own experience and from there infer the authenticity of the teachers, the authenticity of the commentaries, and finally the authenticity of the Buddha's word. In my own case, understanding this has been very useful in developing faith and confidence in the Buddha and his teachings.

My modest experience of the Dharma, which has been valuable in my life and brought me peace of mind, occurred due to hearing teachings from my teachers and in some cases while studying the commentaries, such as those of Nāgārjuna and Asaṅga. If I had received an education that did not mention these teachers and commentaries, these experiences would never have occurred. Thus I naturally admire and venerate these teachers and commentaries and know through my own experience that the teachings of Tsongkhapa and the great practitioners who followed him are indeed wonderful. Tsongkhapa has great respect and admiration for Nāgārjuna and his writings, and this, together with my own studies of Nāgārjuna's works, inspires me to respect Nāgārjuna and his treatises. Nāgārjuna, in turn, praised the Buddha highly, so ultimately my respect and admiration must go to the Buddha, who is our actual teacher. He is truly a trustworthy guide on the path to awakening. Therefore, when I encounter teachings given by the Buddha about very obscure topics, I trust them.

Although we may not have had any extraordinary spiritual experiences, each of us has had some ordinary experiences. Reflecting deeply on the teachings on bodhicitta strongly affects our heart and mind, and contemplating the teachings on emptiness induces a change in our perspective. Although these are not full realizations, they are spiritual experiences that give us a taste of these realizations.

Based on these preliminary experiences, we have an idea of the spiritual realizations described in the biographies of the great practitioners and, in this way, develop belief in the authenticity of these great teachers. This leads us to develop trust in and admiration for the commentaries written by past sages upon which these teachers have relied. Admiration for the commentaries that explicate these teachings propels us to trust the validity of the Buddha's scriptures themselves. In his *Treatise on the Middle Way*, Nāgārjuna pays homage to the Buddha by praising him as the one who taught the nature of reality of all phenomena—their emptiness of inherent existence—by revealing dependent arising. Toward the end of this text, Nāgārjuna again pays homage to the Buddha as the one who embodies compassion for all sentient beings, and for that reason, reveals the path to help us overcome all erroneous philosophical views. Reflecting on these homages enables us to employ inference by authoritative testimony, a type of inference that enables us to gain confidence in the validity of obscure teachings that are not knowable by other means of reliable cognition. In Buddhist epistemology, inference must eventually be founded upon and traced back to direct experience. In this case, based on our own initial spiritual experiences, we infer the scope and quality of the spiritual experiences of the great masters, the commentaries they relied upon, and finally the Buddha's word.

REFLECTION

1. Contemplate the development of the Dharma in time, beginning with the Buddha's delivery of authentic sūtras, which led to the writing of

authentic commentaries by the great Indian masters. This led to the emergence of authentic teachers, who by giving teachings, made possible the authentic spiritual experience of their disciples.

2. To develop conviction in these four factors, reverse the contemplation. Begin with whatever small Dharma experiences you have had and infer that authentic spiritual experiences exist in the mindstreams of the great spiritual mentors. This will lead you to have confidence in the authenticity of the commentaries, which in turn will inspire your faith in the Buddha's sūtras.

Four Buddha Bodies

If we have had certain spiritual experiences, we will be able to relate to the accounts of spiritual realizations in the biographies of the great practitioners. These accounts give us some sense that high levels of spiritual experience may be possible. This, in turn, leads to an appreciation of the Buddha's qualities. If we think of the Buddha's awakening in purely ordinary terms, understanding his marvelous qualities is difficult. In the common historical view, Siddhārtha Gautama was an unenlightened being at birth. In the six years from the time he began meditating to his awakening under the bodhi tree, he traversed the path to awakening, from the path of preparation to the path of no-more-learning. While seeing the Buddha as an unenlightened being who attained awakening in this life is very inspiring, from another perspective it may seem limited.

Viewing the Buddha's awakening within the framework of the Mahāyāna doctrine of four buddha bodies provides a different perspective. In this context, "body" does not refer to a physical body but a collection of qualities. The four bodies are the emanation body (*nirmāṇakāya*), enjoyment body (*saṃbhogakāya*), wisdom truth body (*jñāna dharmakāya*), and nature truth body (*svabhāvika dharmakāya*). An *emanation body* is a buddha's physical appearance as an ordinary being, which he assumes according to the spiritual dispositions and needs of particular disciples. An emanation body manifests from a subtler body, an *enjoyment body*, which is the form a buddha assumes in order to teach ārya bodhisattvas in the pure lands. An enjoyment body, in turn, emerges from the omniscient mind of a buddha, the *wisdom truth body*. The wisdom truth body arises within the underlying nature of reality, a buddha's *nature truth body*. This is the emptiness of a buddha's mind and the final true cessation actualized by that buddha. Both the mind of a buddha and its emptiness are called *truth* bodies because a buddha's wisdom is the ultimate true path and the emptiness of that mind is the ultimate true cessation.

Viewing this in the reverse order gives us a deeper understanding of Śākyamuni Buddha. The nature truth body—which, as emptiness and true cessation, is an ultimate truth—is nondual with the wisdom truth body—the Buddha's omniscient mind that clearly and directly knows all ultimate and conventional phenomena. Motivated by compassion, from this union of the nature and wisdom truth bodies appears a subtle form, an enjoyment body, a person who guides highly realized bodhisattvas. To guide other sentient beings whose minds are more obscured, an emanation body manifests from the enjoyment body. This is the appearance of a buddha as an unenlightened being who can communicate and interact with ordinary beings. Śākyamuni Buddha was such an emanation body. Because he appeared from the enjoyment body and ultimately from the truth body, he did not cease to exist when he passed away. The continuity of his awakened mind remains. That means that if our own inner spiritual experience reaches a certain level, we will be able to see and speak with the Buddha. From the Buddha's side, he is always ready to help, but because of our lack of merit and spiritual experience, we can't see him. For example, microscopic organisms have existed for a long time, but until the microscope was developed, we couldn't see them. When we develop spiritually, we will be able to perceive things that until now have been inexplicable to our limited way of thinking.

At first, experiences described in the biographies of great masters, such as receiving teachings from the Buddha seen in a vision, seem beyond our imagination. Although they are inexplicable to our ordinary rational mind, these exceptional spiritual experiences do occur, some during my lifetime. The great practitioner Taklung Shabdrung Rinpoche (1918–94) once told me that when he was giving the empowerments of practices of the Taklung Kagyu lineage to Dilgo Khyentse Rinpoche, he had a direct vision of the great lineage masters of that particular practice, who appeared vividly on the beams of the room where he was giving the empowerment. Taklung Shabdrung Rinpoche was an old lama when he told me this. Having suffered in Chinese prison for many years, he would have had no ambition to impress me by lying or inflating his experience.

A few years ago I met students and colleagues of Khenpo Acho (1918–98), a practitioner from the Nyarong region of Tibet. He was a Nyingma practitioner who studied at Sera, a Geluk monastery, and later he lived as a hermit. His primary practice was reciting the mantra of Avalokiteśvara, *Oṃ maṇi padme hūṃ*, although he also practiced Vajrayoginī and Vajrakīlaya. His close students and colleagues told me that before he passed away, he asked them not to touch his body and to keep the room closed after he died. After about a week, when they opened the door, they discovered that his body had dissolved into rainbow light. Only his monastic robes were left behind.

Although great Tibetan masters in India do not display supernatural feats during their lifetime, some do at the time of death. After he passed away in 1983, my teacher, Yongzin Ling Rinpoche, remained in the clear-light state for thirteen days without any trace of bodily decay. Some years later, a Sakya abbot remained in the clear light for seventeen days. These extraordinary experiences are not only recorded in the biographies of the past masters but also occur in the present generation.

Ajahn Mun (1870–1949), a well-respected and highly realized monk and meditator in the Thai forest tradition, had visions of Śākyamuni Buddha and the arhats. Even though many people following the Pāli tradition say that Śākyamuni Buddha ceased to exist at the time of his parinirvāṇa, Ajahn Mun clearly saw him surrounded by many arhats. Such experiences are possible when our mind is purified of defilements.

The varying explanations of the Buddha presented above need not be a point of confusion for us. We do not have to choose one view and abandon the other. Rather, at a particular time one or another view may be particularly helpful. When we feel discouraged and think that buddhahood is too high, the path is too difficult, and we are inadequate, it is helpful to think of the Buddha as someone born an ordinary being who experienced the problems involved in career and family life. He chose to practice the Dharma diligently and attained buddhahood. We see we are the same kind of sentient beings that he was and have the same potential to attain full awakening.

At other times, seeing Śākyamuni Buddha as someone who attained awakening eons ago and appeared in our world as an emanation body is more helpful. This perspective gives us the feeling of being cared for and supported by many buddhas and bodhisattvas who manifest in immeasurable worlds for the benefit of sentient beings. These realized beings have accomplished what we aspire to do and can guide us on that path.

We may also think of the Buddha as the physical embodiment of all excellent qualities. Since we limited beings cannot directly perceive the inconceivable qualities of awakening, they appear in the form of the Buddha to communicate with us.

Buddhism in Tibet

To understand Buddhism in Tibet, we must trace its roots back to the Buddha through the Nālandā masters. When Mahāyāna became increasingly more widespread in India, great monastic universities such as Nālandā were constructed. These monastic universities attracted brilliant scholars from all philosophical systems and esteemed practitioners as well. Although Nāgārjuna and his student Āryadeva may have preceded the establishment of Nālandā Monastery, their teachings were studied and debated there. From them sprang the *profound lineage* that widely explained teachings on the ultimate nature. These included the works of Buddhapālita, Bhāvaviveka, Candrakīrti, Śāntideva, Śāntarakṣita, and Kamalaśīla. The *vast lineage*, which emphasized the bodhisattva practices, also flourished there, including the teachings of Maitreya, Asaṅga, Vimuktisena, and Haribhadra. Dignāga and Dharmakīrti, whose teachings on logic and reasoning enabled Buddhists to refute the wrong views of non-Buddhists, also flourished at Nālandā, as did study of the Vinaya—the monastic code of discipline—as expounded by Guṇaprabha and Śākyaprabha. Vasubandhu and Sthiramati elaborated on the Abhidharma.

Buddhadharma first came to Tibet during the reign of Songtsen Gampo (d. 649). Among his wives, Bhṛkuṭī was a Nepali princess and Wencheng a Chinese princess. Both brought with them statues of the Buddha. Bhṛkuṭī also brought Buddhist scriptures of the Sanskrit tradition, and Wencheng brought Buddhist scriptures in Chinese.

Buddhism flourished during the time of King Trisong Detsen (r. 775–800). Having a farsighted vision for the development of the Dharma, Trisong Detsen invited the great monk, Madhyamaka philosopher, and logician Śāntarakṣita from Nālandā to come to Tibet. Although he was already in his seventies when he arrived, Śāntarakṣita took full responsibility for establishing the Vinaya and the monastic system in Tibet. He ordained seven Tibetan men to see if they could keep the prātimokṣa precepts well. This experiment was successful, and in 779 Samye Monastery was founded. In addition to teaching Madhyamaka, Śāntarakṣita encouraged the Tibetan king to have Buddhist texts translated from Sanskrit into Tibetan so that people could learn the Dharma in their own language. Trisong Detsen also invited to Tibet the great tantric yogi Padmasambhava, who gave tantric initiations and teachings and subdued interferences to the spread of the Dharma. I feel very moved when I think of the hardships these masters underwent to bring Buddhism to Tibet. We should feel profound gratitude to the past masters who set up our current systems of study.

In the early ninth century, many Buddhist texts were translated into Tibetan, and a commission of Tibetan and Indian scholars standardized many of the technical terms and compiled a Sanskrit-Tibetan glossary. However, Buddhism met with drastic persecution under the reign of King Langdarma (r. 838–42). During this time the monastic institutions, which were the central repositories for Buddhist learning and practice, were almost totally decimated. With monastics no longer able to live together, the continuation of the Dharma from teacher to student was disrupted, scriptures were scattered, and practice became fragmented with a group in one place practicing sūtra teachings and another group in another place practicing tantra. In this way, people no longer knew how to practice all the various teachings in a unified manner free of contradictions.

The king Yeshe Ö invited the great sage Atiśa (982–1054) to Tibet to remedy this difficult situation. Arriving in 1042, he taught extensively, and to rectify the misconception that the sūtra and tantra teachings were contradictory, Atiśa wrote *Lamp of the Path* (*Bodhipathapradīpa*), showing how a person could practice both sūtra and tantra in a systematic and noncontradictory fashion. As a result, people came to understand that the monastic discipline of the Vinaya, the bodhisattva ideals of the Perfection Vehicle, and the transformative practices of the Vajrayāna could be practiced in a mutually complementary way. Monasteries were again built and the Dharma flourished in Tibet.

The Buddhist teachings that were established in Tibet before Atiśa became known as the Nyingma, or Old Translation, school. The new lineages of teachings that came into Tibet beginning in the eleventh century were called the New Translation schools, and these slowly crystallized to form the Kadam (which later evolved into the Geluk), Kagyu, and Sakya traditions.

All four of these traditions go back to Nālandā. The Nyingma lineage stems from both Śāntarakṣita and Padmasambhava. The Kagyu tradition came from Nāropa, a great yogi who was previously an astute scholar at Nālandā. The Tibetan translator Marpa went to India and brought his lineage back to Tibet. The Sakya tradition came to Tibet via Virūpa, who began as a Nālandā scholar specializing in Cittamātra philosophy. He had many mystical experiences, and one evening the disciplinarian heard women's voices in his room. Opening the door, he found a group of female tantric practitioners there. They were actually the sixteen *ḍākinīs* (highly realized female tantric practitioners) of the Hevajra tantra, but because monastic rules had been transgressed, the monk Dharmapāla was expelled and became the yogi Virūpa. Atiśa was from Vikramaśīla Monastery in India, but he is considered part of the Nālandā tradition because the curriculum at the two monasteries was the same.

All four Tibetan traditions present the stages of practice in the Perfection Vehicle in a similar way, as seen in their major Tibetan treatises on this topic. In the Nyingma tradition, Longchenpa's (1308–64) *Mind at Ease* and his commentary *Great Chariot* resemble Atiśa's *Lamp of the Path*, especially in terms of the outlines and structure of the texts. The Nyingma master Dza Patrul Rinpoche (1808–87) wrote *Words of My Perfect Teacher*, the Kagyu master Gampopa (1079–1153) authored the *Ornament of Precious Liberation,* the Sakya master Sakya Paṇḍita (1182–1251) authored *Clarifying the Sage's Intent*, and the Geluk master Tsongkhapa (1357–1419) composed his *Great Treatise on the Stages of the Path*.[41]

There has been a rich tradition of debate among the various branches of Tibetan Buddhism. For example, some people think that Tsongkhapa's writings about emptiness are his own creative invention. In fact, they are firmly rooted in Nāgārjuna's texts; he relies on Nāgārjuna in his discussion of every important topic. I have found some explanations are slightly different from those of Sakya, Kagyu, and Nyingma masters, but the difference is not of great significance.

The main difference among the Tibetan traditions of Geluk, Sakya, Nyingma, and Kagyu is the principal deities they rely on in tantric practice. The Nyingma principally rely on Vajrakīlaya, the Sakya on Hevajra, the Kagyu on Cakrasaṃvara, the Geluk on Guhyasamāja, and the Jonang on Kālacakra. Their explanations of the teachings preliminary to tantric practice are very similar. All rely on the lineage of Maitreya and Asaṅga for the methods to cultivate love, compassion, bodhicitta, and the six perfections. Their elucidations of emptiness are all rooted in the works of Nāgārjuna and his followers.

As a great scholar and logician, Śāntarakṣita introduced his students to the process of using reasoning to examine the teachings, and from then until now, Tibetans have engaged in rigorous study and debate in addition to meditation. With Tibetan scholar-practitioners studying, contemplating, and meditating on the words of the Buddha as well as the great Indian treatises and commentaries, Tibet came to hold the complete Nālandā tradition.

I have two purposes for calling Tibetan Buddhism the Nālandā tradition. First, this shows that it is not Lamaism, a term early Western visitors to Tibet called our form of Buddhism. Lamaism implies that the teachings were created by lamas who pretended to be the Buddha and that people worshiped their lamas. This term created much misunderstanding. Second, many Tibetans don't know the origins of their own teachings and practices and simply follow their own lama or the texts written by teachers of their own monastery. They lack fuller knowledge and a wider perspective. In Nālandā, in addition to studying various Buddhist tenet systems, they also studied non-Buddhist thought. In this way, they developed their critical thinking and gained real knowledge; reading just one text or learning one system doesn't bring that. Having studied many texts and engaged in serious meditation, the most excellent teachers are able to give extensive explanations.

Due to the social context in India at the time Nālandā and the other great monastic universities flourished, their scholar-practitioners focused on refuting non-Buddhist misconceptions. However, once the great majority of Tibetans became Buddhist, Tibetan scholar-practitioners took it for granted that their audience was Buddhist. For these reasons, although Indian sages wrote texts employing reasoning to refute wrong views, Atiśa emphasized integrating the knowledge of Buddhist practices into daily life. Nowadays the audience is more diverse than ever, and both reasoning to refute wrong views and practice techniques for subduing the mind need to be emphasized.

Sometimes people mistakenly think that Tibetan practice, especially Vajrayāna, is a practice all to itself, separate from the rest of Buddhism. When I first visited Thailand many years ago, some people seemed to think that Tibetan Buddhism was a different religion. However, when we sat together and discussed the Vinaya, the Abhidharma, and such topics as the four truths of the āryas, the thirty-seven aids to awakening, and the four immeasurables (love, compassion, joy, and equanimity), we saw that our Theravāda and Tibetan Buddhist traditions have many common practices and teachings.

With Chinese, Korean, and many Vietnamese Buddhists, Tibetans share the monastic tradition, the bodhisattva ethical restraints, the Sanskrit scriptures, and the practices of Amitābha, Avalokiteśvara, Samantabhadra, and Medicine Buddha. When Tibetan Buddhists meet Japanese Buddhists, we discuss the bodhisattva ethical restraints, the method to generate serenity, and sūtras such as the *Lotus Sūtra* (*Saddharmapuṇḍarīka Sūtra*). The Japanese Shingon sect practices Tantrayāna, and with them we share the yoga tantra practice of Vajradhātu Maṇḍala and the performance tantra practice of Vairocanābhisaṃbodhi. Here we see that Tibetan Buddhist practitioners share many common points that they can discuss with all other Buddhists. For this reason, we can say that Tibetan Buddhism is a comprehensive form of Buddhism.

6 | Investigating the Teachings

B EFORE A WISE PERSON buys a needed but costly item, he thoroughly investigates the quality of the product. Similarly, if we are to invest our time and energy in practicing a path, it is important to investigate the teachings that explain this path and how to practice it. In this chapter, we will examine the factors that make a teaching reliable. Being able to trace a teaching back to the Buddha is a key element in this, so we must know the criteria to do that, especially regarding teachings that have appeared many centuries after the Buddha.

Once we have found reliable teachings, our task is to understand them correctly. Some of us may take all the statements and stories we read in scriptures or hear in oral teachings literally and find them confusing. It is important to discern the intended purposes of certain statements and the points of particular stories in order to avoid reaching the wrong conclusion. To do this entails taking cultural factors into consideration.

Since the Buddha's teachings are now spreading in new locations and interacting with unfamiliar cultures, the question arises, "Is it desirable or possible to change the Dharma teachings?" To answer this, it is essential to be able to differentiate the actual Dharma from its cultural forms and expressions. If we change the teachings of the path, we will not reach the goal of the path—nirvāṇa. If we do not alter external forms, we may spend a lot of time trying to mimic people from another culture without transforming our minds in any meaningful way.

Once we become clear on the path and the goal, we have to set about creating the causes necessary to attain full awakening by practicing the path. Without creating the causes capable of producing a certain result, that result will not come about, so we must be practical and realistic. If we wait until every one of our questions has been answered to our satisfaction, we will miss out on engaging in genuine spiritual practice.

The Kālāmas' Experience

The *Kālāma Sutta* in the Pāli canon tells the story of the Kālāma people from Kesaputta, who were confused by the stream of religious teachers visiting their place, each espousing his own doctrine and deprecating those of others. At the outset of the sutta, the Kālāmas are not the Buddha's disciples. Hearing of his qualities, they seek his guidance about how to determine which teachers speak the truth and which are mistaken. The Buddha recommends (AN 3.65):

> It is proper for you, Kālāmas, to doubt, to be uncertain; uncertainty has arisen in you about what is doubtful. Come, Kālāmas. Do not go upon what has been acquired by repeated hearing; nor upon tradition; nor upon rumor; nor upon what is in a scripture; nor upon surmise; nor upon an axiom; nor upon specious reasoning; nor upon a bias toward a notion that has been pondered over; nor upon another's seeming ability; nor upon the consideration, "The monk is our teacher." Kālāmas, when you yourselves know: "These things are bad; these things are blamable; these things are censured by the wise; undertaken and observed, these things lead to harm and ill," abandon them... when you yourselves know: "These things are good; these things are not blamable; these things are praised by the wise; undertaken and observed, these things lead to benefit and happiness," enter on and abide in them.

Knowing that the Kālāmas are reasonable and sensible people, the Buddha encourages them to investigate the various teachings they hear and not simply accept them because of the flimsy reasons that people too often give for their beliefs. The Buddha does not recommend that the Kālāmas discard statements because they do not understand them. Rather, he encourages them to test the assertions and see if those assertions affirm what the Kālāmas know is true and beneficial from their own experience.

Accepting a teaching simply because it was spoken a long time ago and is part of a lengthy tradition is not wise. However, rejecting old beliefs simply because they don't agree with our present opinions isn't wise either. Remaining open and continuing to examine is judicious. It is our responsibility to use our intelligence to question and test a teaching before accepting it. Having done that, our knowledge will be firm because it will be based on firsthand experience or correct reasoning.

Reliable Teachings

Whatever Buddhist teaching we listen to, study, or practice should be authentic. For centuries people like us have learned and practiced the Buddha's teachings, thereby transforming their minds and hearts and attaining higher spiritual levels, including buddhahood itself. We can be confident that if we learn and practice these teachings correctly, we too can attain the same results as the past great masters did. To ensure that a teaching is effective and reliable—not a recent, untested invention of an unenlightened person—we should be able to trace its roots to the Buddha himself. Three criteria will help us to evaluate a teaching and gain a clearer idea whether it is authentic.

First, teachings given by the fully awakened Buddha himself can be accepted as reliable. To validate commentaries and teachings given by masters of subsequent generations, we investigate if their meanings accord with what the Buddha taught.

Second, a teaching that has been subjected to and affirmed by the logical scrutiny of the great Buddhist sages can be accepted as authentic. These sages were not intellectuals who simply discussed the teachings without practicing themselves. While great sages such as Āryadeva, Candrakīrti, and Śāntideva are usually depicted as actively debating, they were also accomplished practitioners who sincerely put the teachings into practice and transformed their minds.

Third, a teaching that has been practiced and realized by the great *mahāsiddhas*—highly realized yogis and yoginīs—is authentic. These great practitioners have sincerely practiced the Buddha's teachings, internalized their meaning, and gained significant spiritual realizations. This demonstrates that the teachings they practiced are reliable.

Some people hold the mistaken assumption that monastics in India and Tibet only studied and debated, while the tantrikas, whose appearance and behavior did not correspond to monastic discipline, did not study and yet were the real practitioners. Before becoming a tantric practitioner, Nāropa was a well-respected, learned practitioner and the abbot of Nālandā. He did not become a tantric practitioner as a newcomer to Buddhism but only after many years of study in which he gained an excellent conceptual understanding of the Dharma. While he saw that this alone was insufficient to accomplish buddhahood, his extensive scriptural knowledge was a necessary foundation for successfully actualizing the tantric path as a yogi.

Many of the seventeen great Nālandā adepts[42] were not only debaters and teachers but were also among the eighty mahāsiddhas. In Tibetan the term *khedrup nyenten*—which applies to both the sage-scholars from the monastic universities and the mahāsiddhas—indicates a practitioner endowed with learning as well as realizations derived through practice. Without study, we do not know how to meditate correctly; without meditation, our studies remain dry. Both are necessary.

We can compare a teaching to the texts that are commonly accepted by everyone in either the Theravāda or the Mahāyāna tradition as authentic, and if their meaning is compatible, they may be accepted as accurate. For example, in the Mahāyāna tradition, texts by Nāgārjuna, Ārya Asaṅga, Śāntideva, Candrakīrti, and Dharmakīrti are commonly accepted as accurate explanations of the Buddha's word. These works of the great masters have already been proven to be reliable because they have been investigated by the sages and the mahāsiddhas have attained realizations by depending upon them.

This analysis cannot be made on the basis of words alone but must include meanings. For example, the terminology in various tantric commentaries may differ considerably from that in the root texts. However, if their meaning accords with the root texts, the commentaries can be accepted as reliable.

We should avoid disparaging teachings that we disagree with or do not fully understand by declaring, "The Buddha didn't teach this." For example, what is to be gained by saying, "The Buddha didn't teach rebirth" simply because the idea of rebirth makes us uncomfortable or does not immediately make sense to us? It is best to remain neutral toward such teachings and put them aside for the time being.

Nor should we ignore teachings simply because they may not be of immediate use to us. For instance, some people have deep respect for the Buddha and his teachings and are concerned about becoming a more compassionate person. At this time, they are not very attracted to investigating emptiness by means of logical analysis. It is fine for these people to focus on the teachings that are most relevant to their aims. They do not need to study the complex works that the monastics delve into. However, this does not mean that those more complicated texts are irrelevant, unnecessary, or inauthentic.

The Buddha gave some teachings provisionally to benefit a particular individual or group. The scripture is authentic, but its meaning requires interpretation; it is not definitive. For example, one sūtra says, "Father and mother are to be killed." This clearly is not to be taken literally, and its meaning must be interpreted. The Buddha said this to console a king who had taken the lives of his father and mother and was overwhelmed with remorse. In the Buddha's mind, "father and mother" referred to craving and existence, two of the twelve links of dependent origination that describe how we take rebirth in cyclic existence. Once the king had overcome his remorse and his mind was open to hearing more teachings, the Buddha taught him the actual meaning of the Dharma.

In sūtras designed for trainees who would benefit from the Cittamātra presentation, the Buddha taught the three natures, saying the imputed nature does not exist by its own characteristics, but the other-powered nature and the consummate nature both exist by their own characteristics. Although the text is to be understood as expressed above by those with the Cittamātra disposition, the teaching is provisional because it does not present the final mode of existence. The Buddha had another, deeper meaning in mind when he spoke this.

Another example of a provisional teaching is one in which a spiritual mentor instructs a particular disciple, "To meditate on emptiness, simply withdraw your mind from focusing on any object whatsoever." By hearing this advice and applying it in his meditation, the disciple realizes the correct view of emptiness. This instruction, however, is not entirely correct, because even emptiness is an object to be focused on. Meditation on emptiness is not simply emptying the mind of all thoughts. If such a teaching were given to a general audience, many people would misunderstand it and do blank-minded meditation, such as the Chinese monk Hashang Mahāyāna taught in Tibet in the eighth century. The understanding of emptiness in the minds of people in general would, in fact, be hampered because they would mistake not focusing on any object whatsoever for meditation on emptiness; the two are quite distinct.

Why, then, was this instruction given to that disciple? Under those particular circumstances, that individual was ripe and able to benefit from hearing it. Instead of generating the wrong view mistaking blank-minded meditation for meditation on emptiness, this person's unique mental state made him an appropriate pupil to hear that explanation and understand the correct view.

Because such a view can be damaging if taught publicly, Kamalaśīla came from India to Samye Monastery in Tibet to debate with Hashang Mahāyāna and to refute his view. I wonder if Hashang Mahāyāna had initially taught this view to a particular disciple for whom it was suitable and later started teaching it to a general audience. Śāntarakṣita, Kamalaśīla's guru, was at Samye at that time, and had Hashang taught that view publicly in Tibet from the beginning, Śāntarakṣita surely would have spoken up and rejected it, especially since Hashang said studying and contemplating the teachings were not necessary.

The great Nyingma master Longchenpa once commented that due to Tibetans' lack of merit, Hashang's view did not become dominant in Tibet. Another lama then said that was tantamount to Longchenpa saying that his view was the same as Hashang's. Personally speaking, I'm a follower of both Kamalaśīla and Longchenpa and have faith in both of them. As explained above, a statement such as "withdraw the mind from focusing on any object" may be suitable for a specific individual with particular karma and a certain mental state. Kamalaśīla refuted it when it was taught publicly due to the damage it could cause if accepted literally. However, Longchenpa accepted it as applicable to specific individuals. Therefore their positions are not contradictory.

Some statements in sūtras or Indian treatises are explained differently in each of the four philosophical schools, and there are levels of profundity within the sūtra and tantra systems. The Buddha taught certain points with skillful means to benefit a particular type of disciple and gradually lead her to the final, correct view. Thus we accept differing statements in the scriptures and differing interpretations of some statements as indicative of the Buddha's skillful means. However, we should not take this to an extreme and think that the Buddha was so vague that anyone can interpret his statements in any way that she likes! Rather, one statement may have many explicit and implicit meanings that can be drawn out in various ways. In the highest yoga tantra specifically, a phrase may be interpreted in four ways—in accord with its literal meaning, general meaning, hidden meaning, and final meaning. It may also be interpreted in six modes: interpretable and definitive, implied meaning and non-implied (direct) meaning, literal and nonliteral. Here interpretable and definitive do not mean the same as in the sūtra context.

REFLECTION

Three criteria can enable us to discern a particular teaching as reliable:

1. It was given by the fully awakened Buddha himself.

2. It has been subjected to and affirmed by the logical scrutiny of the great Buddhist sages.

3. It has been practiced and realized by the great mahāsiddhas.

Treasure Teachings and Pure Vision Teachings

In Tibetan Buddhism, in addition to teachings spoken by the Buddha in sūtras and by the great masters in their writings, there are "treasure" teachings (terma or tercho) and other teachings that arise from pure visions. How are these traced back to the Buddha, and what is the process for ascertaining their validity?

Termas are teachings discovered centuries after their composition either concealed somewhere in the environment or revealed as visionary teachings. These were hidden as termas because they were not suitable for the practitioners at the time of the initial guru but would benefit practitioners at the time of the *terton*, the later practitioner who discovers them. When the terma is hidden, the guru who hides it often prophesizes where, when, and by whom it will later be discovered.

There are two main kinds of termas: earth treasures and mind treasures. *Earth treasures* are objects such as texts and ritual implements that are discovered in nature—in rocks, mountains, or trees—or in a temple or stūpa. Earth termas are not ordinary books but are often written in another script or language. Sometimes they contain symbols that trigger the terton to recall a teaching, which he then writes down. *Mind treasures* are found in space—that is, they appear to the mind of the terton. Guru Padmasambhava, the most prolific creator of termas, or another guru placed them in the mindstream of the terton, who experiences them in meditation and then writes the teaching down from memory. Sometimes the terton himself holds the teaching in his mindstream and reveals it in a future life.

A treasure teaching enhances the teachings the Buddha already gave. In content and purpose, it is in line with the teachings of Śākyamuni Buddha contained in the sūtras and tantras. In this way it is traceable to the Buddha.

In the Tibetan Buddhist community, some treasure discoveries are considered false and others authentic, indicating that some claims may be forged or simply erroneous. There is not an appointed committee or person who is responsible for checking the accuracy of termas. Rather, a prominent and authoritative master that is well known in the Tibetan community usually comments on a terma. He and others take into consideration three factors: whether the terton and/or the terma were prophesized by the Buddha or another lineage master, chiefly Padmasambhava; how this treasure teaching compares with those well-known, authentic treasure teachings discovered in the past; and the characteristics of the person who claims to be the treasure discoverer.

In most cases, an authentic treasure discoverer conceals a new treasure teaching for some years while he or she practices it to determine whether it is reliable. That person's teacher also practices and evaluates the teaching. Sometimes an explicit statement in the terma says that the terton will encounter a specific, reliable student to whom he should first give this teaching. This student is called the "owner of the teaching," and the discoverer may wait to see if this student appears. As I understand it, when Dilgo Khyentse Rinpoche experienced something akin to intuition in which a teaching appeared in his mind, he explained this to his teacher Khyentse Chokyi Lodro. Then both of them would practice this teaching and, if they both gained some deeper experience, then they considered it authentic.

There are other teachings that derive from a pure vision appearing in the mind of a realized master in deep meditation. Unlike termas, they are not transmitted by mind from Padmasambhava. Rather the pure vision of the deity appears directly to the practitioner. Here the deity who appears is in fact a buddha. As with termas, the teachings given in a pure vision should accord with original teachings traceable to the Buddha. If the deity in the vision taught that an inherently existent soul existed, that clearly would not be an authentic pure-vision teaching!

The Fifth Dalai Lama had visions of several deities, and thus certain initiation lineages trace back to him. He practiced the teachings from his pure visions and had good results. Later masters also did this, with similar results. The Fifth Dalai Lama was a good monk, an excellent scholar, and an outstanding practitioner. He had no reason to lie.

I received some of the initiations coming from the pure vision of the Fifth Dalai Lama from my teacher Takdrak Rinpoche when I was around ten or eleven years old. At that time, I wasn't very interested in them, although I did have some auspicious dreams during that time. Now when I do retreat on the Fifth Dalai Lama's pure visions here in Dharamsala, some indications of success appear during each retreat. They may not be obvious signs, but still they come, so these plus my experience in practicing these teachings leads me to believe they are authentic. The Second Dalai Lama also had many pure visions, as did the First Dalai Lama, although he kept them concealed.

Each Tibetan Buddhist tradition has guru-yoga meditations centered on prominent lineage holders or founders of that lineage. For Nyingma, it is Padmasambhava; for Kagyu, Milarepa; for Geluk, Tsongkhapa; and for Sakya, the five founders of the Sakya order (Sachen Kunga Nyingpo, Sonam Tsemo, Jetsun Drakpa Gyaltsen, Sakya Paṇḍita, and Chogyal Phakpa). We may wonder: Since these masters were later historical figures, the guru-yoga practices centered on them were written long after the Buddha lived. How do we know that these practices are valid?

Upon examination, we see that these guru-yoga *sadhanas* (ritual texts) contain the important elements of any tantric practice: taking refuge and generating bodhicitta, the seven-limb prayer, requesting inspiration, dissolution of the guru into the meditator, and meditation on emptiness. Although the central figure varies—instead of being a deity it is now a lineage lama—the practice is still authentic because it follows the basic meditation procedures for this type of practice.

Exaggerated Statements?

Sometimes we encounter statements in the sūtras or commentaries that appear exaggerated, and we doubt whether we should take them literally. Using the criteria mentioned above as well as our common sense, we can evaluate whether they are accurate if understood literally.

For example, statements in some scriptures say that by reciting a particular mantra once, one will never be born in an unfortunate realm or one will attain awakening easily. If such statements were literally true, there would have been no need for the Buddha to teach us to avoid destructive actions and create constructive ones. If we could be reborn in a pure land by reciting a few mantras, why would the Buddha spend so much time teaching the importance of counteracting ignorance and afflictions by applying the antidotes to them? If we could gain realizations simply by reciting mantras, the Buddha would not have taught the three higher trainings and the cultivation of method and wisdom. We can see that such statements are not consistent with the Buddha's teachings in other scriptures. Therefore we cannot take these statements literally. Reciting mantras must be conjoined with other virtuous practices to bring the desired results. So why does the scripture say this? In part, the benefits of reciting a mantra were extolled to inspire certain people who are embarking on the practice.

In addition, the results of reciting a mantra differ according to the person doing it and how it is done. A constructive action done by a person adhering to Buddhist precepts is far more powerful than the same action done by one not living within the precepts. The potency of mantra recitation done by a person contemplating the emptiness of the mantra, reciting it with a bodhicitta motivation, or visualizing sending out emanations to benefit sentient beings is much more powerful than the same recitation by someone whose mind is distracted. The power of the mantra does not operate independent of these other conditions.

On the flip side of these benefits, some scriptures state, for example, that we will be reborn in the hell realm for the same number of eons as the number of moments we are angry with our spiritual master; that one moment of anger destroys the merit of generosity and other practices accumulated over one eon; or that anger toward a bodhisattva leads to experiencing unfortunate rebirths and great suffering for eons.

Some people may think that the Buddha made such statements to instill fear in us so that we will behave ethically. This is not the case. The Buddha had no reason to threaten us with punishment: the law of karma and its effects is not a system of punishment and reward. Rather, with compassion the Buddha was reminding us that a small action can bring a large result, just as in the physical world a tiny seed can grow into a huge tree. Such seemingly exaggerated statements aren't only about the bad effects of small unwholesome actions. They are also found on the positive side; great beneficial results may come about by doing small constructive actions. For example, it is said that if a person shoots a sinister look to a bodhisattva, the karmic impact is like gouging out the eyes of all sentient beings. However, it is also said that if we pay respect to or venerate a bodhisattva for even one moment, we accumulate merit as vast as the universe. One text says that even if an enraged person glances at the image of the Buddha, he accumulates merit by the power of having contact with an image representing awakening. As a result of this, he will be able to see ten million buddhas in the future. But remember, glancing at a Buddha statue alone will not yield the result of seeing ten million buddhas. We also need to purify our minds, create merit, generate bodhicitta, and understand emptiness.

In statements about the effects of our interactions with buddhas, bodhisattvas, and their images, the heaviness of the karma is primarily due to what is called the "power of the object." That is, buddhas and bodhisattva are remarkable beings who have accumulated merit for countless eons and have continually engaged in benefiting sentient beings. Venerating such beings, making offerings to them, and assisting them in their various works create powerful karma because, being weighty in virtue, holy beings are powerful objects. Similarly, interfering with their good deeds or scorning them leaves heavy harmful latencies in our mind.

Whether our actions regarding holy objects have the potency to bring strong or weak effects also depends on the context of the action. Let's say a person who is not a bodhisattva gets angry at a bodhisattva for whom she usually holds great admiration. Her anger is not rage; rather she lost her temper over a small thing. If she immediately regains mindfulness and regrets her anger, I don't think she will experience suffering for countless eons. However, another person has no regard for bodhisattvas in general and is antagonistic toward one in particular. If he gets very angry toward that bodhisattva, the harsh consequences mentioned above may apply.

Results arise in dependence upon a multiplicity of causes and conditions, so scriptural statements must be understood in that light. The intensity of our intention, whether getting angry or generating compassion, makes a big difference in the strength of the result. Also, if a person performs an action repetitively—be it constructive or destructive—the result will be heavier. Another factor affecting the heaviness is whether a counterforce is present: if we purify destructive actions, their effects will be lighter, whereas generating anger or wrong views hinders the ripening of our constructive karma. The strength of the regret and the strength of the wrong views will also affect the heaviness of the karma.

In short, many factors are involved in the weight of a karma. In *Blaze of Reasoning* (*Tarkajvālā*) by Bhāvaviveka and in the *Great Treatise on the Stages of the Path* by Tsongkhapa, it is said that the intricacies of karma are very profound. How specific actions bring their specific results is a very obscure phenomenon that only omniscient buddhas know with complete accuracy. Nevertheless, we can still evaluate scriptural statements regarding cause and result based on our limited knowledge by comparing quotations on a similar topic to see if they are consistent. In the case of the efficacy of reciting a mantra once, other scriptures present a divergent view and stress the necessity of purifying destructive karma and practicing both wisdom and method for eons. But in the example of a small instance of anger bringing a large result, we find complementary statements that small constructive actions may ripen in significant results. In this case, the claims are consistent with each other.

If we do not feel comfortable believing some of the scriptural statements about karma and its results, we can leave them aside. No one is forcing us to believe what the Buddha said or to become a Buddhist. In matters of religion, a great diversity of beliefs is natural. While everyone—animals and human beings alike—agrees that drinking water is necessary, we disagree on what food is delicious. Similarly, although the search for meaning in life is shared, we may differ regarding religious beliefs. There is room for a variety of views.

REFLECTION

1. Are there scriptural statements that you feel uncomfortable with or doubtful toward? If so, what are they?

2. Are there other scriptures that either reinforce, contradict, or give another interpretation of the meaning of that statement? How does that change your thought?

3. Was religion used as a tool of coercion or intimidation when you were a child? If so, could that experience now affect your perspective on Buddhist scripture?

Correctly Understanding the Point

The meaning of certain stories found in Dharma texts is not always obvious, especially since they were told for a specific purpose and are related to the author's cultural context. A few examples will illustrate this.

There is a story of the Buddha in his previous life giving away his wife and children as an act of generosity. This seems to contradict not only modern values of gender equality but also the ancient principle of caring for one's family.

We may be confused or even incensed by the values and assumptions underlying such a story. It is helpful to step back and ask ourselves what Dharma meaning is being expressed in the story. Most people cherish their family more than anything else. Attachment to our loved ones is often so strong that the thought of being separated from them brings us great anguish. That someone was willing to offer what they cherish the most testifies to the depth of that person's faith and veneration for the Three Jewels. He is willing to separate from his most cherished objects to create merit. This story also illustrates that when attachment has been conquered, the mind does not cling even to those we cherish the most. The mind is so free that we are not overwhelmed with distress when separated from our dear ones.

We don't need to agree with the social values of an ancient culture in order to learn a valuable point from an ancient story. While in ancient times—and to some extent even today—a wife and children being a man's property was acceptable to Indian sensibilities, clearly it is not acceptable now in other countries. We can maintain our contemporary social values and still appreciate the Dharma meaning of a story.

Aśvaghoṣa, a great Indian sage of the first century, wrote the *Acts of the Buddha* (*Buddhacarita*) in which he related the Buddha's deeds when he was a bodhisattva. One of these was the well-known story about the Buddha offering his body to a starving tigress so she could feed her cubs. After writing this, Aśvaghoṣa had a strong aspiration to practice just as the Buddha did, so when he encountered a starving tigress one day, in a pure act of generosity, not expecting anything in return, he gave the tigress his body. The moment he did this, he composed a prayer of seventy verses about the bodhisattva practice, using his own blood as ink. This prayer is really wonderful, but it seems that no one was there when he did this, so I'm not sure where the oral transmission of the prayer came from.

Some people may initially be horrified by the idea of feeding their body to a tiger and wonder why Buddhists would glorify such a suicidal act. "Isn't it better to stay alive and work for the welfare of human beings rather than feed our body to an animal?" they ask. The purpose of this story is to emphasize the depth of bodhisattvas' compassion: they are willing to give even their body and life without any attachment to benefit others. This illustrates the strength of compassion we want to cultivate as aspiring bodhisattvas. Although having no attachment to our body may seem almost impossible at our current level, by training our mind in non-attachment and compassion we will gradually be able to cultivate the attitude that can give our body and life as easily as giving an apple to someone.

In another story, a nonbeliever asked Āryadeva for one of his eyes, and

Āryadeva happily offered it to him. This person then crushed the eye. We may wonder: "Does the generosity demonstrated by this holy being mean I should give away everything indiscriminately, even to someone who doesn't value the gift?"

Some background to this story is needed. At that time, non-Buddhist scholars were challenging Buddhist views, and a big debate was about to occur to determine whose views were correct. Āryadeva was to represent the Buddhist view, and in order to train him, his spiritual mentor, Nāgārjuna, took the position of the non-Buddhists and debated with Āryadeva. Nāgārjuna did this so well that Āryadeva began to think, "My teacher is not actually a Buddhist!" and disparaged him during the practice debate. This disrespect toward his mentor was a destructive act, but because Āryadeva had high realizations, the karmic seed of reviling his spiritual master did not fester in his mindstream but ripened quickly. En route to the debate site, he encountered someone who asked for one of his eyes. In an act of consummate generosity, with no expectation of receiving anything in return, Āryadeva happily complied and continued on his journey. However, as he was walking away, he looked back and saw the person crushing his eye and regretted his generosity. For that reason, his sight was not restored, whereas otherwise it would have been.

There are many lessons in this story: the importance of always maintaining a respectful attitude toward our spiritual mentor, the possibility of compassionately giving away our body with no expectation of return, and the disadvantage of regretting an act of generosity.

From this story, we should not draw the conclusion that we must sacrifice our body or material resources indiscriminately without making sure that they will be properly utilized. The perfection of generosity entails giving an appropriate object to a suitable person at the right time; good judgment is indispensable. Giving a bottle of liquor to an alcoholic is not an act of generosity. In his text, *Bodhisattva Grounds* (*Bodhisattvabhūmi*), Asaṅga gives a detailed explanation about the practice of generosity describing appropriate and inappropriate times, objects, recipients, places, and motivations for giving.

From another perspective, Nāgārjuna and Āryadeva were highly realized ārya bodhisattvas. Thus this story seems odd, for it appears to ignore Āryadeva's mastery. Surely someone with his realizations would never have behaved like that toward his spiritual mentor. Nor would he have given one of his eyes to someone for whom it was of no benefit. Similarly, he would not have regretted his generosity afterward. Because this story makes Ārya-deva appear imprudent, I question whether these events should be taken literally.

There is the story of an old woman whose son was making a pilgrimage to a holy site. She asked him to please bring a relic of the Buddha back for her. He remembered this only on his way home, and not wanting to disappoint his mother, he took a tooth from the carcass of a dead dog he found along the way and presented this to her, saying it was the Buddha's relic. She had great faith and worshiped this tooth devoutly. As a result, the tooth produced many relics, and she experienced miraculous occurrences.

It is easy to conclude from this story that blind faith is necessary on the path. This is clearly contrary to the Buddha's emphasis on developing discriminating wisdom. I do not see much point in this story and propose replacing it with the following, more suitable, account to illustrate the benefit of having confidence in the Three Jewels.

Two or three centuries ago, a great teacher and sincere practitioner named Togyen Lama Rinpoche lived in Tibet. He had a small clay image of Tsongkhapa on his carefully tended altar. One day, due to Togyen Lama's genuine practice and heartfelt aspirational prayers, that image of Tsongkhapa actually spoke and gave teachings to him. This came about not from the side of the statue, but mainly due to Togyen Lama's excellent practice. Due to his spiritual experiences and confidence in Tsongkhapa, this clay image became the real Tsongkhapa and spoke to him. However, for ordinary people who lack that kind of spiritual experience and faith, the statue just looked like clay.

These are just a few examples. When we read stories in texts it is helpful to reflect on them in order to discern the meaning the author intended; we can ignore the social values or other elements of the story that don't make sense to people in our day and age or in our culture. It's also good to remember that not all aspects of an analogy apply to the point being established. Many stories or analogies are useful in one area but cannot be generalized to all situations. When doubts remain, it is helpful to discuss the meaning with Dharma friends or ask our teacher so that we will understand teachings, stories, and analogies in the way that they are intended.

REFLECTION ⸻

1. Recall a story you have heard or read in a Dharma teaching that left you feeling confused, disturbed, or irritated.

2. Realizing that the story is from another culture that had different social values than you do now, set the details of the story aside and ask yourself, "What is the point of this story?"

3. Consider how that point relates to your Dharma practice.

Can the Dharma Change?

Some people ask if the Buddha's teachings can be changed in order to make them more relevant to our historical period. While they want to make the Dharma more understandable to others, they are concerned that altering the teachings would impact their authenticity and efficacy. This question requires much careful thought.

It's important to differentiate between the essence of the Buddha's teachings—the determination to be free, bodhicitta, and the correct view of reality—and the external forms of Buddhism, such as the color and style of monastic robes, the design of the altar, the types of offerings that are made, and the language and melody of chants. External forms have changed each time Buddhism has spread to a different place, and this does not affect the essence of the Buddha's message. However, changing the teachings of the Buddha that describe duḥkha, its origin, its cessation, and the path to nirvāṇa would alter the fundamental perspective and principles of the Buddhadharma, making it no longer the teachings of the Buddha.

Regarding the development of Buddhist thought in ancient India and in the classical period in Tibet, many of the debates in the texts center on issues in epistemology, cognitive processes, and the relationship between body and mind that were important to people at that time and place. In ancient India, Buddhist thinkers had to respond to philosophical claims made by non-Buddhist Indian schools. While some of those debates may, upon first glance, not seem important to us, if we look closely we may see that some versions of those views might exist today. In that case, studying their refutations could help us when speaking with our contemporaries who assert the existence of a universal mind, an absolute creator, predetermination, and so forth. Understanding the reasons disproving the theses of non-Buddhists may also help us dispel similar kinds of beliefs that we may have.

In Tibet, many of the debates center around the two truths: what they are and how they relate to each other. Here Buddhists debate with each other—not with non-Buddhists—in order to distinguish the Middle Way view from views of nihilism and absolutism. Some of the views expressed by earlier Tibetan Buddhists are held by people today, so studying the pros and cons of these various views can be relevant to our practice.

In ancient times, people lacked a sophisticated understanding of the brain and neural processes and of their role in perception, emotions, and other cognitive processes. Since now we have a much better scientific understanding of the brain and its role in our experiences, it would be helpful to bring that knowledge into Buddhist thinking. Buddhist dialogue with science raises a number of other issues that need to be discussed and debated—issues that would not have occurred to people in ancient India or in classical Tibet. Previously people naturally accepted that mind and body were different entities; these days they don't, so Buddhists need to prove the existence of the mind, its difference from the brain, and the relation of the two. The great Buddhist debaters of the past were not concerned with the issue of predetermination and free will, but when Buddhism enters into cultures influenced by theistic religions, those topics become crucial. In these and other such areas, Buddhists need to learn and contemplate the views of scientists and people of other religions and know how to apply Buddhist principles to them and to respond with wisdom. There is much room for us to grow in these areas.

However, with respect to the teachings on afflictions and how they cause suffering, sentient beings today have the same kind of afflictions as they did thousands of years ago. The specific objects of attachment and anger may change in different times: in ancient times human beings weren't attached to their smartphones and didn't become angry when their computers or cars broke down. However, the general objects of attachment and anger are still very much the same—whatever gives us happiness or interferes with that happiness. Furthermore, the processes of getting angry by exaggerating the negative aspect of someone and of subduing anger by means of applying counterforces are the same now as before. The antidotes to individual afflictions such as anger and clinging attachment remain as relevant today as they were then.

It is feasible that after several hundred thousand years, our brain may change through an evolutionary process to the point where even the shape of our head or the functioning of our nervous system will be radically different. In those cases, it is conceivable that sentient beings' preoccupations and ways of thinking may change. However, as far as the problem of self-grasping is concerned, I don't think it will change. Since this root of our suffering will not change, neither will its antidote—the wisdom realizing emptiness. As far as the view of emptiness is concerned, it remains relevant at the beginning, the middle, and the end of our practice, in all historical periods, in all places, and for all sentient beings.

When adopting new cultural forms, we must ensure that we neither intentionally nor inadvertently discard or change vital teachings. Should that happen, the liberation and awakening of future generations would be rendered impossible. Thoughtfulness, care, and slow change are preferable to a rush to make Buddhism more attractive to the present public.

Being Practical

Researching the teachers and teachings before making a commitment is a good idea. However, sometimes we go too far and think that all of our doubts must be resolved and questions answered before we can engage in practicing the path to freedom. One sūtra (MN 63) tells the story of Bhikkhu Mālunkyāputta, who has a surge of doubt because the Buddha did not respond to his questions: Is the world eternal or not eternal? Is the world finite or infinite? Is the soul the same as the body or are they different? After death, does a Tathāgata exist, not exist, both, or neither? In his confusion, Mālunkyāputta thinks that he cannot continue to practice the Dharma unless those pressing issues are resolved, and so he approaches the Buddha.

To instruct his disciple, the Buddha uses the simile of a man shot by an arrow. Suppose someone is wounded by a poisonous arrow and taken to the doctor. The wounded man arrives at the clinic, in pain and bleeding profusely, but rather than letting the doctor treat him, he insists on first knowing the social class of the person who shot the arrow, the name and clan of that person, his height and complexion, where he lived, and the type of bow, shaft, feathers, sinews, and arrow that were used. Clearly he would die before all his questions were answered. And even if he were successful in obtaining that information, it would not stop the bleeding nor extend his life. Similarly, if we think, "I will not practice the Dharma until all my questions are answered and doubts resolved," this life will end and no practice will have been done.

For that reason, the Buddha told Mālunkyāputta that he teaches, "This is dukkha, this is the origin of dukkha, this is the cessation of dukkha, this is the way leading to the cessation of dukkha." The Buddha teaches the four truths because they are beneficial to learn, they will help people to live the holy life, and they lead to disenchantment with cyclic existence, the giving up of sensual craving, cessation of dukkha, peace in the mind, direct knowledge of the way things are, and nibbāna. He leaves other topics aside because learning them is not necessary or conducive for this purpose. Whether the world is eternal or not has no relevance to the important task of eliminating afflictions and ceasing saṃsāra. The Buddha recommends that Mālunkyāputta leave aside his questions and focus on the path that leads to liberation. In that way, Mālunkyāputta will not waste time on senseless doubts.

Like this, we should focus on what is important and not be distracted by pointless speculation. If we do not instantly understand a Dharma topic, we can temporarily put it aside and focus on those Dharma topics that help us here and now. Later on we can return to those other topics. Not all our questions can or will be answered at once. Let's be practical and remove that poisonous arrow of the afflictions before it takes our life.

In this chapter, we have learned the criteria to discern reliable teachings. Now we must study those teachings and understand them as they are meant to be understood. This may entail looking beyond cultural overlays and detecting the point of a story or analogy. To attain the goals of liberation and awakening, we must follow the path as the Buddha taught it, without altering it to suit our fancies and predilections. While the outer "packaging" of the teachings—the cultural forms in which they exist—may be changed, we must take care not to change the essential teachings just because they don't agree with our opinions. The challenge is to differentiate between the packaging and the essence. Great skill is needed to do this.

Having reached the point where we are ready to engage in serious study and practice of the Buddha's teachings, let's not be waylaid by doubts. Instead, let's approach the teachings with curiosity, sincerity, and intelligence.

7 | The Importance of Kindness and Compassion

A Peaceful Mind

SIMPLY TAKING CARE of our body and tending to its physical comfort but neglecting the state of our mind and heart is not wise. Just as we nourish our body and care for its health each day, we should also invest effort and time into cultivating our mind and ensuring its spiritual health. Doing so will bring us great peace and happiness now as well as in the future.

Whether or not you accept future lives, counteracting disturbing emotions and cultivating our good qualities are still extremely important. We are all subject to frustration, disappointment, and loss in life as well as to aging, sickness, and death. Such conditions plague us simply because we are human. No external method to eliminate them exists; the only way to face these trials gracefully and lessen the suffering that accompanies them is to prepare for them by transforming our mind. Then, when such inevitable sufferings come, we will be able to handle them more easily, with less anxiety and fear, and even with some joy at the special opportunities they provide for our spiritual development.

Medical researchers are taking more interest in studying emotions because they see there is a relationship between positive emotions and good health. Having a positive attitude sustains good health as well as increases our ability to heal after injury and surgery. Destructive emotions, such as anger, fear, and anxiety, can eat away not only at our emotional well-being but also at our health. The link between these emotions and ulcers, high blood pressure, and so forth has long been known. Some scientific studies have found that destructive emotions weaken our immune system while constructive emotions boost it.

Constructive emotions help people better weather the natural process of the body's aging and eventual demise. People with a positive attitude are able to face these events with inner balance and acceptance—this illustrates that although the body may be ill or painful, the mind can remain peaceful and people can still enjoy a sense of purpose in life. My mother was a good example of this. She experienced many hardships, including fleeing her homeland and becoming a refugee, but she maintained a positive and kind attitude throughout. Due to this, she was appreciated and loved by others.

From the time we are born, constructive emotions affect our physical, social, and emotional development. Studies have shown that when infants receive compassionate care from their parents, it facilitates the proper development of their brains. We all know from our own experience that a child who is treated with kindness and compassion has more self-confidence and better relationships with others.

Sometimes we think that animals and insects may be happier than we are: they have no fear of layoffs at work, financial woes, or broken relationships. This may be true, but their lack of anxiety is not due to spiritual practice and mental transformation but to the clouds of ignorance and confusion that obscure their minds. There is nothing to admire about this state; contrary to the popular saying, ignorance is not bliss. Fortunately, we human beings, by using our intelligence and reason, have the ability to consciously cultivate constructive mental states and the path to peace and happiness. We have the ability to actualize our unique potential to its fullest.

From the beginning of the Buddhist path to the end, each practice is aimed at developing virtuous qualities of mind. The qualities we attain through disciplining and cultivating our mind are vast and extensive, as illustrated by sincere practitioners and highly realized beings.

For our spiritual practice to bear good results, kindness, tolerance, and compassion for other sentient beings are essential. Practicing any spiritual path motivated by habitual self-absorption won't do, because that attitude is a principal cause of our unhappiness. Seeking wealth, social status, or fame is hardly a spiritual motivation, nor is arrogance, jealousy, or competition. To progress on the path to awakening, we need to begin with and maintain a sincere attitude that deeply cherishes others and that cares for ourselves in a healthy way, without being either self-indulgent or self-denigrating. Such a mental state is necessary both to live happily in this life and to make our spiritual practice effective. This is because our motivation is the chief factor determining the long-term results of our actions. In this chapter, we'll learn contemplations that lead to a compassionate attitude and altruistic intentions, and then we'll discuss mind training, a skillful method to help us maintain a compassionate outlook even in the face of adversity.

The Importance of Motivation

The Buddhadharma is a method to train our mind that aims at eliminating afflictions—disturbing emotions and incorrect views. *Nirvāṇa* is true freedom—the elimination or cessation of these afflictions. Our physical, verbal, and mental efforts directed toward this goal are included in Dharma practice.

What is and is not Dharma practice is determined by our motivation. A spiritual motivation must be different from our ordinary wish to seek well-being by way of possessions, money, reputation, and the sweet words of our loved ones. In short, a spiritual motivation must go beyond seeking the happiness of only this life. There are three levels of Dharma motivation that correspond to the three capacities of practitioners: the first seeks a favorable rebirth, the second aims for liberation from cyclic existence, and the third aspires for full awakening in order to benefit all sentient beings.

We may wonder, "What about the happiness of this life? Everyone wants that." That is true, but we often employ misguided means in our attempts to be happy and wind up creating more causes for misery instead. To get what we want, we may lie or cheat. When our efforts to procure what we desire are frustrated, we become angry and blame the people around us. We talk behind their backs, stir up others against them, and speak harshly to them. In this way wars begin, be they our personal wars against a colleague, acrimony among racial, ethnic, or religious groups, or wars between countries. In short, attachment to the happiness of this life brings about more problems in the present, creates the causes for future problems by transgressing our ethical values, and impedes our spiritual goals.

For these reasons, the demarcation between a Dharma action and non-Dharma action is whether our principal aim is only the happiness of this life. An activity done exclusively with strong grasping for the happiness of this life is limited in its scope. A motivation focused on my happiness now cannot act as a cause for good rebirths, liberation, or awakening. In fact, it is antithetical to spiritual aims. On the other hand, actions motivated by kindness and compassion, actions done with the thought to abandon harming others, and actions done with the motivation to attain a good rebirth, liberation, or awakening enable us to transform even the simplest actions in our daily life into Dharma practice.

While the happiness of this life is not the principal aim, it comes as a byproduct of Dharma practice. By restraining from harmful actions, we immediately get along better with others. When we act with kindness and compassion, we feel good about ourselves and our self-esteem improves. Others reciprocate our kindness. Interestingly, people who relinquish the preoccupation with the happiness of only this life experience more happiness in this life.

A motivation seeking good rebirth, liberation, or full awakening helps us to overcome clinging attachment, hostility, confusion, jealousy, and arrogance, which are the source of so much unhappiness. We experience a great sense of purpose in our lives, and our minds become more peaceful now, even as we create the causes to actualize our long-term spiritual goals.

We can't evaluate the spiritual value of an action by how it looks on the outside because the same activity can be done with different motivations. Giving millions of dollars to charity with the aim of increasing our fame or wealth in this life is not Dharma practice, no matter how much acclaim we may receive, whereas giving a small donation with a kind heart is. Meditating with the motivation to reduce our stress will bring that result, but it is not Dharma practice because our motivation is focused solely on our own happiness in this life. To ensure that our practice brings the spiritual results we seek in the long term, we consciously generate a Dharma motivation before engaging in any activity, especially prior to meditating and giving or attending teachings.

Before going to work, take time to cultivate the motivation to help others. For example, think, "May the work I do serve the clients or customers and bring happiness in their lives. May I contribute to a feeling of harmony among my colleagues." Changing our motivation changes our actions, and that in turn changes the dynamics in our family and workplace. One person cultivating kindness has a strong effect on a group.

It is important to observe our mind and ensure that our kindness is sincere. When I was a child in Lhasa, I had a parrot that would bite anyone who put his finger in its cage. My calligraphy teacher would give nuts to the parrot, who was always excited to see him. My teacher would put his hand in the cage and pet the parrot, and the parrot would eat nuts from his hand. I was jealous and wanted the parrot to like me just as much as it liked my teacher, so I gave it some nuts. The parrot took them to the other side of the cage and ignored me. It knew I didn't have a good motivation. One day I was so angry when it didn't respond to me that I hit it. Afterward, whenever I came near, it would cry out in fear. Even animals know if we're hypocritical or sincere.

Mindfulness and introspective awareness are indispensable to maintain a compassionate motivation or a motivation that looks beyond our immediate gain. Because we have strong habits underlain with the thought "I want what I want when I want it," we need to continually reinforce mindfulness of our values so we act ethically. With introspective awareness, we monitor our physical, verbal, and mental actions to make sure they correspond with our motivation. In this way, we treasure, protect, and enhance our noble motivations so that they will manifest in constructive actions.

A good intellectual understanding of the Dharma path helps us refine and improve our motivation. Although conceptual knowledge is not the final goal of the path, it gives us the tools to begin to counteract corrupt motivations. When we feel lazy, we will know to meditate on impermanence and the unsatisfactory nature of cyclic existence to instill a sense of urgency to practice. If we are angry and upset, we meditate on love or fortitude to calm and center ourselves.

REFLECTION

1. Our motivation is the principal factor determining the value of our actions.

2. For an action to be Dharma, the motivation must be more than seeking our immediate happiness of this life.

3. We are not "bad" for seeking the happiness of this life, but if we seek only this, we often create the causes for misery now and in the future.

4. Expanding our hearts to care for others and training our minds in long-term motivations such as seeking fortunate rebirth, liberation, and full awakening bring a sense of inner fulfillment.

Cultivating a Compassionate Intention

Developing a genuinely compassionate attitude is based on being aware of others' duḥkha as well as their kindness. To be aware of others' misery, we must first be aware of our own, and to cultivate compassion that wishes ourselves and others to be free from duḥkha, we must identify the causes of duḥkha and know they can be eradicated. Ignorance—a state of unknowing that misapprehends how phenomena exist—is the root cause of duḥkha. "Unknowing" implies the existence of its opposite—a state of knowing or wisdom. This gives us confidence that it is possible to eliminate ignorance and overcome duḥkha. Understanding this, we naturally want to learn the path to bring it about. Once again, we see the Buddha's teachings on the four truths of the āryas, the framework for the Buddhist path. The first two of the four truths pertain to the cause and result of birth in cyclic existence—ignorance and suffering. The last two truths pertain to the cause and effect of freedom from that duḥkha—the path and the attainment of nirvāṇa.

As discussed earlier, there are three levels of duḥkha. The *duḥkha of pain* is the physical and mental pain that all beings abhor. The *duḥkha of change* refers to experiences and sensations that we usually identify as pleasurable. These are harder for ordinary people to identify as unsatisfactory, but when we think about them in greater depth, we see that they do not bring us lasting happiness, ultimate satisfaction, or security. In fact, they often leave us disillusioned or despondent.

The deepest unsatisfactory condition is the *pervasive duḥkha of conditioning*, the fact that our very existence is conditioned by ignorance and polluted karma. When the Buddha spoke about the disadvantages of duḥkha, he was principally referring to this form of duḥkha. When we can recognize the nature of cyclic existence in such terms, we will be able to develop the genuine aspiration to seek freedom from it.

Cultivating the wisdom that counteracts ignorance is the path to freedom. This wisdom that knows reality must be cultivated by the subtlest level of consciousness, a state of mind that is beyond our everyday, gross mental processes. Highest yoga tantra refers to eighty conceptions that are indicative of the gross level of mental processes. When these gross levels of mind gradually dissolve, we experience three increasingly subtler levels of consciousness—called the white appearance, red increase, and black near-attainment. When these, too, have dissolved, the innate mind of clear light dawns. It is at this subtlest level of consciousness that the wisdom that is the true antidote to our innate ignorance needs to be cultivated.

Therefore the demarcation between being fully awakened or imprisoned in cyclic existence is a function of this fundamental mind of clear light. If the fundamental innate mind of clear light remains obscured by the afflictions, we are in the state of cyclic existence. When the afflictions as well as their seeds and latencies have been removed from the fundamental mind of clear light, we attain liberation, and when the fundamental mind of clear light is freed from even the latencies of the afflictions, we attain buddhahood. So we can see that liberation and awakening are actually functions or states of the fundamental innate mind of clear light.

At first we understand saṃsāra and awakening in terms of our own duḥkha and our own minds, which inspires our renunciation of saṃsāric duḥkha. When we extend our perspective to see all other sentient beings in this light, compassion arises. Although we are not always aware of it, we are closely connected to all these sentient beings. Since we have been reborn for infinite lifetimes, they have been our parents and raised us with kindness in previous lives. In this life, too, our ability to stay alive depends on them. They grow our food, make our clothing, build our homes, treat our illnesses, and teach us everything we know. When we look deeply, we see that their kindness to us is limitless. Automatically, compassion and a sense of concern for their well-being arise within us.

Just as all of our experiences of mundane happiness—prosperity, security, friendship, or simply having enough to eat—come in relation to other sentient beings, the fruits of spiritual practice also rely on other beings. Cultivating compassion, practicing generosity, living in ethical conduct, and developing fortitude are all done in relation to other sentient beings. When we cultivate single-pointed concentration or wisdom, our underlying motivation has to do with other sentient beings. Likewise, our attainment of buddhahood depends on sentient beings: it can only occur when we truly dedicate ourselves to their welfare. Without sentient beings serving as the object of our compassion and care, there is no way for us to create the causes for supreme awakening. Therefore we can see that when it comes to our own happiness, be it mundane or transcendental, the presence of other sentient beings is indispensable. Seeing this, Śāntideva wonders in *Engaging in the Bodhisattvas' Deeds* why we revere the buddhas but not sentient beings. Shouldn't we try to forsake our self-preoccupation and cultivate a sense of endearment and compassion toward them?

One line in the *Seven-Point Mind Training (Blo sbyong don bdun ma)* of Geshe Chekawa (1101–75) says that emptiness is the supreme protection. The idea is that when we are confronted with an obstacle, we should reflect upon the emptiness of the person who is harming, the act of harm, and ourselves as the recipient of the harm. By contemplating that none of these has any independent self-nature but exists in dependence on the other two, we are able to counter the obstacle. Similarly, meditating on compassion toward the agent of harm is a strong method to cut the intensity of our sense of injury. Instead of harboring malice toward that person, cultivating a sense of concern, caring, and compassion for him is the most powerful kind of protection.

The tremendous benefits of altruism are evident in both our daily lives and our spiritual lives. When we cultivate an altruistic attitude toward colleagues, family members, or even people whose actions are repugnant to us, immediately fear, insecurity, and anxiety decrease. This occurs because underneath fear and insecurity is a suspicious attitude that looks at others as a threat. When we view others as being truly like ourselves—as living beings who naturally aspire for happiness and wish to overcome suffering—and on that basis develop concern for them, it has the immediate effect of releasing us from the grip of tension, mistrust, and jealousy.

Here it is evident that right away altruism creates ease and joy within us. We can mentally relax, sleep more deeply, and the taste of our food even improves. In a sense, as a byproduct of cultivating an altruistic attitude and engaging in altruistic action, our own interests are served, everything from temporary happiness to the long-term joy of full awakening. All of these are a function and result of altruism. If we think and act with compassion now, eventually, as buddhas, we will be able to benefit other sentient beings in the most effective way possible.

Although the wisdom realizing emptiness is very important on the path, it is bodhicitta that makes this realization a cause for us to attain the fully awakened mind of a buddha. Without great compassion and bodhicitta, the wisdom realizing emptiness alone cannot bring buddhahood.

REFLECTION

1. The altruistic intention of bodhicitta encompasses all sentient beings. Generating it uplifts our hearts and gives meaning to our lives.

2. Generating bodhicitta begins with wanting to free ourselves from the three kinds of duḥkha or unsatisfactory conditions—the duḥkha of pain, the duḥkha of change, and the pervasive duḥkha of conditioning.

3. Like us, other sentient beings are afflicted by the three types of duḥkha. Like us, they want to be happy and avoid misery. In addition, they have been and will continue to be kind to us. Generate compassion wishing them to be free from all duḥkha.

4. Based on this compassion, generate the altruistic intention to become fully awakened so that you can bring this about.

Mind Training

One of the practices I cherish and enjoy the most is mind training. Many texts have been written on this, and I myself often teach them. Mind training presents techniques for transforming adverse circumstances into the path. From a Buddhist perspective, all the misfortune we experience can be traced back to our own destructive actions—negative karma—which were motivated by our self-centered thought and self-grasping ignorance. The self-centered thought believes that our own happiness—including our own liberation—is more important than that of others, and self-grasping ignorance misapprehends the actual way all people and phenomena exist.

At the moment, our idea of success is that all external events unfold according to our wishes and all people behave in accordance with our ideas. We are happy when our desires and needs are fulfilled, but when we encounter adversity, we crumble and revert to old habits like complaining, sulking, or attacking those who interfere with our desires.

However, if our happiness depends on the behavior of others, we have no recourse and little control when things do not go as we wish. But if our happiness is rooted in our own thoughts and actions, we have the means to determine the nature of our future experiences. Remembering this, we resolve to subdue self-centeredness and self-grasping ignorance and the actions that are motivated by them. In short, not only is it counterproductive and futile to blame others for our problems and unhappiness, it is also unrealistic: they are not the true cause of our misery. By accepting responsibility for our unrealistic expectations and our previous harmful actions, we can transform their undesirable results into factors that help us to progress on the path to awakening. We do not deliberately seek out suffering, but when it comes our way, we can benefit from it by practicing mind training.

One method to transform adversity into the path to awakening is to contemplate cause and effect by understanding that our difficult experience is the result of our own past destructive actions, which were motivated by afflictions. In this meditative technique, we reflect that the karmic seeds created by those actions could have ripened as horrible suffering in an unfortunate rebirth, but now they are ripening as a suffering we can actually manage. That brings a sense of relief: "This is nothing compared to what it could have been." Then we understand that if we don't like this suffering, we must stop creating the causes for it. We renew our determination to live ethically and abandon harmful actions, because we know that harming others also brings suffering upon ourselves.

The practice of transforming adversity into the path sees difficulties as opportunities to learn and grow. If someone criticizes us unjustly or if we experience a painful physical injury, we contemplate the benefits of problematic situations. Adversity strengthens our renunciation because we see no lasting happiness is to be found in cyclic existence. Our conviction in the law of karma and its effects becomes stronger because we see that difficulties arise from causes that we ourselves created. Our compassion increases because we can empathize with the suffering of others. Bodhisattvas even look forward to problems because they are focused on the benefit that can be accrued from experiencing them with a virtuous attitude. That this can happen illustrates dependent arising: when we introduce new ways of thinking, our resultant mental state changes from unhappiness to appreciation. We are no longer constrained in our choice of emotional responses to difficult situations to fear, anger, or self-pity.

The mind-training practice instructs us on the development and implementation of the two bodhicittas. *Conventional bodhicitta* is the altruistic intention to attain awakening for the benefit of all sentient beings, and *ultimate bodhicitta* is the wisdom directly realizing the ultimate nature that relies on the extraordinary method of conventional bodhicitta. Practitioners of mind training generate compassion and conventional bodhicitta whether or not things are going well in their lives. They cultivate ultimate bodhicitta by meditating on emptiness. When doing so, in addition to using reason, they emphasize the practice of seeing all phenomena as like illusions as a way to approach the correct view of emptiness and to deal effectively with adversities. When we see a difficult situation as illusory and remember it is only an appearance to the mind—not an inherently existent problem—then our mind is more relaxed. Recalling impermanence also eases the mind. When we remember that everything is in a state of constant flux, we see that even our painful feeling is changing in every moment and will not endure forever.

Since we live in times when anger, wrong views, and violence abound, mind-training techniques are especially valuable. Sometimes we have difficulties procuring material requisites for life—food, shelter, clothing, and medicine. Other times we are beset by abuse and insult from others. Due to political or economic situations, we may find ourselves impacted by conflict or corruption against our wishes. We may face prejudice and oppression, and in extreme situations even war or genocide. Of course, if we can do something to avoid or escape horrible situations without harming others, we should definitely do it. But when we can't change our environment or the people in it, practicing mind training can lessen our misery and help us find inner strength we didn't know we had. If we don't practice mind training and remain stuck in our old views and emotional habits, these situations torment us. We may even be in danger of giving up Dharma altogether due to discouragement.

Mind training enables us to turn all these situations around so that we can benefit from them. If we change our way of thinking to make it more in tune with reality, most of our mental unhappiness will be dispelled. Fear comes from the self-centered attitude that fabricates a thousand worst-case scenarios. Recognizing the scenarios are fictions of our own mind and are highly unlikely to happen alleviates stress. Even if those scenarios do occur, we will have inner strength to deal with them and know that resources also exist in the community to help us. Of course, if we take sensible precautions to avert harm or disaster, that is wise, but being crippled by unrealistic fears does not help us prepare for the future.

Many Tibetans practiced mind training when they were imprisoned or tortured by the Communist Chinese after 1959, and for this reason, few of them suffer from post-traumatic stress disorder. Cultivating the two bodhicittas through mind training was the chief practice I relied on when I became a refugee in 1959, at age twenty-four, and it is the practice I have relied on since to maintain a peaceful mind despite not being able to return to my homeland and seeing the suffering of my people, the destruction of our culture, and the denigration of Tibet's pristine environment.

Mind training is very useful for dealing with psychological problems as well, for it gives us alternate perspectives on situations, so that we can break out of the rusty mental and emotional patterns that perpetuate unhappiness. To understand these techniques properly, receiving teachings on them and then applying these instructions to our own situation are important.

REFLECTION

1. Since problems are inescapable in cyclic existence, transforming adversity into the path to awakening is a skillful and useful technique to make every situation we encounter an asset to our spiritual practice.

2. How do we learn from misfortune? We practice thinking that unpleasant situations result from our own destructive actions and we make a strong determination not to perform those actions again in the future.

3. Consider other benefits we can derive from accepting an unpleasant situation—increasing our determination to be free from saṃsāra, enhancing compassion and bodhicitta, and developing the wisdom realizing reality.

Eight Verses

I recite the "Eight Verses of Mind Training" by Langri Tangpa (1054–1123) every day and regularly apply it to my life. When I'm delayed at an airport, I reflect on these verses, and before going into potentially difficult situations, I contemplate them as well. I will briefly explain this poem and encourage you to read it daily. Beyond just reading or reciting the eight verses, try to practice what they say by transforming your emotions and thoughts.

> 1. With the thought of attaining awakening
> for the welfare of all beings,
> who are more precious than a wish-fulfilling jewel,
> I will constantly practice holding them dear.

Imagine looking at sentient beings—friends, enemies, strangers, humans, animals, the sick, the healthy, the young, and the old—and seeing them all as equally precious. Such an attitude takes time to cultivate, but it is both realistic and beneficial because other sentient beings are a major source of our happiness and prosperity. Recall, as we explored above, that all the experiences that we value and seek depend upon cooperation and interaction with others. We depend on their efforts: they grow the food we eat, make the clothes we wear, construct the buildings and roads we use, and remove the trash we no longer want. Our feelings of comfort and security are due to sentient beings' help and support. Our knowledge comes from those who teach us; our talents depend on those who encourage us and provide us with opportunities. Even our progress on the path and our Dharma realizations depend on others, for without cultivating the aspiration to attain full awakening for their benefit, we cannot progress on the bodhisattva path. At buddhahood, too, buddhas' compassionate activities occur spontaneously and effortlessly in relation to sentient beings, who are the beneficiaries of their awakening influence. Without sentient beings, there would be no reason for bodhisattvas to work hard to become buddhas.

Our internal well-being depends on others as well. As we train our minds to see others in a more positive way, feelings of closeness and caring arise in us, which allow us to relax. On the other hand, if we dwell on others' faults and despise them, we are unhappy. A sense of goodwill toward others gives us inner strength in our daily lives, even in the face of difficulties.

When we experience pain, we are often weak-minded, feeling angry or overwhelmed because we lack control over a situation we did not choose. However, while we may feel some discomfort when empathizing with or feeling compassion for another's pain, it is accompanied by a certain inner stability and confidence, because we have accepted that pain voluntarily. Intriguingly, if we imagine taking on the suffering of others when we feel wretched, it alleviates our feelings of misery.

Buddhist teachings on compassion and altruism contain instructions such as, "Disregard yourself and cherish others." Understanding this advice properly is crucial, for it is given in the context of training the mind in compassion and used as an antidote to self-obsession. Compassion for others must be cultivated on the basis of self-respect, not out of guilt or feelings of unworthiness. We and others are equal in wanting to be happy and avoid pain. On that basis, it is suitable to care for and benefit everyone.

Self-preoccupation brings us misery: viewing everything—whether large or inconsequential—in terms of ourselves, we become overly sensitive, easily offended, irritable, and difficult to be with. The self-centered thought clouds our judgment and makes us foolish. If people are kind to us—even if they have the motivation to manipulate or deceive us—we like them. But if people who care about us point out one of our faults or try to prevent us from making a bad decision, we get angry. Skewing our interpretations of situations and people, self-centeredness is the cause of many mistakes and bad choices. Expanding our focus to care about others alleviates this unhealthy self-preoccupation and enables us to connect better with others. As social animals, healthy interactions with others gives meaning and purpose to our lives.

To be happy ourselves, we have to care about the welfare of others. We live in relation to others, and if they are distressed or oppressed, we will be surrounded by unhappy people, which is certainly not pleasant for us. If we care for others' well-being, they will be happy, and living among people who are content is more pleasant for us, too! In short, our own happiness comes about as a byproduct of genuinely caring for others. For this reason, caring for others' welfare is a wise way of caring for ourselves.

2. Whenever I am with others,
   I will practice seeing myself as the lowest of all,
   and from the very depth of my heart,
   I will respectfully hold others as supreme.

Building on the instructions in the first verse to see others as precious, the second verse points out that our arrogance is an obstacle to doing this. Love and compassion are based on seeing others as worthwhile and respecting them. These virtues are unbiased and go beyond the ordinary attitudes of cherishing those who help us and feeling pity for those less fortunate. The foundation of impartial love and compassion is knowing that we and others are equal in wanting happiness and not suffering.

To remedy our arrogance and partiality, we practice seeing ourselves as the lowest of all. This must be understood in the proper context. It does not mean denigrating ourselves or succumbing to low self-esteem. Thinking we are worthless certainly can't lead to compassion for others.

Seeing ourselves as lower is done in relative terms. In general, human beings are considered higher than animals because we have the ability to distinguish virtue and nonvirtue and understand the long-term results of our actions, whereas the ability of animals to do this is limited. From another perspective, however, we could say that animals are superior to human beings because they kill only because they are hungry or to protect their life when they are personally threatened, whereas human beings kill for sport and pleasure or when caught up in an ideology or wrong views.

This verse encourages us to cherish others and appreciate their good qualities. When we invite guests to our home, we respectfully regard them as supreme, prepare a delicious meal for them, and serve them first. In our workplace and family life, we respect those in leadership positions. Similarly, here too we regard others as "supreme" regardless of their or our social status.

When greed, hatred, or arrogance overwhelms us, we usually act without restraint, often in ways that we later regret. However, cultivating the thought that others are valuable and that we are just one among many people enables us to curb this behavior.

> 3. In all actions I will examine my mind
> and the moment an affliction arises,
> endangering myself and others,
> I will firmly confront and avert it.

The essence of the Dharma is liberation, the state of freedom from duḥkha and the afflictions that cause it. Afflictions are the real enemy that destroys our happiness, and the task of a Buddhist practitioner is to defeat this inner enemy. Confronting and averting afflictions does not mean suppressing them or pretending they do not exist, which can be psychologically unhealthy. Rather, we must notice afflictions and apply an antidote so that they cease, like tossing water on a fire to extinguish it.

Cultivating *introspective awareness*, which identifies afflictions the moment they arise, and *mindfulness*, which recalls their faults, helps us to exercise restraint, curtailing the harmful influence of the afflictions. Without applying mindfulness and introspective awareness, we risk giving afflictions free reign to wreak havoc in our lives. They will increase in strength to the point where they overwhelm common sense and reason, and we will find ourselves in dangerous, bewildering, or painful situations.

This verse describes how to apply antidotes to the afflictions at the level of manifest and felt experience. Since only very advanced practitioners are able to cut off afflictions at their root by meditation on emptiness, we must train ourselves in the easier technique of applying the antidote that counteracts a specific affliction. To counteract anger, we contemplate love and compassion; to oppose strong attachment, we reflect on the disgusting aspects or undesirable aspects of the desired object. To dissolve arrogance, we reflect on our shortcomings and all that we don't know or understand to increase our humility. Whenever I have a little tingling sense of conceit, I think of computers, about which I know next to nothing. That really calms my conceit!

REFLECTION

1. Contemplate the disadvantages of the afflictions.

2. Make a strong determination to notice and counteract them.

3. Spend time familiarizing yourself with the antidote to each affliction so that you will be able to recall and apply it easily whenever that affliction begins to arise.

4. Whenever I meet a person of bad nature
   who is overwhelmed by negative energy and intense suffering,
   I will hold such a rare one dear,
   as if I had found a precious treasure.

Difficult people challenge our ability to maintain compassion and peace of mind. When we encounter such people, the temptation is to react with strong anger or even violence. Some people may simply appear to us as hateful or offensive, and we need to be especially mindful in their presence to counter the afflictions that arise in our mind. Not only should we restrain from disdaining them, this verse advises us to hold them dear.

We can apply this teaching to larger social issues. We may have prejudices about certain groups of people—for example, people branded as criminals—and not want to include them within the scope of our compassion. In the case of the incarcerated, it is important for us to release our biased antipathy and make an extra effort to give them a second opportunity to become accepted and productive members of society and restore their self-esteem.

Likewise, we may habitually ignore or avoid those with disabilities and the terminally ill. We may be afraid we will contract the illness—even if it is not contagious or the chances of our getting it are slim—or we may feel uncomfortable witnessing their suffering. In these cases, too, we need to consciously cultivate empathy and compassion, remembering that we could one day find ourselves in similar circumstances and need the kindness of others.

Since we have the opportunity to overcome our deep-seated biases only by meeting people who are oppressed by negative energy and intense suffering, for us they are like precious treasures, giving us the chance to enhance our fortitude, empathy, and compassion. We may even be surprised by how much we can learn if we open our hearts and minds to their experiences.

> 5. When others, out of jealousy,
>   mistreat me with abuse, slander, and so on,
>   I will practice accepting defeat
>   and offering the victory to them.

From a conventional legal viewpoint, if we are wrongfully accused, we feel justified in reacting with righteous indignation. However, vehement outrage is not in our best interest—it simply stirs up an already contentious situation, forcing people to form factions and making genuine communication impossible.

Accepting defeat does not mean we make ourselves the world's doormat or accept responsibility for the wrongdoing of others. In some conflicts, capitulating could damage others or ourselves. Here, "offering the victory" to others means we don't have to have the last word in an argument or continually correct every small error others make. We can become more open and tolerant and less vindictive. When we are calm, we can try to clarify the situation and reach a resolution suitable to all.

Some people like to quarrel and enjoy picking a fight. In such a situation, it is best not to bite the hook. When we refuse to argue, the squabble can't continue. Giving the victory to others means restraining ourselves when we want to dominate others physically or verbally. Seeking to control or have power over others does not bring happiness to ourselves or others in the long term.

This is not to suggest that practitioners should simply yield to whatever harm or injustice is being inflicted upon them. In fact, according to the bodhisattva precepts, we should respond to injustice with a strong countermeasure, especially if there is danger that the perpetrator will continue acting destructively in the future or if others will be adversely affected. We need to be sensitive to the situation, and know when to let a situation pass and when to confront it. But whether we say something to the person or let it go, it is vital that our own mind harbors no resentment. That is what we are releasing when we offer up the victory.

> 6. When someone I have benefited
>   and in whom I have placed great trust
>   hurts me very badly,
>   I will see that person as my supreme teacher.

After helping someone, we usually expect at least a "thank you" in return, if not their help later on. Especially when we are close to someone, we tend to expect a lot from them. When, instead of responding to us in the way we would like, the other person is inconsiderate or inflicts harm, we often react with hurt and anger. Our sense of disappointment and betrayal is so deep that we may ruminate on the situation for a long time and plan our retaliation, wanting that person to hurt as much as we do. Such thinking can be all-consuming as we alternate between feeling sorry for ourselves and indignant toward the other person. However, taking revenge does not eliminate our pain; it only masks it temporarily by giving us a false sense of power. The only way to free ourselves from pain and anger is through forgiveness.

Forgiveness does not mean we condone the other person's action. It simply means that we are tired of being hurt and angry and are releasing those emotions because they're making us miserable. To do this, we practice seeing the other person as our teacher of fortitude. He is like a rare gem, because people who give us the opportunity to practice fortitude and forgiveness are rare.

Also helpful when we feel pained due to the betrayal of trust is to reflect that in the past we have behaved in such ways toward others. Although it is unpleasant to admit to ourselves, it is true that we have not always been exemplars when it comes to treating others fairly or keeping our promises and commitments. Since we have acted in hurtful ways to others, why are we surprised, incensed, or devastated when such behavior is done to us? It is wiser to accept the situation, forgive the other person, and work on making ourselves more reliable and trustworthy in the future so that we avoid creating the karmic cause to receive such treatment ourselves.

In the future, instead of throwing a blanket of mistrust over everyone to protect ourselves from being hurt, we should slow down and evaluate which areas and to what extent each individual can bear trust. We trust the pilot of a plane, who is a stranger, with our life when we board the plane, but we may not trust him to do our accounting. We may trust a friend to speak to us honestly but not to fix our car. One reason we experience pain from broken trust is that we mistakenly trusted people in areas where they cannot bear trust, or perhaps we had expectations of them that they could not fulfill or never agreed to fulfill. In the future, it is wiser to get to know others better and not have so many unverified assumptions about how they will think or act. In addition, even when people make promises, circumstances change, and they are unable to keep them or no longer want to. Human beings make mistakes and change their minds. Our expectations have to include space for these possibilities as well.

REFLECTION

1. Acknowledge your pain in situations when a betrayal of trust has occurred.

2. Contemplate that in the past you have acted in ways that others saw as breaking a commitment.

3. Extend compassion and forgiveness to yourself for such behavior.

4. Extend gratitude to those who betrayed your trust for the opportunity they gave you to practice fortitude and forgiveness.

7. In short, I will offer directly and indirectly
   every benefit and happiness to all beings, my mothers.
   I will practice in secret taking upon myself
   all their harmful actions and sufferings.

This verse describes the taking-and-giving meditation, where at the level of thought, we cultivate compassion so strong that we imagine taking upon ourselves the suffering of others as well as the afflictions and destructive karma that caused it. Upon taking these, we think that they destroy our own ignorance and self-centeredness. Then, with a loving heart, we imagine transforming our body, possessions, and merit into whatever others need and giving those to them. This meditation can be practiced in conjunction with our breathing, inhaling the suffering of others with compassion and exhaling with love all that they need to be happy.

To paraphrase the Kashmiri sage Paṇchen Śākyaśrī, "When I'm happy I dedicate this well-being for all sentient beings throughout space to be filled with happiness and its cause, merit. When I am miserable, may my suffering desiccate the suffering of all sentient beings. Through my experiencing difficulties, may all others be free of these." These are the thoughts of a true mind-training practitioner, someone who is at peace with himself and with others.

Practicing "in secret" may be understood in two ways. It suggests that this practice of love and compassion may not be suitable for beginners and should be taught only when someone has a certain depth of courage and commitment to the mind-training practice.

"In secret" also refers to how we should do this practice—discreetly, with humility and integrity, without drawing attention to ourselves. Geshe Chekawa advises that we radically transform our inner thoughts and emotions but act normally. When a person with little knowledge succumbs to the temptation to show off and assumes an air of importance, it cheapens his or her true experience and deceives others. We should definitely avoid this.

8. Without these practices being defiled by the stains of the
   eight worldly concerns,
   by perceiving all phenomena as illusory,

I will practice without grasping to release all beings
from the bondage of the disturbing, unsubdued mind and karma.

The eight worldly concerns consist of four pairs:

- Delight at receiving money and possessions and dejection at not receiving or losing them
- Delight with receiving praise and approval and dejection when receiving criticism or disapproval
- Delight with fame and a good reputation and dejection when infamous and notorious
- Delight with pleasurable sights, sounds, smells, tastes, and tangible objects and dejection with those that cause unpleasant feelings

These eight worldly concerns pollute our virtuous activities. For example, when I sit on the Dharma throne, if in the back of my mind there is the thought, "Did I give a good Dharma talk? Will people praise or criticize me?" my mind is polluted with the eight worldly concerns.

Perceiving all phenomena as illusory is one method to prevent the eight worldly concerns from contaminating our mind. Before we can see all phenomena as like illusions, we have to realize they are empty of inherent existence. The realization of emptiness does not come about through repeating this verse in our mind or chanting "empty, empty" while imagining nothingness. To develop a genuine insight into emptiness, we must employ reasoning to investigate how phenomena exist.

One of the most effective and convincing ways to understand that everything is empty of inherent existence is to contemplate dependent arising and interdependence. A unique quality of this approach is that it enables us to find the middle way between total nonexistence and independent or inherent existence. By understanding that things are dependent, we know they are not independent. Since independent existence and inherent existence are synonyms, we then know that they lack inherent existence. However, things are not totally nonexistent because they exist dependently. Contemplating in this way, we will not be lost in either absolutism or nihilism and will generate the correct view.

Once we gain insight into emptiness in our meditation, there is a new quality to our interactions with the world and the people in it. This is due to our awareness of the illusory nature of veil objects we encounter in daily life. With an understanding of both the empty and the illusory natures of persons and phenomena, we can work with compassion to skillfully lead others on the path so they, too, will be free from the unsubdued mind of afflictions and karma and will experience the joy and peace of full awakening.

8 | A Systematic Approach

AWAKENING REFERS TO the ultimate qualities of the mind; the path to awakening eliminates the impediments and enhances the qualities leading to this state. Tibetans translated *bodhi*, the Sanskrit word for awakening, as *jangchup*. *Jang* means "to cleanse" and in this case refers to true cessation, the cleansing or elimination of afflictions, their seeds, and latencies. *Chup* refers to having cultivated all positive qualities. *Jang* highlights the buddhas' abandonment of all faults, while *chup* denotes their qualities and realizations. Awakening is not granted by an external being but is attained through the process of cleansing and cultivating our minds. The potential to attain it is already within us: the nature of the mind is clarity and cognizance, so the capacity to perceive all phenomena is already there. We need to eliminate obstacles to doing so by realizing the empty nature of all phenomena.

Newcomers to Buddhism occasionally ask me what it feels like to be awakened. I don't know, but I think it must be a sense of deep satisfaction and fulfillment due to knowing reality. To use an analogy: When we are ignorant about something, we feel uncomfortable and try to understand it. Once we have understood it and that obstacle has lifted, we feel tremendous relief. We feel pleased because we are fully confident that our understanding is correct. When we become fully awakened, we will directly realize all that exists, so imagine the deep satisfaction we will experience then. This gives us an idea of the mental joy a buddha experiences.

Paths for Spiritual Development

To attain a buddha's qualities, we need to develop many diverse aspects of our body, speech, and mind. Throughout the ages, Buddhist masters have used various paradigms that set out a progressive path to do this, and in this chapter, we will explore some of these. These step-by-step presentations outline a systematic path that allows each person to practice at his or her own level and progress in a comfortable and gradual way.

We'll begin with Āryadeva's presentation of three stages of the path (CŚ 190):

> First prevent the demeritorious;
> next prevent self;
> later prevent views of all kinds.
> Whoever knows of this is wise.

This verse may be understood in two ways. In the first way, "First prevent the demeritorious" indicates the necessity of abandoning the ten paths of nonvirtue and practicing the ten paths of virtue in order to prevent an unfortunate rebirth and gain a fortunate one. "Next prevent self" means to abandon grasping at the coarse self of persons—a self-sufficient substantially existent person. While abandoning this grasping does not bring arhatship or buddhahood, it does stop the coarse afflictions, which is beneficial. "Later prevent views of all kinds" indicates realizing the emptiness of true existence and employing this wisdom to eradicate all afflictions from the root.

The second way to approach this verse is to start with the final goal and work backward. To attain full awakening, all cognitive obscurations must be eradicated, as indicated by "Later prevent views of all kinds." To eliminate these, it is not sufficient to contemplate the *object clear light*—the ultimate nature, emptiness—based on subtle dependent arising. From the viewpoint of highest yoga tantra, we must make manifest the *subject clear light*—the subtlest mind that arises after the eighty conceptions and three appearances have dissolved—and use it to realize suchness. Prior to this, we must realize emptiness and eradicate the afflictive obscurations, as indicated by "next prevent self." In order to do this, we need a continuous series of good rebirths in which we can practice the Dharma. The way to attain these is to "first prevent the demeritorious," the ten paths of nonvirtue.

In *Lamp of the Path*, Atiśa sets out three stages of the path according to three levels of practitioners: great, medium, and initial. The path of the person of great spiritual development eliminates the cognitive obscurations so that he or she can become a buddha in order to benefit all sentient beings most effectively. This individual aims for the highest, longest-lasting bliss and peace for self and others—full awakening—and thus wants to extinguish duḥkha and its causes for both self and others. The cognitive obscurations that impede full awakening are the subtle latencies of ignorance and the appearance of inherent existence that they create. To remove these, a person must cultivate bodhicitta, practice the six perfections, and unite serenity and insight on subtle emptiness. This is the path of the practitioner of great capacity.

The path of the person of medium spiritual development eliminates the afflictive obscurations—the afflictions, their seeds, and polluted karma that cause rebirth in cyclic existence. This person seeks liberation—the peace of nirvāṇa that is free from the cycle of uncontrolled rebirth. To do this, he or she practices the three higher trainings motivated by the determination to be free from cyclic existence and attain liberation.

The path of the person of initial spiritual development eliminates coarse negativities, such as the ten paths of nonvirtue—killing, stealing, unwise and unkind sexual conduct, lying, divisive speech, harsh words, idle talk, covetousness, malice, and wrong views. These ten cause unfortunate rebirths in the future as well as constant problems in this life. The beginning practitioner seeks the happiness in cyclic existence that comes from pacifying her gross mistaken thoughts, words, and deeds.

To express this path in a forward sequence, a practitioner must first and most urgently reduce his or her gross afflictions and harmful actions and practice the path of the ten constructive actions. Although his ultimate goal may be nirvāṇa or awakening, he must first deal with the most blatant obstacles to happiness by taking a defensive stand against them. He must especially prevent taking an unfortunate rebirth that would forestall his being able to practice the path for a long time.

The second level is the actual combat, going on the offensive to destroy the afflictions. A practitioner who is victorious over them attains nirvāṇa.

The third step is to remove the latencies or stains left on the mindstream by the afflictions. Having eliminated these, a practitioner becomes a fully awakened buddha.

LEVEL OF PRACTITIONER	THEIR DIRECT AIM	WHAT THEY PRACTICE	WHAT THEY ELIMINATE
Initial	Fortunate rebirth	Pacifying coarse harmful thoughts, words, and deeds and practicing the ten virtues	Ten nonvirtues
Middle	Liberation (arhatship)	The three higher trainings	Afflictive obscurations: afflictions, their seeds, and polluted karma causing rebirth in saṃsāra
Advanced	Full awakening (buddhahood)	The six perfections, four ways of gathering disciples, Vajrayāna	Cognitive obscurations: latencies of afflictions and appearance of inherent existence

These three levels or capacities of practitioners form the basic outline for the presentation of the teachings in this book. Certain meditations are prescribed to cultivate the motivation specific to each level and other meditations to actualize the intended result of that motivation. The meditations on precious human life, death and gross impermanence, and the possibility of taking an unfortunate rebirth help us generate the aspiration to have a fortunate rebirth. We attain such a rebirth by taking refuge in the Three Jewels and observing the law of karma.

Meditations on the first two of the four truths inspire the aspiration for liberation within us. Generating true paths by practicing the three higher trainings will bring about true cessations and liberation.

Meditation on the seven-point cause-and-effect instruction and the meditation on equalizing and exchanging self and others are the methods to generate bodhicitta, the aspiration for full awakening to benefit all sentient beings. The method that leads to awakening is the practice of the six perfections, four ways of gathering disciples,[43] and Vajrayāna.

LEVEL OF PRACTITIONER	MEDITATIONS THAT LEAD TO THE MOTIVATION OF THIS LEVEL	MOTIVATION	PRACTICES DONE TO ACTUALIZE THE RESULT OF THIS MOTIVATION
Initial	Precious human life, death and impermanence, unfortunate rebirth	To have a fortunate rebirth	Take refuge in the Three Jewels, observe the law of karma and its effects
Middle	The first two truths: true duḥkha and true origins	To attain true cessation, nirvāna	True paths: the higher trainings in ethical conduct, concentration, and wisdom
Great	Equanimity, seven-point cause-and-effect instruction, equalizing and exchanging self and others	Bodhicitta	Six perfections, four ways of gathering disciples, Vajrayāna

There are two types of initial-capacity practitioners, one superior and the other inferior. Superior initial-capacity practitioners seek higher rebirth as a human or a celestial being. Although they also seek the betterment of this life, their main focus is to create the causes for fortunate future lives. Lesser individuals think only of the betterment of this life and do not prepare for future lives, although they may still create virtuous karma through being generous, living ethically, and so on.

Those of you who grew up in cultures where the belief in rebirth is not prevalent may initially come to Buddhism with the motivation simply to improve the quality of this life. At the moment, you are ordinary initial-level individuals who would like to experience less stress and anger, better relationships, improved health, and more peace of mind in this life, and you look to the Buddha's teachings as a way to that end. By using the Dharma to become a more balanced person, you will engage in fewer destructive actions and more constructive ones. As time goes on, you will learn about the existence of future lives, cyclic existence, liberation, awakening, and the paths leading to them. As you think about these topics and gain conviction in them, your perspective will expand, and you will want to create the causes to have a peaceful death and a good rebirth. You will become aware of the dangers of cyclic existence and aspire to free yourself from it. As your heart opens to others more and more, the thought of attaining awakening for the benefit of all beings will grow in your heart. In this way, you will progress on the path in an organic way.

While Buddhism speaks about the importance of preparing for future lives, this does not mean we should disregard this life. If we want to have favorable future lives, properly taking care of this life by being an honest person who refrains from harming or cheating others is important. By keeping good ethical conduct, we will have fewer problems in this life and will create the causes for fortunate future lives.

The paths practiced by these three levels of practitioners are not separate paths. One person passes through all three stages as he or she progresses. To remove the cognitive obscurations preventing full awakening, we first must remove afflictive obscurations and free ourselves from the sufferings of cyclic existence. To attain liberation by severing the afflictions from their root, we must first rein in the attachment to the happiness of this life, which stimulates us to engage in the ten destructive paths of action. In this way, the practitioners of initial, middle, and advanced capacities refer to one person at three different times in their spiritual journey. Such a practitioner gradually and sequentially develops the three different levels, each one indispensable for those that follow.

On the other hand, the practice for each of these three individuals is complete. If, at present, we wish only for a fortunate rebirth, we will find a complete method to actualize our aspiration in the path of the initial-capacity practitioner. On the basis of first practicing the initial level, middle-level practitioners will find a complete path to fulfill their aspiration for liberation in the practice of the middle level. If we seek full awakening, we will proceed through all three stages by first practicing the first two stages, which will lead us to practice the advanced path. For advanced practitioners, the first two paths are said to be "paths *in common with* initial-capacity practitioners and middle-capacity practitioners" because they are not exclusively for the initial- and middle-capacity practitioners.

"In common with" also indicates that advanced practitioners aiming for full awakening do not practice the initial and middle paths exactly the same way as initial and middle-level practitioners do. While initial-level practitioners are satisfied with aspiring to improve the quality of their lives in cyclic existence, practitioners aiming for full awakening have a more extensive aspiration right from the beginning. Although they lack the realization of bodhicitta, they do all the initial and middle-level practices with some degree of bodhicitta.[44]

As a commentary on the *Lamp of the Path*, Tsongkhapa's *Lamrim Chenmo* followed Atiśa's presentation. The Sakya tradition also follows Atiśa's sequence when it presents abandoning four attachments. The first Sakya patriarch, Sachen Kunga Nyingpo, in "Parting from the Four Clingings" says:

> If you cling to this life, you are not a Dharma practitioner;
> if you cling to the three realms, that is not renunciation;
> if you cling to self-interest, you are not a bodhisattva;
> if grasping arises, it is not the view.[45]

Here, we begin by freeing ourselves from the eight worldly concerns that focus on the happiness of only our present life. By abandoning them, we will become an actual Dharma practitioner. We then cultivate renunciation of saṃsāra and the determination to be free from birth in all three saṃsāric realms. Contemplating that all other sentient beings suffer in saṃsāra just as we do, we broaden our perspective and generate the altruistic intention of bodhicitta. To fulfill bodhicitta's aim of attaining full awakening, we must gain the correct view of the two truths and abandon all grasping at the two extremes of inherent existence and total nonexistence by realizing emptiness. In this way, this short verse from the Sakyapas reflects the same approach of three ascending levels of motivation for Dharma practice presented by Atiśa.

The fifth-century Theravādin master Buddhaghosa thought along the same lines when he described inferior, medium, and superior levels of ethical conduct (Vism 1.33):

> . . . that [ethical conduct] motivated by craving, the purpose of which is to enjoy continued existence, is inferior; that practiced for the purpose of one's own deliverance is medium; the virtue of the perfections practiced for the deliverance of all sentient beings is superior.

Ethical conduct and other Dharma practices motivated by a desire for a good rebirth in cyclic existence, while virtuous, are inferior. Practices done with the wish to liberate ourselves from cyclic existence are excellent but not supreme; the perfections that are done with the wish to liberate all sentient beings are superior. While initially our motivation may be limited, as our wisdom and compassion expand, our motivation will as well.

The Four Truths and Three Levels of Practitioners

Describing the four truths from the perspective of the three levels of practitioners helps us understand the motivation, aim, and practice of each level.

For an initial level person who aspires for a good rebirth and happiness in cyclic existence, true duḥkha refers to coarse suffering, especially the misery involved in unfortunate rebirths. The true origins of this duḥkha are the ten nonvirtues and the coarse afflictions that motivate them, such as covetousness, malice, and wrong views. True cessation is the temporary freedom from an unfortunate rebirth, and the true path to attain that is abandoning the ten nonvirtues and engaging in the ten virtues.

For a person of middle capacity, who aspires for liberation, true duḥkha is the five aggregates of a saṃsāric being that are taken under the influence of afflictions and karma. True origins are the afflictive obscurations that cause rebirth in cyclic existence. True cessation is the freedom from all such rebirth, or more precisely the ultimate nature of the mind that has abandoned all afflictive obscurations by applying the true paths. True paths are āryas' realizations held by the wisdom that directly realizes emptiness.

For a person of advanced capacity, who aspires for full awakening, true duḥkha is one's own lack of omniscience and the duḥkha of all sentient beings. True origins are the cognitive obscurations and the self-centered attitude. True cessation is the cessation of cognitive obscurations at buddhahood, or more exactly the ultimate nature of the mind that has abandoned all cognitive obscurations by applying the true path. True paths are āryas' realizations held by the wisdom directly realizing emptiness and bodhicitta.

More Than One Approach

Our ultimate goal is to attain buddhahood and become the Three Jewels ourselves. The Dharma Jewel consists of the last two of the four truths—

true paths and true cessations. Our mind becomes the Dharma Jewel when we gain true paths and actualize true cessation. At this time we become the Saṅgha Jewel. When, motivated by bodhicitta, we fully actualize all true cessations, we become the Buddha Jewel. Thus, to understand the meaning of refuge in the Three Jewels, we need a deeper understanding of the Dharma Jewel, and this is based on understanding the four truths. Full understanding of the subtle aspects of true cessations depends on understanding the two truths—veil and ultimate—especially the ultimate truth, the emptiness of inherent existence.

While Atiśa's *Lamp of the Path* presents one sequence of steps to become the Three Jewels, the Prajñāpāramitā sūtras present another. Maitreya's *Ornament of Clear Realizations*, a treatise on the Prajñāpāramitā sūtras, presents this sequence by means of eight clear realizations[46] that are characterized by seventy topics. The first clear realization—the exalted knower of all aspects (omniscience)—has ten principal characteristics that define a buddha's mind: bodhicitta, instructions, and so forth.[47] The topic of instructions begins with the two truths, which encompass all phenomena, followed by the four truths, which are the objects of practice. After this, taking refuge in the Three Jewels is discussed, followed by nonclinging, tireless effort, and so forth.

Haribhadra wrote *Clear Elucidations* (*Sphuṭārthā*), the most widely used commentary on the *Ornament of Clear Realizations*. In it he speaks of two kinds of practitioners: those of sharp faculties who are very intelligent and deeply analyze the meaning of the teachings, and those of more modest faculties who follow due to faith in the Buddha and the scriptures. The principal audience for Haribhadra's commentary is sharp-faculty practitioners, and the above sequence is especially useful for them.

The audience for Atiśa's *Lamp of the Path* is different. He wrote this text at the behest of the prince Jangchup Ö, who requested a teaching that was suitable for Tibetans—the vast majority of whom were Buddhists. He wanted instructions they could easily put into practice that would enable Buddhism to flourish once again in Tibet. In response, Atiśa outlined the sequence of the three levels of practitioners.

When I give general instructions on the Buddhadharma to educated people who are new to Buddhism, I prefer to use the sequence in the *Ornament of Clear Realizations* to present the overall structure of the Buddhist path, starting with the compassionate bodhicitta motivation and moving on to the instructions. This helps them to understand how various points fit into the framework. While I can't go into depth on these points with beginners, everyone appreciates the notion of compassion, so I speak of that first. I then briefly introduce the two truths so that people will be aware that the way things appear and the way they actually exist differ. From there, I go onto the four truths of the āryas, which establishes the framework for the path to liberation. In this context, turning to the Three Jewels for refuge and guidance makes sense. For this reason, in this series taking refuge in the Three Jewels will be presented in conjunction with the four truths rather than in the context of the initial-level practitioner, as in the lamrim presentation.

I encourage those of you who have completed philosophical studies and appreciate the sequence of instruction in the Prajñāpāramitā sūtras and the *Ornament of Clear Realizations* to integrate that sequence into your lamrim teachings. This will benefit your students. I also suggest you teach the tenet systems. Lamrim is more practical, while tenets are more academic. If your students study both, they will develop a clear sense of purpose for Dharma practice and a deeper understanding of emptiness.

A teacher will vary his or her approach depending on the audience. When Nāgārjuna taught *Precious Garland,* his audience was a king—a person who was interested in the Dharma but also had worldly responsibilities. To him, he first presented the method to secure fortunate rebirths followed by the method to attain liberation. On the other hand, when he taught *Commentary on Bodhicitta* (*Bodhicittavivaraṇa*), which explains a verse from the *Guhyasamāja Root Tantra,* the audience was of advanced capacity—specifically practitioners of highest yoga tantra—and this approach suited them.

When instructing a large group, spiritual mentors give teachings designed for the public. Here they usually follow a particular text and give a broad presentation of the path to address the needs of many people in general. When teaching a small group or an individual, spiritual mentors give instructions according to the needs of those specific individuals. It is important not to confuse these two situations and think that because our spiritual mentor gave one instruction to a specific individual that everyone should follow it.

The order of presenting topics may differ as well. The *Ornament of Clear Realizations* briefly mentions the wisdom realizing emptiness and then proceeds to bodhicitta; the *Commentary on Bodhicitta* presents emptiness first, followed by the cultivation of bodhicitta and the bodhisattva practice. This is the approach for intelligent disciples. Although bodhicitta comes later in the lamrim sequence, Śāntideva teaches it at the beginning of *Engaging in the Bodhisattvas' Deeds* so that all subsequent meditations and practices will be directed toward awakening.

No matter which order we learn bodhicitta and emptiness, it is helpful to cultivate an understanding of both even as we emphasize the practices of the initial and middle levels in our personal practice. In this way, our meditation on precious human life, death and impermanence, and so forth will be supported by some degree of bodhicitta and the wisdom understanding emptiness. In addition, our meditations on the topics of the initial and middle levels will increase our appreciation of and urgency to cultivate bodhicitta and practice the six perfections.

Teachings for a Contemporary Audience

Atiśa composed the *Lamp of the Path* with the needs of eleventh century Tibetans in mind. He did not go into detailed philosophical debates or extensive reasonings when writing that text because his audience already believed in the Buddha's teachings. They simply required a concise, straightforward teaching explaining how to practice from the beginning of the path up to awakening.

With Buddhism now spreading internationally, the audience is very different. These people need to hear the rational arguments proving rebirth, liberation, the existence of the Three Jewels, and karma and its effects that are found in the treatises of the great Indian sages. Without a clear understanding of these topics, their comprehension of the path to awakening will not be complete.

I read some lamrim notes written by the respected Geluk master Tseten Shabdrung (1910–85). He commented that when we contemplate a lamrim topic, we should integrate points from the major treatises on the Perfection of Wisdom and the Middle Way into our reflection. In this way our study of the great philosophical treatises and our lamrim practice will complement each other. This is the method used by the Kadam Shungpawa—the Kadam "great text" tradition headed by Geshe Potowa.[48]

An understanding of the principal subjects studied in the great monastic universities—the Perfection of Wisdom, Middle Way, Reasoning and Epistemology, Abhidharma, and Vinaya—is most helpful to facilitate our practice of lamrim. When Tibetans first began teaching Westerners, very few philosophical texts were translated into Western languages. Nowadays, more translations and study guides are available, making the study of these classical texts possible.

Some people may have heard that since lamrim encompasses all the teachings of the Buddha, it is sufficient to rely on it alone. This is true in the sense that the lamrim summarizes the meaning of the great treatises so that someone who has spent years studying them can easily identify the important points for meditation. Those who have not studied these important texts will benefit from learning something about them.

Modest-faculty disciples rely more on faith, seeing the Buddha as a perfect spiritual master and lineage teachers from Nāgārjuna up to their own teacher as reliable spiritual mentors. These people are not as interested in in-depth study, whereas those of sharp faculties are curious and want to learn more. They question the meaning of the teachings they hear and read; they want to know why a particular sage explained the Dharma the way he did. Buddhism encourages us to investigate and explore. People who are curious, with a genuine wish to investigate the Dharma, are real followers of the Buddha. For these students, lamrim alone is not sufficient; they must rely on the great treatises.

If we lack proper understanding of the exact meaning of emptiness, true cessations, nirvāṇa, and awakening, what is the basis of our devotion? If we understand how it is possible to eliminate ignorance and afflictions completely, our conviction in the Buddha and reliance on his teachings will be firm. Without learning and contemplating the Buddha's teachings, it is difficult to clearly distinguish the Buddhist path from paths espoused by other teachers, and as a result our faith in the Three Jewels will not be firm. We see people who change beliefs from one day to the next. Although they may attribute their changeability to open-mindedness, it seems to me that it is due more to confusion. If they learn and contemplate the Buddha's teachings, especially the philosophical treatises that describe emptiness and dependent arising, this confusion will give way to clarity.

The lamrim teaches us how to go for refuge in the Three Jewels by understanding their unique qualities that are not possessed by other spiritual guides. When we have such an understanding, we naturally take refuge in the Three Jewels: no one needs to encourage us to do so, and no one can discourage us from taking refuge in them.

We may hear about pith instructions and ear-whispered teachings that are transmitted orally from teacher to disciple.[49] Do not think that these instructions are separate from Nāgārjuna's texts and the other classical treatises. Whatever is in the ear-whispered teachings and the pith instructions is also in these texts. There are no secret teachings apart from what we study in the classical treatises. If we don't know how to integrate the teachings in the great treatises into our practice, the fault is our own, and it is up to us to rectify it.

Value of the Stages of the Path

The lamrim's gradual, systematic approach to the path has many advantages.

We will see that the Buddha's teachings are not contradictory. If we compare the Buddha's advice to various disciples, we may think he contradicted himself. In some sūtras the Buddha said there is a self, in others he spoke of selflessness. In some scriptures he spoke of the importance of abandoning alcohol, in others he allowed it in particular, rare circumstances.

These differences occur because the Buddha guided sentient beings with vastly different dispositions and tendencies, at different levels of the path. His motivation was the same in all instances: to benefit the person and to gradually lead him or her to awakening. To fulfill this purpose, he tailored his instructions to suit the current capacity of each disciple. Saying that a self exists was a skillful way to guide people who fear selflessness. Later, when they were more spiritually mature, he clarified that there is no inherently existent self. For the vast majority of people, consuming intoxicants harms their spiritual practice and should be given up. For highly accomplished tantric practitioners who have renunciation, bodhicitta, and the wisdom realizing emptiness, consuming a small amount of alcohol may benefit their meditation in particular circumstances.

This advice is not contradictory because the Buddha's motivation is the same in all cases. If a person walking on a narrow path with precipices on both sides is too close to the left precipice, a skillful guide will call out, "Go right!" But if she is too close to the right precipice, the guide will direct, "Go left!" Taken separately, these may seem to be contradictory instructions. However, when we understand the context and the long-term purpose, we see there is no contradiction and only benefit.

Not only does the Buddha give different teachings for different individuals, his advice to one person will vary according to the circumstance at different times, depending on the distortions most prominent in that person's mind. Initially, someone may conceive of the self as a permanent, unitary, independent soul, in which case the Buddha will teach how to refute such a self. If at another time in her practice, she may conceive of the external world as independent from perception, the Buddha will teach the Cittamātra view that there is no external world distinct from the mind to help her dissolve that false grasping.

We will comprehend all of the Buddha's teachings as personal instructions. Some people mistakenly believe some scriptures are for study and others for meditation and practice. When we understand the step-by-step approach of the lamrim, we see that all teachings relate in one way or another to subduing defilements and cultivating good qualities and thus are relevant to our practice. Our mind is so complex and the afflictions are so powerful that one practice alone cannot eliminate all afflictive mental states at once. The stages of the path is a systematic strategy for gradually overcoming destructive attitudes and emotions by instructing us in a variety of topics and meditation techniques to develop many different aspects of our minds.

Although the realization of emptiness is the ultimate antidote to all afflictions, at the beginning of the path our understanding of emptiness is too weak to be an effective remedy. Applying some of the techniques that are specific to each affliction, such as those found in the mind-training teachings, enables us to subdue our gross anger, attachment, and confusion. This more pacified state of mind, in turn, is more conducive to meditating on emptiness.

The broad layout of the lamrim enables us to understand how all the various teachings fit together in a cohesive whole designed for one person to practice. This helps us to avoid pitfalls and detours, and to know how to integrate all the key points of the path into our practice in a balanced way so that we will be able to fulfill our spiritual aspiration.

We will discover the intention of the Buddha. The Buddha's ultimate intention was to fulfill all beings' aspirations for fortunate rebirth, liberation, and full awakening. The structure of the stages of the path clearly illustrates how to actualize these aims.

We will be deterred from the great error of rejecting the Buddha's teachings. Since buddhas and bodhisattvas teach all aspects of the path to lead diverse sentient beings to awakening, we should respect all of the Buddha's teachings. Nowadays we unfortunately find people who criticize not only other religions but also other Buddhist traditions. While debate increases our understanding, deprecating teachings that are helpful to others is not beneficial. If we say we respect the Buddha and want what is best for others, how can we disparage teachings meant for disciples whose dispositions and interests differ from our own?

Knowledge of the stages of the path enables us to understand and respect the practices of other Buddhist traditions as well as the people who engage in them. Knowing the three spiritual aims of sentient beings—fortunate rebirth, liberation, and awakening—as well as the meditations to cultivate these aims and the meditations to actualize them, we will know where in this schema a specific teaching belongs.

Two Aims and Four Reliances

In this chapter, we have focused on the broad perspective of the lamrim and how that gradually leads a person to full awakening. Now we will synthesize the path into two aims and then examine the four reliances that are important for fulfilling the lamrim's ultimate purpose, the attainment of full awakening.

Nāgārjuna says (RA 5–6):

Due to having faith, one relies on the practices;
due to having wisdom, one truly understands.
Of these two, wisdom is foremost,
but faith must come first.

One who does not neglect the practices
through attachment, anger, fear, or confusion
is known as one with faith,
a superior vessel for the highest good.

These verses express the two aims of the Buddhadharma—the attainment of higher rebirth and the highest good (liberation and awakening). Attaining a higher rebirth corresponds to the initial motivation in the lamrim, while attaining the highest good fulfills the middle or advanced motivation. As the means to attain these, the Buddha taught two methods: faith and wisdom respectively. The obstructions to these two goals are two kinds of ignorance: the ignorance of the law of karma and its effects and the ignorance of the ultimate nature of reality. To eliminate these, the Buddha instructed us to cultivate understanding of two types of dependent arising: the understanding of causal dependence and the understanding of dependent designation.

By meditating on causal dependence, we understand that our happiness and suffering arise from virtue and nonvirtue. Faith is required to accept the subtle details of karma and its effects, which is an obscure phenomenon that cannot be known directly by our senses. With trust in karma and its effects, we will rein in gross attachment, anger, fear, and confusion, and thus will cease nonvirtuous actions and engage in virtuous ones. In this way, we will attain a fortunate rebirth in the future.

The understanding of dependent designation leads to the realization of emptiness. That wisdom is the antidote to the ignorance of the ultimate nature and will eradicate all obscurations completely. By cultivating our understanding of the complementary nature of dependent designation and emptiness, we will be able to attain liberation and awakening.

AIM	MEANS	OBSTACLES THAT ARE PACIFIED	MEDITATION ON DEPENDENT ARISING
Higher rebirth	Faith	Ignorance of karma and its effects, gross afflictions	Causal dependence leading to ethical conduct
Highest good	Wisdom	Ignorance of the ultimate nature of reality, all obscurations	Dependent designation, complementing the realization of emptiness

There is a lot to contemplate in these two short verses by Nāgārjuna. When we examine them carefully, we find that they contain the entire path to awakening.

Of the two purposes for engaging in the Buddhist path, the highest good is foremost. To attain it, the wisdom realizing the empty nature of phenomena is essential. This wisdom is not gained through blind belief or through prayer but by reason. The four reliances—found in the *Sūtra on the Four Reliances* (*Catuḥpratisaraṇa Sūtra*) and the *Sūtra Unraveling the Thought*— guide us in doing this.

1. Rely principally not on the person but on the teaching.
2. With respect to the teaching, rely not on mere words but on their meaning.
3. With respect to the meaning, rely not on the interpretable meaning but on the definitive meaning.
4. With respect to the definitive meaning, rely neither on sense consciousnesses nor on conceptual consciousnesses but on the nondual wisdom that realizes emptiness directly and nonconceptually.

The four reliances illustrate a gradual progression in a practitioner's development. Here "rely" means to mentally rely on that which is a source of reliable knowledge, nondeceptive and reasonable to trust. Throughout the path, we must rely on a teacher, learning first the words of the teaching and then understanding their meaning. Regarding the meaning, we rely first on the meaning of the interpretable teachings that describe the stages of the path and the coarser views of selflessness, and then the meaning of the definitive teachings that describe the complete view of emptiness. When we meditate on emptiness, our initial understanding is with a conceptual consciousness. Through familiarization with emptiness, we break through the veil of conception and attain direct, nonconceptual, nondualistic perception of emptiness.

To explore these in more depth:

1. Rely principally not on the person but on the teaching. Here "person" refers chiefly to ordinary beings who teach many different paths that they have heard from others, misunderstood, or made up. Rather than depend on people whose minds are under the influence of ignorance, it is wiser to depend on scriptures taught by the Buddha that explain nondeceptive methods to attain awakening. Instead of using "The person who taught this is exceptional" as the reason to follow a teaching, we should apply reason to examine the words and meaning of the teaching.

Even with the Buddha, not everything he said should be taken literally. Sometimes he taught a provisional view as a skillful means to lead a particular individual or group to the final path. To some people, he taught the tathāgatagarbha theory, which, taken literally, seems to affirm the existence of a permanent self. However, the meaning in the Buddha's mind was the ultimate nature of the mind—its emptiness of true existence—which is permanent. Although such teachings are not to be taken literally, they are considered nondeceptive in that the meaning in the Buddha's mind is true and reliable. Similarly, when the Buddha taught nihilists that there is a self-sufficient substantially existent person, his words are not to be taken literally. He taught this so that they would not deny karma and its effects and would understand that there is a self that carries karma to future lives and experiences its effects.

2. With respect to the teaching, rely not on mere words but on their meaning. If we are attentive to only the words of a teaching, we may neglect its meaning. This inhibits its ability to guide us on the right path. Instead of thinking we understand a topic simply because we can use complex academic terminology and language, we should use our intelligence to understand the meaning of the teaching. We should also focus on the meaning in the Buddha's mind, not on words that can be misunderstood when taken literally.

When we want to understand the nondeceptive mode of existence of all phenomena, rather than rely on teachings about bodhicitta and the Buddha's qualities, we should rely on teachings on the emptiness of inherent existence, which is the object of exalted wisdom. This wisdom has the ability to cut the root of saṃsāra. Furthermore, we should rely on reason and cultivate reliable cognizers—nondeceptive minds that know their object correctly.

While the four reliances are taught specifically in relation to realizing emptiness, the first two apply to learning any Dharma topic. Instead of being charmed by an ordinary person's charisma, we must listen to what he or she teaches. In addition, rather than becoming enchanted with lofty sounding words, we must contemplate their meaning and try to understand them.

3. With respect to the meaning, rely not on the interpretable meaning but on the definitive meaning. "Interpretable meaning" refers to veil truths—which include all the objects that exist and function in the world. To understand the liberating teachings on emptiness, we must rely not on texts that speak about veil truths such as the defects of cyclic existence or the benefits of bodhicitta. While these teachings are important and necessary to actualize the path to full awakening, they do not express the ultimate nature. We should also avoid taking veil truths—such as the multifarious objects of the senses—as the true mode of existence but understand that they mistakenly appear inherently existent, although they are not. The meaning to rely on is phenomena's subtlest mode of existence, their mere absence of inherent existence. Since all phenomena lack inherent existence, their emptiness is called the "one taste" of all phenomena.

4. *With respect to the definitive meaning, rely neither on sense consciousnesses nor on conceptual consciousnesses but on the nondual wisdom that realizes emptiness directly and nonconceptually.* When progressing on the path to liberation in accord with the Buddhadharma, we should not be satisfied with conceptual understanding of emptiness but continue to meditate until we gain an unpolluted wisdom consciousness that directly and nonconceptually realizes emptiness. From the perspective of this wisdom, there is no dualistic appearance of a cognizing subject (the person or the consciousness) or of a cognized object (in this case emptiness). While gaining the correct conceptual, inferential realization of emptiness is essential, it is not the culmination of the process of realizing the ultimate nature. Ordinary beings as well as āryas can have profound conceptual understanding, but we must seek to gain an ārya's nonconceptual wisdom that arises in the wake of analytical meditation on emptiness. To do this, we must look beyond the appearances to our sense consciousnesses and our conceptual mental consciousness of the aggregates and so forth that are the substrata of emptiness—that is, the objects whose ultimate nature is the emptiness of inherent existence. Instead we must cultivate a direct, yogic reliable cognizer of emptiness—a mind that perceives emptiness free of conceptual appearances. This mind knows its own ultimate nature. Emptiness directly appears to this mind, and the mind nonconceptually ascertains it. At this time, the appearance of subject and object ceases, and the mind and emptiness become undifferentiable, like water poured into water.

The progression illustrated by the four reliances indicates that we must not be complacent with one level of understanding but continue until we gain direct experience of the path and actually free our mind from defilements.

9 | Tools for the Path

To practice the Dharma successfully, more than information and a meditation cushion are required. We need a proper motivation and good, practical advice that will help to overcome hindrances. This chapter speaks of the mental tools we will need to progress along the path, such as faith and wisdom. We'll also explore the role of prayers and rituals, of purification and the collection of merit, and of memorization and debate in cultivating the three wisdoms: the wisdoms arising from learning, reflecting on the teachings, and meditating on them.

General Advice

Learning the Dharma is different from learning subjects in school. Not only is our motivation different—we seek the method to attain fortunate rebirths, liberation, or awakening—but also the methodology is different. Our spiritual mentors present topics that are comparatively easy to understand as well as those that are more challenging in the same Dharma talk. Sometimes their response to our questions leads to more confusion. Our mentors instruct us to think about the topic and discuss it with others, but we want them to give us the right answer. Unlike academic studies in the West, where we are expected to remember and understand everything our teacher says so that we can pass a test, this is not necessarily the case in Dharma education. While we should try to remember and reflect on the salient points of a lecture, we are not expected to understand all the intricacies of a topic at once. Teachers explain a topic to "plant seeds" in our mindstreams so that we will become familiar with the vocabulary. Having heard the topic once, the next time we hear it, we will be able to focus on the concepts being presented. By hearing and reflecting on a teaching repeatedly, our understanding and ability to integrate the meaning into our lives will gradually increase.

Understanding the Dharma is not dependent on worldly intelligence. Some people who are brilliant in academic studies or worldly affairs have great difficulty understanding Dharma principles. On the other hand, some people who do not do well in school quickly catch the intent of the Buddha and practice diligently. For this reason, we should not be arrogant because we have worldly intelligence and not put ourselves down if we lack it.

We need to be patient with ourselves and let go of unrealistic expectations of quick attainments. We should also avoid comparing ourselves to others and feeling proud that we are more advanced than our friends or lamenting that we lag behind them. Each person has different predispositions from previous lives, so no two people will progress at the same speed or in the same way. Comparison of this sort only breeds jealousy, arrogance, and competition, qualities that waste time and are not conducive for transforming our mind.

Similarly, due to karmic connections in previous lives, our friends may be drawn to a particular teacher who does not particularly inspire us and vice versa. Rather than be influenced by peer pressure, we must choose our teachers depending on the quality of guidance we receive from them and the depth of connection we feel with them. We should avoid comparing the practices our teachers instruct us to do with those our friends are prescribed. Because no two sentient beings are identical, the Buddha taught a wide variety of practices so people could find those suitable for them. That does not make one practice better and another worse; it simply means that one practice is more suitable for one person and a different practice for another person. At a buffet dinner, one person may like rice and another noodles. Debating which is best, trying to convert our friends to our preference, or feeling out of place because we aren't attracted to the one our friends like are useless. The point is for each person to eat food that nourishes his or her body. We should study with the teachers who inspire us and practice in the way that works best for us.

Strong, continuous, and stable spiritual experiences are more reliable than powerful, fleeting ones. Some beginners have a strong emotional feeling that they must renounce everything and meditate in solitude for the rest of their lives. Instead of immediately searching for an isolated retreat hut, they should keep practicing and see if after a year the feeling still has the same intensity. If it does, they should consult their teacher for guidance.

For most people, meditating in isolated retreat for years is not an option or even a preference. The vast majority of us need to balance Dharma study and sitting meditation with our daily-life activities. Formal, daily sitting practice enables us to deepen and integrate our understanding of the Dharma in a concentrated way, but the actual determining factor of the effectiveness of our practice manifests in our behavior. There's the story of someone who meditated in an isolated cave for years and thought his practice was progressing well. But when he went down to the town to get supplies, someone criticized him; his anger immediately flared, and he began shouting at the other person. Similar incidents in our life show us which disturbing emotions we need to put more energy into taming in our sitting practice.

People often ask how to balance formal Dharma practice with actively engaging in projects that benefit others. If you are a householder, "fifty-fifty" is a good balance. But remember that how this balance manifests in your life will change according to circumstances, so be flexible. Stabilize your compassion through formal practice and express it through active service to others. Work at transforming your motivation, thus making your daily activities part of the Dharma path.

If you feel stressed by your service work for others or become angry at or disappointed in the people whom you are trying to help, step back, rest, and take more time for personal practice. During your meditation practice, focus on developing a compassionate motivation, fortitude, and joyous effort. Learn to accept the limits of the change you can enact in a world under the influence of afflictions and polluted karma.

Sometimes we go too far in the other direction, becoming complacent in our Dharma studies or in a stagnant meditation practice. In these cases, contemplate impermanence and death as well as the suffering of sentient beings to reinvigorate your compassion.

REFLECTION ——————————————————————————

1. A balanced life entails sharing our time among many activities: Dharma practice, socially engaged projects that benefit others, work, caring for friends and family, exercise, and other activities.

2. What is a practical way to prioritize these activities in your life?

3. Given your talents and limitations, think of a realistic way to apportion your time and energy that will bring you satisfaction, not stress.

———————————————————————————————————————

Wisdom and Faith

Wisdom and faith complement and reinforce each other on the path. Whereas faith enables us to be inspired and receptive, wisdom gives us a clear mind that understands both conventional existence and ultimate reality.

Wisdom is an analytical mind that deeply understands its object, such as impermanence or selflessness. Analysis is not intellectual gymnastics used to impress others; it involves deep investigation into the nature of objects and leads to understanding and knowledge.

The English word *faith* does not have the same connotation as the Sanskrit word it translates, *śraddhā*. To understand what faith is, we must look beyond our previous associations with the word to its meaning. Faith is confidence and trust in the Three Jewels; it is not blind belief. A virtuous and joyous mental factor, it enriches our spiritual practice and arises when we admire the Three Jewels, aspire to be like them, or deeply understand the teachings. Accordingly, the Mind and Awareness texts speak of three types of faith or trust: admiring faith, aspiring faith, and believing faith.

Admiring faith arises when we learn about the excellent qualities of the Three Jewels or witness the good qualities of our spiritual mentors and admire them. It may also arise from reading the biographies of previous practitioners, contemplating their diligence and determination, and reflecting on the difficulties they overcame to practice the Dharma. This faith clears away mental distress and makes the mind joyful. In extreme cases, admiring faith could degenerate into blind faith, which has little value and may be dangerous. But authentic admiring faith is a vital aid on the path that serves to orient our efforts in a positive direction.

Aspiring faith arises when we develop the wish to attain the excellent qualities of the Three Jewels. It arises from reflecting on the possibility of removing defilements and attaining liberation, and it gives purpose and energy to our practice. When we know the benefits of serenity and concentration, we have faith in them and aspire to attain them.

Believing faith is of two kinds. The first believes the truth of the Buddha's teachings because they were taught by the Buddha and our spiritual mentors and we trust them. This faith may arise due to reasons that we have only partially verified or without applying reasoning.

The second type of believing faith is based on conviction and arises after having examined and understood a teaching. Because it often involves a reasoning used to verify the topic, this faith is stable. Having contemplated the four truths for a long time, we become convinced that they accurately describe our predicament and how to remedy it. After studying and using reasoning to investigate the ultimate nature of phenomena, we experience a calm conviction that all persons and phenomena are empty of inherent existence. We are confident that by realizing this directly, we will be able to uproot the self-grasping ignorance that is the source of all duḥkha. In these examples, believing faith is directed toward the Dharma Jewel—true paths and true cessations. From this, firm confidence in the Buddha and the Saṅgha Jewels easily follow. Such faith borne of conviction stabilizes our practice, enabling us to pursue the Dharma in depth.

Tsongkhapa illustrates this second type of believing faith arising from reason in his "Praise to Dependent Arising":

> Having seen the truth, you taught it.
> Those following you will leave all troubles far behind,
> for they will cut to the root of every fault.
>
> However, those outside your teachings,
> though they practice long and hard,
> are those who beckon back faults,
> for they are welded to views of self.

Ah! When the wise see the difference,
how could they not revere you
from the very depths of their hearts![50]

The second type of believing faith arises from deep conviction that is born from clearly knowing and analyzing the distinction between the Buddha's teachings and those of masters who adhere to views of inherent existence. After examining both teachings with discerning wisdom and clearly seeing the truth in the Buddha's teachings, the wise have no choice but to feel great faith, trust, and respect for the Buddha. Tsongkhapa expresses this with these moving words:

Alas! My mind was defeated by ignorance.
Though I've sought refuge for a long time
in such an embodiment of excellence,
I possess not a fraction of his qualities.

Nonetheless, before the stream of this life
flowing toward death has come to cease,
that I have found slight faith in you—
even this I think is fortunate.[51]

In the first verse, "qualities" refers chiefly to insight into emptiness. Tsongkhapa acknowledges that for a long time ignorance has obscured his mind. Yet due to gaining some understanding of emptiness, he experienced faith based on conviction in the doctrine of emptiness taught by the Buddha with great compassion. Considering how few people encounter teachings on emptiness and among those, how few gain even a modest understanding of it, Tsongkhapa felt fortunate to trust the truth of non-inherent existence. Pondering this will increase our aspiring faith and motivate us to practice like the Buddha did and attain the same depth of realization.

Learn the teachings well and use reason to reflect on their meaning. If you do not find any logical fallacies or contradictions, you will have believing faith in the path and the possibility of attaining it. That faith, in turn, will help increase your trust in those topics that cannot be understood completely through factual inference, such as the intricacies of karma and its effects. Believing that actions bring concordant results is sufficient to help us curb destructive actions and act constructively, thus accumulating merit, which aids the increase of wisdom. In Buddhism, wisdom and faith are not contradictory, and when properly cultivated, they increase each other.

Haribhadra, in a commentary on Maitreya's *Ornament of Clear Realizations*, speaks of having faith not only in the Three Jewels but also in the treatises that take the Three Jewels as their subject matter. While many people have admiring faith in the Three Jewels, not many have faith in the treatises that discuss them. Faith in the treatises and their authors leads us to study the texts, which increases our knowledge of the Three Jewels. This, in turn, promotes contemplating and then meditating on the meaning that we learned, thereby deepening both our wisdom and believing faith. These, in turn, are essential factors for our awakening.

There is no fixed order in which faith and wisdom arise. According to individual tendencies, faith may give rise to wisdom, wisdom may lead to faith, or these two may occur simultaneously.

Stabilizing our faith increases our resilience. Stable faith is not affected by the opinions of others and prevents discouragement when viewing others' wrongdoings. Our faith in the Buddha's teachings will not falter should we find a statement in the scriptures or one said by our teacher with which we initially disagree. Instead, we will continue to investigate.

REFLECTION

1. Find examples in your own experience of the three types of faith.

2. How does each one contribute to your internal happiness?

3. How can you gently increase your faith and trust in the Buddha, Dharma, and Saṅgha?

Proper Practice

I am concerned that these days people rely too much on admiring faith and, even then, do not understand or cultivate it properly. Some people have great devotion but minimal interest in study. Many years ago I went to Singapore, and the Buddhists there greeted me with so much devotion. Some of them touched my clothes or my body believing they would receive some blessing, but when I explained the Buddhadharma, few of them were interested. I prefer when people are very attentive at teachings and want to learn. They take notes and record the teachings and refer to them later.

Buddhism is a path of self-reliance not one of propitiating an external god or deity to give us material goods, reputation, or spiritual realizations. Tibetans often have statues of protector deities on their altars and store their valuables in the cabinets below. I joke with them that it appears that they pray to the protectors on top of the cabinet to protect the worldly goods inside the cabinet! This is not Buddhist practice.

Expecting an external holy being to remove our suffering and make us a buddha is a wrong view. Improper understanding of prayers in Tibetan liturgy can lead to this idea; we request to the assembly of holy beings, "Please grant me blessings to generate compassion." This is a skillful way of focusing our energy and identifying what is important. However, we cannot simply make offerings to the gurus and deities, request them to grant us blessings, and then sit back and have a cup of tea, thinking they will do all the work!

The buddhas have such great compassion for sentient beings that if they could have eliminated our suffering and given us realizations, they would have done so by now. However, our progress along the path depends on our creating the appropriate causes. Our own effort is crucial. Just as another person cannot sleep for us so that we'll feel well rested, no one else can transform our mind for us. Nevertheless, innumerable holy beings are trying to assist and guide us on the path. But do we pay attention to their guidance— the teachings they give us?

If we call ourselves Buddhists and seek protection from suffering, we should rely on the Buddha's teachings. The principal way the Buddha protects us is by teaching us the Dharma. By putting the teachings into practice, we abandon harmful actions, purify those done in the past, and engage in constructive actions—this is the best protection. If we do not observe the law of karma and its effects, we may make extensive offerings to protectors, chant innumerable *pūjās* in deep, melodic voices, beat drums, and ring bells, but misery will still befall us because we have created the cause for it. On the other hand, if we act ethically, even if others try to harm us, they will not succeed because we will have removed the causes that make us vulnerable to it.

The Tibetan word *byin rlabs* that is translated as "blessing" or "inspiration" literally means "to transform into magnificence" or "to transform by magnificence." We receive a blessing not through an external power causing us to have an extraordinary experience, but through a combination of the holy being's teachings and our practice. The real sense of "blessing" is a transformation of mind from an unwholesome state to a wholesome one. Indications that our mind has been inspired and transformed are that our fear lessens, our temper calms, and our tolerance and respect for others increase.

As a sincere Buddhist, do not seek magnificent mystical experiences to boast about to your friends but instead try to become a better human being. If you do that, you will automatically benefit others and improve the world.

Purification and Collection of Merit

Merit is virtuous karma or goodness created by restraining from harmful actions and cultivating constructive ones. It leads to good results in cyclic existence and enriches our minds with positive energy that facilitates gaining spiritual realizations. Merit cannot be seen with our eyes or measured with scientific instruments, yet it acts as the support for both wisdom and faith to grow in our minds and enables our practice to be successful.

If we lack merit, our efforts to cultivate wisdom may result in a corrupt intelligence that reaches the wrong conclusions. Some people are extremely intelligent, but because they are excessively skeptical and critical, they reflexively criticize reasonable theories and beneficial practices. Nihilistic and cynical, they act in ways that harm themselves and others.

A lack of merit also impedes integrating the Dharma in our lives. Some Buddhists study the scriptures extensively and are excellent debaters and great logicians. They can explain the meaning of many scriptures, but their knowledge has not transformed their minds, and their everyday conduct lacks discipline. This indicates the corruption of intelligence due to lack of merit and proper faith. To cultivate wisdom that is capable of transforming our mind, we must accumulate merit and generate faith based on understanding the meaning of the teachings.

In ancient India, the great non-Buddhist masters who debated complex issues with the Buddhists must have had well-developed knowledge of the Buddhist view of these topics, otherwise they would not have been able to debate them. However, they had no conviction in the veracity of the Buddhist views; knowledge does not always lead to conviction. Gaining a deep understanding of the Buddha's teachings that goes beyond intellectual comprehension depends on having accumulated merit.

Purifying ourselves of negativities—destructive actions and harmful thoughts—is also important. Done by means of the four opponent powers—regret, taking refuge and generating bodhicitta, resolving not to do the action again, and engaging in remedial behavior—purification cleanses the mind of impediments. The mind is like a field. Just as we must remove debris from a field and add fertilizer so that the seeds we plant can grow, we perform purification and collect merit so that the seeds of Dharma planted in our minds during teachings can grow into a vast harvest of Dharma realizations. To do that, the great masters advise us to do certain preparatory practices, such as the seven-limb prayer, at the beginning of meditation sessions to purify and collect merit. These seven limbs are (1) performing prostrations, (2) making offerings, (3) confessing our misdeeds, (4) rejoicing in our own and others' virtue, (5) requesting our teachers to teach the Dharma, (6) imploring the buddhas to remain in the world, and (7) dedicating our merit for the awakening of all beings. In addition, some practitioners engage in specific preliminary practices prior to doing tantric retreats in order to accumulate merit; for example, some do a hundred thousand maṇḍala offerings or recitations of Vajrasattva's mantra. If we do these devotional practices with awareness that the factors composing them—the agent, object, and action—arise dependently yet are empty of inherent existence, we also cultivate wisdom, which is the ultimate purifying agent.

Sometimes we feel stuck in our studies and practice. The mind is bored, unresponsive, and dull, and we have difficulty understanding Dharma topics and focusing the mind on virtue. At such times, engaging in purification and the collection of merit is very effective to open the mind and make it receptive to the Dharma.

This is illustrated in the biography of Tsongkhapa. After practicing for many years, he had a meditative vision of Mañjuśrī, the buddha of wisdom, and was able to converse with him. He consulted Mañjuśrī regarding some difficult points about emptiness. Mañjuśrī answered his questions, but Tsongkhapa still did not understand. Mañjuśrī responded, "There is no way for me to explain it to you in an easier fashion. You will be able to understand only if you enhance your meditation with three factors. First, make heartfelt supplication to your guru, whom you regard as inseparable from your meditational deity. Second, engage in purification practices and accumulate merit. Third, study the treatises written by the great Indian masters and then reflect and meditate on them. With the help of these three, you will have a true insight into emptiness before long."

Tsongkhapa then went to do retreat at a hermitage near Ölka. There he made 3.5 million prostrations—a hundred thousand each to the thirty-five purification buddhas—and many thousands of maṇḍala offerings. In addition, he made requests to his guru, whom he viewed as having the same nature as his meditational deity, and continued to study the great treatises as advised by Mañjuśrī. The obstacles to his understanding of emptiness cleared, and he realized the correct view. Similarly, these three can rejuvenate our Dharma practice whenever our mind feels dry or obscured.

Prayers and Rituals

Many people ask me to pray for them. Thousands of buddhas and gurus already pray for us, but because we do not practice sincerely, nothing happens. Our progress depends on our own effort, and I am always delighted when students sincerely practice to transform their minds. That is the best offering.

Bodhisattvas make a vast variety of aspirations and prayers and then strive to accomplish their aspirations. In contrast, ordinary people pray to have a happy life but ignore Dharma practice, which is the source of happiness. They pray "May I be healthy" but eat junk food; they aspire to have good relationships with others but are careless about their speech. Good relationships will elude us as long as we speak divisively, blame, or criticize others. We should be like bodhisattvas and think about what causes will accomplish our prayers. If we create those causes, our prayers will bear fruit, and we will be receptive to the inspiration of the Three Jewels.

When we request spiritual mentors or monastics to pray for us, we should from our side refrain from nonvirtuous behavior and act constructively. That way their prayers can be effective. The actualization of virtuous prayers and aspirations is a cooperative effort: prayers are made, we engage in virtuous actions, and the Three Jewels send their inspiration. In Prajñā-varman's commentary on the *Udānavarga*, the Buddha says:

> Buddhas do not wash away negativities with water,
> clear away beings' duḥkha with their hands,
> or transfer their realizations to other beings:
> they liberate them by teaching the truth of reality.

Buddhas cannot magically make everything go well in our lives and in the world. The principal way they help us sentient beings is by teaching us how to create the causes for happiness and abandon the causes for suffering. Making our actions accord with their instructions—especially those regarding ethical conduct—is essential to alleviate duḥkha. We may recite thousands of prayers and mantras, but if we do not use the Dharma tools to transform our minds, we are wasting time. As Dza Patrul Rinpoche candidly says (AKC 15):

> Ritual sessions four times a day without the generation and
>   completion stages,
> pounding drums and clashing cymbals without reminding
>   ourselves of pure perception,
> droning mantras without any concentration:
> all that gets us no further on the path to liberation.

The main purpose of rituals involving deity-yoga practice is to generate the union of method and wisdom. It is not to seek blessings, as if nirvāṇa were something external to us that our spiritual mentor or meditation deity could transfer into our mindstream. Tantric practices are very profound, but to derive the greatest benefit from them, we must have a good foundation in general Buddhist teachings and learn how to meditate while performing these rituals. While making offerings to the saṅgha and requesting them to perform pūjās on our behalf create merit due to our sincere motivation, we should not think that we can "hire" someone to create merit, freeing us to continue to deceive customers at work or get drunk with our friends!

People easily believe that the performance of a ritual, not the mental change it is supposed to invoke in the participants, is an end to itself. This is precisely the attitude that the Buddha opposed during his life and that led to his disapproval of rites and rituals done simply for their own sake. Nowadays it seems that some people are going backward into this superstitious way of thinking and not forward to deeper, more genuine practice.

After a large teaching in the West some years ago, the students wanted to offer me a long-life pūjā. Although I appreciated their kind intentions and good wishes, I explained to them that it is their Dharma practice that keeps their gurus alive and ensures the presence of buddhas and bodhisattvas in the world. If they don't practice, there is no need for buddhas and bodhisattvas to appear in the world or for teachers to live long. However, if the students practice even a little of what I teach so that when we meet again they have less anger, jealousy, and attachment, then I will be extremely happy, and the cause for their spiritual mentors to live long will be present.

I was once requested to exorcize a spirit. Not knowing any rituals for this, I meditated on compassion and bodhicitta. Later the people told me the problem stopped, so I felt that perhaps I did something helpful. Another time, customers of a hotel had had bad experiences in a particular room. Not telling me this beforehand, the staff had me stay in that room, where I did my daily practice, which includes meditation on compassion and emptiness. Later they told me that the room had become peaceful and their customers could stay there again. While I haven't realized bodhicitta or emptiness, this attests to the power of meditating on them! Please remember this when you face difficulties.

In the Tibetan community, it is common to ask a spiritual mentor to do a divination when facing an obstacle or beginning a new project. Divination texts often attribute a problem to spirit harm, and usually the diviner will recommend that a particular pūjā be performed to eliminate the obstacles caused by spirits. However, as Buddhists, we should not be attributing our problems to external beings but to our own karma. I prefer that instead of prescribing pūjās, diviners tell people to meditate on bodhicitta and emptiness, to deepen their refuge in the Three Jewels, or to reflect on the law of karma and its effects and engage in purification practices. These will definitely cure the causes of suffering by transforming people's minds.

There is no need to consult a horoscope before starting a project or deciding where to place an altar. I don't have much faith in horoscopes and astrology—my tutor Ling Rinpoche (1903–83) told me he was born on a day of nine bad signs. We don't wait for a good date for the two most significant activities of our life: our birth and death. However, as an ancient tradition that is a part of Tibetan culture and heritage, it's important to continue Tibetan astrology.

Study, Reflection, and Meditation

The sūtras speak of the threefold practice of study, critical reflection, and meditation and the understanding or wisdom that is developed by each one. Individually and together these three enable us to practice skillfully, avoid pitfalls and detours, and gain liberating realizations.

Study. In ancient times, the Buddha's teachings were passed down orally, so the first step in learning was to hear teachings. The broader meaning of "hearing" (*śruti*) includes all forms of study, including reading and new forms of learning. Studying the sūtras and tantras, as well as treatises and commentaries by later sages, gives us the necessary information to know how to practice. Without this first, crucial step, we risk making up our own path or practicing incorrectly.

Many people are eager to meditate, which is commendable; but without proper study, they run the risk of going astray. They will not know how to meditate correctly, even if they have a strong aspiration to do so. Studying the teachings on emptiness, we learn the reasonings that prove phenomena are empty of inherent existence. Study reveals different perspectives on a topic, thereby increasing our mental flexibility and acuity. Then when we contemplate and meditate, we can look at the topic from many angles and see connections among diverse points. Knowing the paths and stages on the path to awakening enables us to assess our own progress when we are not able to consult our spiritual mentor. Hearing is not dry, intellectual learning. It is dynamic and sparks transformation in our mind.

One lama said that it is better to study scriptures one month than to do a one-month retreat meditating on and reciting the mantra of Mañjuśrī. This illustrates the importance of study to gain wisdom. The Dharma is vast, and we should continue to learn its various aspects our entire lives. Our bodies may become old, but our minds can still be young and full of enthusiasm for learning. Whenever I have time in my busy schedule, I read one of the great treatises. Even if I have studied it many times before, new aspects are revealed with each reading.

Something to keep in mind when studying the Dharma is that many words have multiple meanings that differ according to the context. The Tibetan word *rig pa*, for example, is translated as "awareness" or "cognizance" in the context of the Mind and Awareness teachings, but in Dzogchen it refers to the subtle mind. *Bliss* has different meanings in the contexts of serenity meditation and highest yoga tantra.

Reflection. Having studied, we must think about what we learned. This involves investigation and critical analysis to ascertain the correct meaning, which engenders deep conviction in the veracity of the Dharma. Reflection may be done quietly on our own or together with others, discussing and/or debating the teachings. For this reason, Tibetan monastics engage in rigorous debates that are often entertaining as well as educational. Sometimes we believe we understand a topic well but discover we don't because when someone asks us a question or challenges our assertion, we don't know how to respond! The *Sūtra Unraveling the Thought* explains four principles that are useful to understand a phenomenon such as the mind from different perspectives.

The *principle of nature* or *reality* includes examining realities commonly known in the world, such as water's wetness; inconceivable realities, such as the Buddha's abilities; and the abiding reality (emptiness). To understand the mind, we examine its clear and cognizant nature and its impermanent nature. Due to the mind's nature, two contradictory emotions or thoughts—for example anger and love—cannot be manifest simultaneously.

Investigating the *principle of dependence* entails examining causality, the arising of results from their causes. This enables us to understand that because individual phenomena do not have certain qualities or abilities from their own side, when they interact with other phenomena, new properties emerge. Regarding the mind, afflictions depend on ignorance; they cease when ignorance ceases. Virtuous mental factors are not rooted in ignorance and do not cease when ignorance ceases. They depend on other causes that can be cultivated limitlessly.

Some results are material while others are consciousnesses or abstract composites—impermanent phenomena that are neither material nor consciousness, such as the person and karmic seeds. The diversity of results is due to the diversity of causes. There are two types of causal processes. One involves karma; the other is causality that is distinct from karma. Karmic causal processes involve sentient beings' experience of happiness and suffering and depend on their intentions. Causal processes that are distinct from karma involve the physical, chemical, and biological laws of nature.

The *principal of function* shows that each phenomenon has its own function. Understanding the mind's function, we see that wisdom eradicates ignorance and afflictions, and contemplating the kindness of others as well as their suffering stimulates compassion. Afflictions disturb the mind, while wisdom pacifies and calms it. Agent, object, and action function together within any event.

The *principle of evidence* or *logical reasoning* involves examining whether something can be apprehended by any of the three reliable cognizers—direct perceivers (for example, reliable sense consciousnesses), inferential consciousnesses that use reasoning to know their object, and reliable authoritative testimony of experts. By understanding the first three principles, we can then apply reasoning, e.g., because *x* exists, *y* must exist or occur. We can establish a conclusion that cannot be contradicted by any of the three reliable cognizers. Based on understanding the above three principles with respect to the mind, we can conclude that liberation is possible and that a path exists that can bring it about.

These four principles are built one on top of the other. We can use evidence and reasoning to cultivate understanding because they presuppose that phenomena have particular functions. We can understand their functions because underlying them are dependently related phenomena. Why is there a relationship between cause and effect? Because it is the nature of effects to follow their causes; this is the way things are. When we ask why matter has the property of obstructiveness and consciousness has the aspect of subjective experience, the only answer is "that is its nature."

To explain these four in their forward sequence: the principle of nature allows for dependent relationships to occur, and these dependent relationships among phenomena provide the basis for the specific function of each phenomenon. Based on the dependent nature of phenomena and their functions, we can employ the principle of reasoning to understand things that are not immediately evident. "Because there is smoke, there is fire" involves knowing that the nature of fire is hot and burning, that fire produces smoke, and that smoke functions as evidence of fire.

We apply these same four principles when practicing the four establishments of mindfulness. Many of the meditations on the body, feelings, mind, and phenomena involve understanding their nature, causes, and functions or effects. Through that, we can use them as reasons to know that the body, feelings, mind, and phenomena are impermanent, duḥkha by nature, empty, and selfless.

The manner in which scientific investigation proceeds is similar to these four principles. Scientists first endeavor to understand the various properties of their object of study—their nature—and then examine what these objects depend on. Through this, they research emergent properties and their functions and then apply reason to understand characteristics that are not evident.

Meditation. Based on learning and critical reflection on the teachings, our meditation will be effective. The purpose of meditation is to integrate the meaning of the teachings into our mindstream by means of repeated practice. Having a correct and stable intellectual understanding due to applying the four principles, we now engage in absorption meditation to familiarize our mind with the topic and transform intellectual understanding into realization. Here our meditation mainly, but not exclusively, involves stabilizing meditation done with access or full concentration, although analytical meditation may be applied at times.[52] This produces the understanding arising from meditation, which has a powerful ability to transform our minds.

Learning, critical reflection, and meditation complement each other. Some people incorrectly think "These three apply to sūtra practice, but tantra is actualized through devotion and faith, so study and analysis are not necessary." The Kadam geshes, who practiced both sūtra and tantra, used to say, "When I hear teachings, I also reflect and meditate. When I reflect, I also hear and meditate. When I meditate, I hear and critically reflect."

Learning gives us general knowledge of the topic and reduces one level of confusion and doubt. Thinking about and analyzing the teachings gives us a more nuanced conceptual understanding based on reason. Meditating integrates this understanding with our very being. In the case of realizing the nature of reality, hearing and studying the teachings give us a general knowledge about the object of negation, the rational arguments proving that all phenomena lack inherent existence, and the stages of realizing emptiness. By then contemplating and discussing what we have studied, we come to understand that the I does not exist inherently as it appears but exists dependently. The I is empty of inherent existence because it is dependent on the five psychophysical aggregates and on the mind designating "I." The emptiness that we have ascertained by reflection now becomes the object of meditation. In meditation we now cultivate a union of serenity and insight on emptiness.

REFLECTION

1. Why are study, critical examination, and meditation important to gain realizations?

2. Pick a particular thing and contemplate the four principles—nature, dependence, function, and evidence or reasoning—in relation to it.

3. See how the four work together to bring understanding.

Memorization and Debate

In traditional Tibetan monastic universities, the daily schedule includes specified times for group chanting, teachings, memorization, and debate. Private study and silent meditation are done at monastics' own convenience. Since the time of the Buddha, memorization has been a principal way of preserving and conveying the teachings from spiritual mentor to disciple. Memorization has many benefits: students already have some familiarity with a text's contents when they receive teachings on it. After studying a text, they will be able to easily recall its key points. By having quick access to quotations, students can draw attention to these passages when they debate and contemplate. When teaching, they are able to cite passages related to a specific topic from diverse texts, enhancing the breadth and depth of their explanation. In difficult situations, they can easily remember Dharma advice. Many Tibetan monastics who were imprisoned by the Communist Chinese after 1959 silently recited texts in their prison cells. Not only did they spend their time familiarizing themselves with the Buddha's thought, but they also could easily recall advice on how to practice during difficult times. Someone who holds a wealth of texts in their memory is like a cook who has all the ingredients for a delicious meal at her fingertips.

Memorization is also a way of training the mind. Students must learn to concentrate on the material they are memorizing and recall it instantly. In a Tibetan monastery, this requires special focus, since one is surrounded by many other monastics loudly reciting the passages they are memorizing. They build up the ability to not be distracted by external sounds, which is a great aid when they meditate.

Debate is an animated process that helps students to learn the material, think about it, and remember what they have learned. The structure of a debate is formalized, and both participants—the seated respondent and the standing questioner—must be familiar with the syllogistic structure. This format teaches people how to think clearly. The speaker cannot ramble and hope the debate partner understands what he is trying to say. Both parties must be concise and to the point.

A debate begins with the questioner asking the respondent a question. Once the questioner has an idea of the view the responder holds (the thesis), he will ask him what reasons he has to support that. If he sees a flaw in the responder's logic, he will try to refute it either by getting the responder to contradict himself or by establishing the correct view.

In his *Supplement to the Middle Way* (*Madhyamakāvatāra*), Candrakīrti states that the purpose of these philosophical debates is not to generate hostility toward the other person and his view or to arrogantly establish our own view in order to gain a good reputation. The purpose is to eradicate the ignorance that obscures both parties from gaining Dharma realizations, and to establish both self and others on the path to awakening. Bearing this in mind helps debaters maintain a good motivation and also counteracts the supposition that debate is simply intellectual competition.

During the Buddha's time, two monks, Bhaṇḍa and Abhiñjika, were debating the teachings in order to determine who could speak better and have the final word. When news of their activities reached the Buddha, he called for them, and the following dialogue ensued (SN 16.6):

The Buddha: Is it true, bhikkhus, that you have been competing with each other in regard to your learning, as to who can speak more, who can speak better, who can speak longer?

Monks: Yes, Venerable Sir.

The Buddha: Have you ever known me to teach the Dhamma thus: "Come bhikkhus, compete with each other in regard to your learning, and see who can speak more, who can speak better, who can speak longer?"

Monks: No, Venerable Sir.

The Buddha: Then, if you have never known me to teach the Dhamma thus, what do you senseless men know and see that, having gone forth in such a well-expounded Dhamma and Vinaya, you compete with each other in regard to your learning, as to who can speak more, who can speak better, who can speak longer?

Seeing their fault, the bhikkhus immediately prostrated to the Buddha, confessed their error, and asked for his pardon. We, too, must be careful to maintain a wholesome motivation so that our Dharma debates and discussions do not become a purely intellectual and ego-driven pursuit.

One time a famous logician approached the great meditator Milarepa, and trying to embarrass him, asked "What are the definitions of a syllogism of pervasion and a syllogism of contradiction?"

To this Milarepa replied, "Your mind being pervaded with afflictions is a syllogism of pervasion, and your mind being contradictory with the Dharma is a syllogism of contradiction." In this way, he skillfully and compassionately burst the bubble of arrogance of this logician, who pursued debate with a skewed motive. Another time, when a logician asked Milarepa to give the definition of *nonascertaining direct perception*, Milarepa responded, "A person who outwardly assumes the appearance of a Dharma practitioner but inwardly is not ascertained as a Dharma practitioner—that is a nonascertaining direct perception."

Āryadeva says (CŚ 185):

> While attached to your own position
> and disliking others' positions,
> you will not approach nirvāṇa.
> Neither conduct will bring peace.

Someone who is not really interested in Dharma practice may use debate to enhance his arrogance and animosity. I heard a story about a monk who was unable to establish his own position to the responder during a debate. He became so enraged that he stormed off, picked up a stone, and struck the responder.

In another case, I heard of two knowledgeable students whose debates were deep as well as competitive. The questioner and respondent were always eager to defeat each other. This sense of competition continued even after they attended tantric college, sat for their geshe exams, and received their geshe degrees. It seems that for the rest of their lives, they remained antagonistic, continually debating with each other with the thought, "I want to defeat him."

On the other hand, there are those like the respected master Dondrup Tsondru, well-known for his skill in debate, which made his students proud to have him as their teacher. Once a Mongolian monk, a learned new geshe, was debating at the Great Prayer Festival, and Dondrup Tsondru was the questioner. During the debate, nothing remarkable happened; there was no rigorous exchange on any important issue. Afterward his students asked Dondrup Tsondru, "What happened, Master? You weren't successful in bringing about a powerful debate with this responder."

Dondrup Tsondru replied, "The responder was very skilled and learned. Whatever he said accorded with reasoning and scripture, so there was nothing to debate." The Mongolian monk had used debate in the way it was intended—to eliminate ignorance. Dondrup Tsondru honored that and did not try to stir up false debates just to demonstrate his skill and emerge victorious.

Among new students who are learning to debate, there's the saying, "If you can convince the responder that something that is correct is incorrect or that something that is incorrect is correct, then you are learned and skilled in the topic." Candrakīrti discourages this attitude, saying that it is wrong to refute someone's idea simply for the sake of refuting it and being triumphant. Having the reputation of being a good debater does not get one closer to awakening. In the tradition of Nālandā's learned practitioners, we should be objective, honest, and truthful. One physicist told me that a scientist must be impartial and objective when doing research. Being attached to one's hypothesis or the outcomes of one's research is not the correct approach.

Some people have the mistaken impression that Gelukpas only engage in intellectual study and debate, without much meditation, and that Nyingmapas and Kagyupas do not study much but meditate a lot. Such stereotypes are unfortunate, because within each Tibetan tradition we find people who focus on study, others who emphasize meditation, and some who offer service in the monasteries. When I speak at any of the three large Geluk monasteries—Gaden, Sera, and Drepung—I encourage the monks to engage enthusiastically in philosophical studies and debate and then relate what they learn to practice-oriented texts such as those on the lamrim. They should meditate on those teachings, integrating the meaning into their hearts and lives. Similarly, when I teach monastics from Nyingma, Kagyu, or Sakya monasteries, I encourage them to study the great Indian classics as well as the texts from their own tradition, and then reflect and meditate on what they learn.

However, I have witnessed the tendency for some people—teachers and students—to get so accustomed to debating that the way they engage with the Dharma becomes unbalanced. For example, Candrakīrti's *Supplement to the Middle Way* is a key text studied in the monastic curriculum. The initial praise to compassion and the first five chapters are filled with material for practice—compassion, bodhicitta, generosity, ethical conduct, fortitude, joyous effort, and meditative stability. But since there is not much material for debate in these, some people hurry through them to reach chapter 6, which is about emptiness, where they jump into debate with full force. I don't know if they meditate on chapter 6 while studying it. Just learning the terms—object of negation, emptiness of inherent existence, two truths, and so forth—doesn't bring realizations. We need to identify the object of negation within ourselves and then see that it doesn't exist.

Something similar may happen when people study Nāgārjuna's *Treatise on the Middle Way*. They spend more time on the first few chapters where there is a lot to debate, but neglect chapters 18 and 26, which speak about dependent arising and the means to achieve liberation. I like to teach chapters 18, 24, and 26 of this text because understanding how we are reborn in cyclic existence and how to reverse that and attain liberation are essential topics for practice.

A Western professor once commented to me that monastics debate, but in the end they return to scriptural quotations to "prove" their point. He is right. I have suggested many times that people only use reason when debating topics that are slightly obscure. Scriptural authority should only be used concerning very obscure phenomena, and even then, you must show why the scripture you are citing is reliable. In short, we should try to practice wisely.

It is my sincere wish that people emulate the great learned practitioners of the past and develop all three wisdoms of study, reflection, and meditation. Pointing fingers at others and chiding them to both study and meditate is useless; we should evaluate our own activities and examine whether we incorporate all three into our practice in a balanced way.

To investigate the Buddha's teachings in a beneficial way, it is essential to have the qualities of a receptive student—eagerness to learn, intelligence, open-mindedness, and sincerity. As we increase these qualities, our understanding of the Dharma will deepen, and that will arouse confidence in the teachings. This conviction in the truth of the Dharma leads us to have faith in the Buddha who taught it and the Saṅgha who have correctly realized it. This illustrates the interconnectedness of philosophical studies and faith in the Three Jewels.

Role Models

When engaging in a new activity, we naturally look to role models for guidance and inspiration. Spiritual practice is no exception. In the Tibetan Buddhist tradition, the two types of prominent role models we find are the scholar/commentator (such as Asaṅga and Candrakīrti) and the ascetic meditator (such as Saraha or Milarepa). Occasionally we find examples of people who are both, such as Nāropa, Dza Patrul Rinpoche, or Tsongkhapa. Because they are usually depicted in one role or the other, we tend to forget that most of the great scholars were also great yogis, and that the great meditators often became so after years of study and debate in either this or previous lives.

Hearing about these historical figures, we may receive the unspoken message that to be successful in the Dharma, we have to become either a great scholar or a great meditator. But where does that leave people who are drawn to neither role? What about the average practitioner who does her best according to her own disposition? Each of us wants to feel that we are successful in our own way.

We must remember that success in Dharma practice is not dependent on societal recognition. The law of karma and its effects is not duped by hypocrisy. Leaving this life with a great collection of merit, fewer negativities, and the imprints from having heard and practiced many teachings are signs of a successful Dharma practice. Fame is not.

In seeking out role models, I (Chodron) look to the Buddha himself. In sūtra passages and in artwork, he is depicted in a variety of situations: sitting and meditating peacefully; speaking fearlessly to a crowd of non-Buddhists; tending to the needs of a sick monk; talking to merchants, courtesans, royalty, and paupers. He addresses one person gently and scolds a monk with wrong views. He instructs that the food remaining from a meal offered to the saṅgha be given to the poor. In one instance, he praises the merit of a beggar who mentally offered the meal with a good motivation over the wealthy patron who actually gave the food but lacked a generous intention. He consoles a woman whose child died and those fearing the loss of their parents. The Buddha sits under forest trees; he walks in towns. He spends time with others and is often alone. He speaks with men and women, monastics and lay. He knows how to address intellectuals, wandering ascetics, nonbelievers, the grieving, the impoverished, and criminals— the Buddha is everyone's person. He fits no stereotype.

The Buddha engaged in so many diverse activities that he can serve as a role model for many different kinds of people with diverse interests. We can let go of the critical self-judgment that may arise if we aren't among the best of the debaters or the most realized yogis. It's important for each of us to find our own way of living a Dharma life while internally cultivating the same qualities of wisdom, bodhicitta, and so forth.

In thinking of the diversity of Tibetan adepts, the three lineages of Kadam practitioners come to mind. One group practiced mainly lamrim, following Atiśa's *Lamp of the Path* and other texts, without studying philosophy extensively or debating very much. The second group emphasized philosophical studies and debate, integrating this into their lamrim meditation. The third group relied mainly on the personal instructions they received from their spiritual mentors and meditated on those.

Some Kadam practitioners displayed great devotion to their teachers and served them assiduously. Others stayed alone or practiced with a small group of companions. Some were teachers, others were not. Their biographies show that they had very different personalities. They did not squeeze themselves into a predetermined role or persona in order to be successful practitioners.

I often comment on the importance of Buddhists being engaged in social welfare projects, and for some people that is the natural expression of their Dharma practice. Master Cheng Yen, the Chinese bhikṣuṇī who founded the Tzu Chi Foundation, is a good example of this. A Buddhist nun, she practiced in a hut in Taiwan for years, bowing to each syllable of the *Lotus Sūtra*. Villagers recall unusual light emanating from her hut. Later she saw a poor person being turned away from a medical clinic, and she began to construct hospitals for the impoverished. Now she directs an international welfare organization whose volunteers travel around the globe to offer aid when disasters and emergencies occur. Master Cheng Yen remains humble and peaceful in demeanor, yet her firm determination to benefit others has inspired thousands. There is a waiting list to volunteer at her welfare centers in Taiwan!

As Buddhists, we should encourage those who want to live as renounced meditators after completing their studies. We should also support those whose talents lie in study and teaching, compassionate service, or social engagement. Each of us must find a suitable way to combine study, meditation, and service in our own lives.

Dharma practitioners have a variety of personalities. In the early sūtras, we meet Mahākāśyapa, who engaged in ascetic practices allowed by the

216 | APPROACHING THE BUDDHIST PATH

Buddha. He appears austere, aloof, and perhaps a bit rigid as well. Ānanda, the Buddha's personal attendant, is sociable and kind and compassionately looks after others. Looking at a wide variety of role models widens our perspective.

Bodhisattvas are depicted in several ways in the scriptures. Some live in society, helping those they encounter. Some are royalty who affect the welfare of others through promulgating fair policies and sharing their wealth. Some are merchants who support the saṅgha and give generously to those in need. Some live with the most neglected people in society, uplifting them materially and with the Dharma. Some bodhisattvas live in pure lands, where they make elaborate offerings and learn from the principal Buddha there. Some bodhisattvas teach the Dharma to multitudes; others teach to a few through their example. All these ways of living bodhicitta apply now as well.

Tantric adepts are often portrayed living eccentric lives and sometimes acting outrageously, transgressing the social mores of their time. While many of us admire someone who is not constrained by conventions, this image of tantric adepts can be misleading, especially if emulating it feeds our craving for attention, contempt for society, or unhealthy psychological states. Nowadays it is better to practice as the mind-training teachings advise: externally appearing simple; internally living with love, compassion, and bodhicitta; and discreetly practicing tantra.

In short, do not become rigid in your notion of a successful Dharma life. Know that, due to karma, people have different mentalities and interests and different opportunities as well. Encourage yourself and encourage others to abandon negativity, create virtue, and cultivate wisdom and compassion. Respect all practitioners and rejoice at whatever virtue anyone creates.

10 | Making Progress

All of us want our Dharma practice to bear fruit, but even with good intentions it is easy to deviate from the path. We can get sidetracked in several ways. Being aware of potential pitfalls in advance helps us to avoid them, and knowing the signs of making progress on the path enables us to accurately assess our practice.

Realistic Expectations

We have both a useful and a useless sense of self. The unrealistic sense of self operates without sound reason, just on the grounds of "I want this or that." This sense of self is the root of our duḥkha and is eliminated by the realization of emptiness. The positive sense of self operates on the basis of reason. It is the basis for bodhisattvas' strong self-confidence, without which they would be unable to confront and subdue the self-centered attitude.

Afflictions are overcome in stages, not all at once. The first time a layer of them is eradicated is upon gaining a direct, nonconceptual perception of emptiness. Before that, when we encounter circumstances that give rise to our afflictions, we must practice ethical conduct and employ the antidotes specific to each affliction in order to prevent harmful behavior. To develop such self-control, two factors are crucial—a sense of personal integrity and consideration for others. Personal integrity enables us to abandon negativities because we respect our values and precepts. Consideration for others does this because we care about the effect of our bad behavior on others.

Some people mistakenly believe that if they do some spiritual practice for a short time, they will continue to progress even if they do not actively practice. If we practice consistently, progress will definitely occur, but if we do not, our afflictions will arise effortlessly and lead to destructive actions, bringing more misery.

Vajrayāna speaks of awakening in this life. Some traditions or teachers speak of a direct, swift path to awakening. Hearing this, some people develop unrealistic expectations, thinking they will have quick results from doing just a little practice. Personally speaking, all these statements remind me of communist propaganda!

How, then, should we understand the statements in some tantric texts that "one attains awakening in one moment"? If this is the case, why do we need to practice step-by-step, as stated in all other teachings? To understand them correctly, we must know the context within which these statements are made. The meaning of "one moment" and "one short instant" varies in different situations. The duration of a phenomenon is understood in relation to other phenomena. Compared to the beginninglessness of cyclic existence, the age in which we live is like one moment. Likewise, when one attains strong concentration, hundreds of eons may appear to that person as just one moment, and one moment may appear as an eon. If a person has accumulated extensive merit in her previous lives, she may gain realizations or attain awakening in this life. In this case, one lifetime is the meaning of "one moment."

But this does not mean that this person completed the entire path in only one brief lifetime. That person must have collected extensive merit and wisdom during many lifetimes, such that when she meets a particular external situation in this lifetime, realizations or awakening appear to come swiftly. Eons ago, she began the path as an initial-level practitioner and actualized the steps to awakening gradually, life after life. The swift results in the present life are the product of hard work in previous lives.

Westerners are practical and want immediate results. Their eagerness to see results motivates them to practice. However, if they go on retreat and return home at more or less the same level, they may think Dharma practice does not work and give it up. Tibetans may go to the other extreme. They believe in the five paths and ten bodhisattva grounds[53] but tend to be complacent and think these things can be developed later. They lack a sense of urgency and do not exert a lot of effort.

It seems "hybrid" practitioners are best—those who are motivated, enthusiastic, and practice what they learn but who are also relaxed and patient. These practitioners seek awakening quickly for the benefit of sentient beings but accept that it will take a long time to become buddhas and are willing to practice however long it takes.

To illustrate the necessity of gradual training, the Buddha uses a simile about a thoroughbred colt (MN 65). At first the colt is completely wild, so the trainer must get him used to wearing a bit. Because it is something the colt has never done before, he is obviously uncomfortable, but with constant repetition and gradual practice, he gets used to it and is peaceful when wearing the bit. At that time, the trainer introduces the harness, which is new to the colt. Again the colt tries to throw it off, but with repetition and practice, he eventually becomes used to it and wears it happily. Now the trainer progressively trains the colt to keep in step, run in a circle, prance, gallop, charge, and so forth. The colt initially resists each new step but eventually becomes familiar with each task and masters it. When the colt is thoroughly trained and able to do many things that he could not do before, he is fit for the king.

Similarly, when we train as Dharma practitioners, we will come up against many things that are unfamiliar. We may be incapable of doing them at present, be afraid of them, or lack the confidence to try them. But if we have a wise spiritual mentor and like the colt, allow ourselves to be trained and continue to train even when we initially feel some discomfort, good results will come. Eventually, we will accomplish all the causes and conditions necessary to attain awakening.

At present we are ordinary beings whose minds are completely under the influence of the three poisonous attitudes of ignorance, anger, and attachment. Day in and day out these difficult-to-control, unwelcome disturbing emotions and wrong conceptions arise in our mind. Since this is the case, is it reasonable to think that we will be able to quickly remove the cloud of afflictions once and for all? If we tried, it would be difficult. In fact, it is hard to have a peaceful mind for more than a few minutes!

No matter what field of knowledge we want to master, we cannot learn everything at once. We must study step by step and progress gradually. This also applies to gaining transcendental realizations, which are beyond our ordinary understanding.

220 | APPROACHING THE BUDDHIST PATH

Eliminating afflictions depends on generating strong counterforces to them, and this requires time. These counterforces are virtuous qualities, which are cultivated gradually, each successive step depending on its own causes and conditions. It is fruitless to expect an outcome without creating the causes that will produce it.

On the path to awakening, it behooves us to study the teachings well so we'll know how to create the specific causes and conditions for our spiritual goals and the order in which to do the various practices. Then we can practice with delight and enthusiasm, knowing that realizations will come when all the causes and conditions are assembled. Greeting each day with the thought, "Will realizations finally come today?" will only make us agitated. Such impatience is the opposite of the attitude necessary for our practice to be effective.

To grow peas, we first till the ground, fertilize it, plant pea seeds in the springtime, and then water them. When this has been done, we relax and give the seeds time to grow. We don't dig them up every day to see if they have sprouted yet! Instead we remain content knowing that they will grow in their own time.

Once, at a large public teaching, someone asked me what was the quickest and easiest path to awakening. I began to weep because I sensed that the person wanted to attain a lofty goal without engaging in the process of getting there. Thoughts of great practitioners, such as Milarepa, flooded my mind. They practiced joyfully even under difficult conditions because they wanted to attain awakening for the benefit of all sentient beings. They were willing to undergo whatever was necessary to create the causes for awakening, because they were convinced in the depths of their hearts that this was the most worthwhile thing to do. To attain results like these great practitioners did, we must cultivate that same compassionate motivation and enthusiastic effort.

When I cultivate enthusiasm to achieve buddhahood in this lifetime, in the back of my mind I have the idea of numerous lives and many eons. Thus my prayer becomes, "In order to serve sentient beings, may I attain buddhahood—if possible within this lifetime, but more likely after countless lives." If we think of attaining awakening in this life but lack the perspective of many lifetimes, our wish is unrealistic and may lead to despair when we do not progress as quickly as we would like. A view accepting future lives is critical to maintain a long-term joyful motivation free from both idealism and despair.

Some Westerners have genuine interest in Buddhism but have difficulty accepting multiple lifetimes and eons of existence. Thinking that this one lifetime is all that exists, they want to see immediate progress—fast food and fast awakening! But the latter is not possible. I do not know how to help them maintain a joyful motivation given how difficult it is to attain buddhahood in this lifetime.

Some goal-oriented people think of nirvāṇa and awakening as things to achieve, yet they do not want to do what is necessary to get there. They seek transcendental experiences in meditation but are reluctant to change bad habits such as harsh speech, lying, and taking intoxicants. Here, too, it is difficult to guide them.

Transforming our mind is a process. Awareness of this brings our attention to the present moment, for the time to practice is now. A process-orientated approach also rouses us to examine our daily activities in light of the Dharma and to see that progress is made by transforming our thoughts, emotions, speech, and behavior.

Some of my Western students comment to me that Buddhist scriptures talk about either deluded people who consistently create destructive karma or bodhisattvas whose motivation and conduct are pure. They wonder how to practice when they are in between these two extremes.

Bodhisattvas' wonderful deeds are activities to emulate and inspire us to practice. The scriptures always present the ideal; if they didn't, we wouldn't know what to aim for and would think mediocre attainments were the best. But no one—except maybe ourselves—expects us to master the bodhisattva practices instantly. While I admire the abilities of the great bodhisattvas and spiritual mentors, I do not expect myself to practice as they do, given my present situation. By endeavoring to think and act as they do, I am confident that gradually these abilities will take root and grow within me.

Thinking of the Buddha as having always been awakened creates unnecessary obstacles in our mind. The Buddha is not an inherently existent awakened being. He was once an ordinary, confused being like us, and through gradual, consistent practice, he transformed his mind and attained buddhahood. We are no different from him; if we joyfully persevere in creating the causes, we too will become buddhas.

Advanced Practices at the Right Time

In their enthusiasm for the Dharma, some beginners enter into advanced practices without sufficient preparation. They may make serenity and meditation on emptiness the focus of their practice, receive tantric empowerments, and enter a three-year retreat and later become discouraged by their lack of progress.

While the union of serenity and insight on emptiness is the actual path that liberates us from cyclic existence, we must still practice the initial meditations. Without doing that, trying to gain deep concentration while living in the city will only make us frustrated because our minds are unfamiliar with the antidotes to afflictions and the external situation isn't conducive to progress. Tsongkhapa gave some excellent advice in this regard:

> Some say to expend your energy only to stabilize your mind and to understand the view, ignoring all earlier topics, but this makes it very difficult to get the vital points. Therefore, you must develop certainty about the whole course of the path.[54]

In other words, our journey to awakening will be successful if we start at the beginning of the path. When we are ready to cultivate serenity and insight on emptiness, it is imperative to receive instructions on the methods to do so and to practice these correctly. Gaining the correct view is not easy. Emptiness is not nothingness, and meditation on emptiness is not simply resting the mind in a vague nonconceptual state. We must be able to negate all fantasized ways of existence and still establish the conventional functioning of karma and its effects that is the support for ethical conduct. Also, our concentration must be vivid, unclouded by subtle laxity or excitement.

Tantra is an advanced practice that requires lengthy preparation. In their excitement to enter tantra, some people find contemplation of the disadvantages of cyclic existence tedious, meditation on death and impermanence uninteresting, and teachings on ethical conduct inconvenient. They skip over practices to generate renunciation and bodhicitta and take many empowerments, which entail assuming tantric precepts and commitments. After some time, they become confused and find keeping tantric precepts and commitments burdensome. Not progressing as rapidly as they would like, they become discouraged and either neglect their tantric commitments or abandon Dharma practice altogether.

We may ask why Tibetan masters give highest yoga tantra empowerments to relatively inexperienced practitioners. I too wonder about this! It could be to please the students who request them or to plant seeds in their mindstreams so in future lives they will encounter tantra. Perhaps in the audience there are a few people who are able to practice at this level. However, it is sad when this ends with someone giving up the Dharma.

Accomplishing the entire path to awakening is like building a house. A solid foundation is necessary before erecting the walls, and stable walls must be in place to put on the roof. Similarly, beginners would do well to gain an overall understanding of the path by contemplating the four truths, meditating on the practices in common with the initial- and middle-capacity beings, and practicing the six perfections according to the Sūtra Vehicle. Furthermore, doing a lot of purification and collection of merit will eliminate obstacles. If they then receive an empowerment, their tantric practice will bring the desired results.

Some beginners hear about three-year tantric retreats and are eager to do one. However, because they are not well prepared, at the end of the retreat their major accomplishments are being expert in playing ritual musical instruments, chanting pūjās in Tibetan, and making *tormas* (ritual cakes). Not much internal transformation has occurred, and their disturbing emotions remain almost the same. A few who have done many tantra visualizations and recited millions of mantras may boast that they are accomplished tantric practitioners. Some adopt the title "lama" after the retreat, but personally speaking, I believe doing a three-year retreat is insufficient to earn that title. One time I commented upon people entering Vajrayāna too soon to a close disciple of the previous Karmapa, and he fully agreed. The great nineteenth-century Nyingma lama Dza Patrul Rinpoche said (AKC 12):

Any Dharma that does not benefit one's own mind
is just sanctimonious, not meaningful Dharma.
Unless it makes some difference to your mind,
even doing retreat for a hundred years would just be a pain.

These relative newcomers to the Dharma who do three-year retreats have tremendous determination and self-discipline. I would find it difficult to sleep sitting up and then meditate the next day. I respect and admire them for that. However, rigorous physical disciplines do not necessarily transform the mind; they may simply be a test of one's willpower. Someone may have physical and verbal discipline but an unruly mind. Dza Patrul Rinpoche said (AKC 14):

> Even if we have completed our quota of years and
>   months on retreat
> and managed to recite millions and millions of mantras,
> unless attachment, hostility, and ignorance have
>   decreased in our minds,
> that Dharma I consider as just pointless.

These people have put the cart before the horse. Building a proper foundation by learning the four truths and practicing the bodhisattva deeds would do them well.

Checking Our Meditation Experiences

Some students talk of having extraordinary meditative experiences, but when something upsetting happens in life, they are unprepared and cannot handle it. This usually occurs because they have overestimated their meditative experiences. Unusual experiences such as visual appearances, special dreams, or feelings of bliss are not necessarily indications of spiritual realizations. They may occur due to an imbalance of the winds (*prāṇa*) in the body, external interferences, or an overactive imagination. For this reason, it is important to consult our spiritual mentors, who will help us evaluate these experiences.

Some experiences, such as having premonitions of future events, arise due to karma. They are not always accurate, and not everyone will welcome a prediction of future illness when they haven't asked us for advice!

Unusual or exotic forms may appear when we're meditating, or we may experience strange sensations in our body. Most of these are distractions and should be ignored.

Once I met a Westerner who considered himself a tantric practitioner.

In a hopeful voice, he told me of a dream in which he saw many deities and related it to the passage in Candrakīrti's *Supplement to the Middle Way*, "At that time you will see one hundred buddhas," which refers to a bodhisattva on the path of seeing who has a direct perception of emptiness. This person thought that because he dreamed of many deities he must be an ārya bodhisattva and waited for me to confirm that. I replied, "Seeing a hundred buddhas is not the only quality of bodhisattvas on the path of seeing. They have many other qualities as well—they can live one hundred eons and emanate one hundred manifestations. So examine whether you can do these as well."

Remaining humble is an essential quality for genuine spiritual practitioners. A disingenuous person may praise himself or disparage others due to attachment to receiving offerings, fame, or status. We should not be led astray by this. The Buddha described several ways to differentiate a true from an untrue person (MN 113):

> But a true person considers thus: "It is not because of one's renown that states of greed, hatred, or confusion are destroyed. Even though someone may not be well known and famous, yet if he has entered upon the way that accords with the Dhamma, entered upon the proper way, and conducts himself according to the Dhamma, he should be honored for that, he should be praised for that." So, putting the practice of the way first, he neither lauds himself nor disparages others because of his renown.

The Buddha spoke similarly regarding true persons who do not laud themselves and disparage others due to their family's socioeconomic status, how many offerings they receive, how ascetic they are, how strictly they keep their precepts, or what levels of samādhi they have attained. The Mahāyāna mind-training texts emphasize the same points: "Do not be boastful" and "Do not turn a god into a devil" by using Dharma practice to increase our self-centered attitude and self-grasping ignorance.[55]

One Tibetan meditator had a vision of Tārā in retreat. His student became very excited upon hearing this, but the meditator remained nonplussed. Puzzled, the student asked why, to which the meditator replied, "Whether or not Tārā actually appeared to me, I need to continue practicing. Realizing emptiness with the subtle mind is what will actually free me."

226 | APPROACHING THE BUDDHIST PATH

Dreams are illusory, although sometimes they may indicate future occurrences. I have met Tibetans who dreamed of Dharamsala before they came here, and some people dreamed of being at temples before having gone there. However, attachment to dreams increases grasping at true existence, which leads to obstacles, so it's important to remember that dreams are empty of true existence. When we face obstacles due to sentient beings, meditation on compassion is best; when we encounter other obstacles, meditation on emptiness is the best antidote.

Sometimes we meet people who have practiced for years and seem to have deep meditative experience but act in ways that appear ethically questionable. When a contradiction exists between someone's seemingly high realization and their ethical conduct, that realization may not be as high as it seems. Although the ability to remain in single-pointed concentration or in a nonconceptual state is a realization, it is not a very deep one. It is not a realization of emptiness, and the person is still afflicted by ignorance and karma.

An actual realization should bring about a change in our life. The sign of having gained the wisdom of studying the Dharma is that our outward behavior has become calm. The sign of having experientially realized the teachings of the middle level is that our coarse afflictions have diminished in strength. If we meditate properly on bodhicitta, we become kinder human beings who are courageous in practicing the Dharma. In adversity, yogic meditators remain impartial, open, and compassionate. From such behavior we can infer they have subdued their minds through deep meditative experiences. However, this alone is not an indication that they have realized emptiness directly.

REFLECTION

1. Have you inadvertently fallen into any of the above pitfalls?

2. What were the factors that led to this?

3. What must you do now to get back on track?

Signs of Progress

If we devote our lives to familiarizing ourselves with the Dharma, we will definitely see a change in our mind. As a Buddhist saying predicts, "You will be able to see the whole world and everything in it as Dharma instructions." This occurs when, through daily practice, our mind has become familiar with the Buddha's teachings and we are able to practice in most of the situations we encounter. When we have gained some experience of impermanence, we are aware of things changing, arising, and ceasing in each moment. With this understanding prominent in our mind, our clinging to people and things that are unable to provide us lasting happiness decreases. Automatically, our mind is more relaxed and at ease.

When doing analytical meditation on the stages of the path, contemplate each point, considering it logically and relating it to your own experience. While thinking about these points, do not let the mind wander to objects of attachment or become sleepy or dull. Try to have a mind that is clear and concentrated that stays on the points you are contemplating and is able to penetrate their meaning.

Certain signposts along the path help us check whether our meditations are progressing in the right direction and bearing fruit. If we meditate consistently on how to rely on a spiritual mentor and come to a point where we do not pick faults in our spiritual teachers and feel genuine respect for their qualities and gratitude for their kindness, we have achieved a good result from this meditation. If we meditate on precious human life and have a stable feeling, "My present life with so much freedom and opportunity to practice the path is difficult to receive and very precious. I do not want to waste it but direct it toward familiarizing my mind with bodhicitta and emptiness," we are proceeding in the right direction. If we pay less attention to the happiness of this life and prepare for future lives we are experiencing the result of meditation on impermanence. If acting destructively repulses us and we want to avoid it like poison, we have benefited from meditating on the sufferings of unfortunate rebirths. The mark of gaining experience of the meditation on refuge is that we understand the qualities of the Three Jewels and have deep trust in their ability to guide us on the path. Such feelings may arise during a meditation session, but the sign of real progress is when they occur repeatedly.

How do we know we have generated true renunciation of cyclic existence? Tsongkhapa said that when, through habituation, day and night we do not wish for the pleasures of cyclic existence and yearn for liberation, we have developed true determination to be free. Such an attitude has ramifications in our life. We cease being obsessed with the pleasures of cyclic existence, and things that used to irritate us cease to do so. This does not mean, however, that in deep sleep we still aspire for liberation, for that is not possible. Nor is our determination to be free manifest when we are in deep concentration realizing emptiness. Nevertheless, it has not been lost; it is present but latent when our mind is focused on other objects.

We have realized bodhicitta when, through habituation and practice, the great compassion and the aspiration to attain awakening arises spontaneously in our mind whenever we hear, see, or think about any sentient being. As explained in Tsongkhapa's "Three Principal Aspects of the Path" (*Lam gtso rnam gsum*), the measure of having ascertained the correct view of emptiness is seeing that dependent arising and emptiness are not contradictory but are mutually reinforcing, such that the mere reminder of dependent arising brings understanding of emptiness and vice-versa.

Generating virtuous qualities and realizations involves both undistracted focus and analytical discernment. Tsongkhapa says (LC 1: 272):

> Therefore, the Buddha says that any achievement of a virtuous quality in the three vehicles requires a state of mind that is both (1) an actual serenity, or a similitude of it, which rests one-pointedly on its virtuous object of meditation without wandering from it; and (2) an actual insight, or a similitude of it, which carefully analyzes a virtuous object of meditation and distinguishes both the real nature and the diversity of phenomena.

If we take "good qualities" and "realizations" to have similar meanings, serenity and insight or mental states that are similar to them are needed to gain them. This is certainly true for the realization of selflessness, which may be conceptual and inferential (on the path of preparation) or direct and nonconceptual (on the paths of seeing and meditation). For good qualities like renunciation, compassion, or bodhicitta to be definitively achieved, we need serenity or a state of one-pointedness like it. To realize selflessness—be it the conceptual, inferential realization on the path of preparation or the direct nonconceptual realization on the path of seeing—both full serenity and insight are necessary. To realize selflessness before that, similitudes of serenity and insight are required. For those of us who would like to gain attainments quickly, this may seem like a high bar to reach. However, this description makes it clear that a realization is not a flash of understanding that comes and goes. It is a stable state of mind that can be sustained with undistracted focus. Unlike fleeting flashes that are difficult to replicate, the experiences from gradual cultivation can be generated repeatedly and enhanced through single-pointed concentration.

REFLECTION

1. What are realistic expectations for you on the path?

2. What can you do to accomplish them?

3. How can you keep a happy mind and cultivate patience while you go about creating the causes?

11 | Personal Reflections on the Path

My Day

P EOPLE OFTEN ASK ME about my daily schedule and Dharma practice. I am a very poor practitioner, but I keep trying because I am convinced that practicing the Dharma is the path to peace and happiness. In Dharamsala, India, where I live, I wake up at 3:30 a.m. and immediately visualize the Buddha and recite a verse of homage written by Nāgārjuna (MMK 27.30):

> Enthused by great compassion,
> you taught the exalted Dharma
> to dispel all [wrong] views.
> To you, Gautama, I prostrate.

Sometimes I change the last line of the verse to say, "May I be inspired by Gautama Buddha." This verse is especially meaningful to me because it points out the Buddha's compassionate motivation that led him to identify ignorance as the cause of duḥkha and then to attain the wisdom realizing the ultimate nature to dispel that ignorance. Ignorance is not a mere lack of knowledge; it is a distorted apprehension that grasps as existing what doesn't exist—inherent existence. Bodhicitta then spurred him to accumulate merit, purify his mind, and hear, think, and meditate on the Dharma. In that way, he became an awakened teacher with the ability to liberate sentient beings by giving faultless teachings.

Reflecting in this way increases my confidence in the Buddha and in the path I practice to transform my mind. It also helps me to appreciate my precious human life with many fortunate qualities: I live in a place and time where the Buddha has appeared and his teachings still exist, and I have belief in things worthy of respect such as ethical conduct, concentration, and wisdom. Recalling this daily enables me to maintain a joyful attitude immune to depression and discouragement.

After reciting this verse three times, I visualize Buddha Vajradhara dissolving into me and inspiring my mind. This gives me a feeling of courage and the willingness to persevere in my practice. I then generate bodhicitta and remind myself that I can surely see transformation happening within myself, although it may be small. This encourages me to rejoice in my virtue and continue practicing.

To clear the fogginess of sleep from my mind, I recite Mañjuśrī's mantra, *Oṃ a ra pa ca na dhīḥ*,[56] and then recite *dhīḥ* as many times as possible with one breath, imagining Mañjuśrī's wisdom in the form of the syllable *dhīḥ* absorbing into a *dhīḥ* at the back of my tongue. While meditating on Mañjuśrī like this, I reflect on the four truths of the āryas, especially the liberating power of true paths and the peace that comes with actualizing true cessations.

Then I begin prostrations and daily recitations followed by a glance meditation, in which I recite and contemplate verses sequentially outlining the complete stages of the path to awakening. After that, I do formal meditation, predominantly analytical meditation to increase my understanding of the Buddha's teachings. Here my efforts are mainly directed to meditation on dependent arising and emptiness as well as on compassion and bodhicitta. I also do the tantric practice of deity yoga, which involves imagining transforming death, the intermediate state between one life and the next, and rebirth into the three bodies of a buddha.

I continue meditating, taking a few breaks, including breakfast and exercise, until about 8:30 a.m. If there is no office work, then I study Dharma texts. I take delight in reading the Indian and Tibetan treatises and commentaries repeatedly, each time discovering something new in them. There's a Tibetan saying, "If you read a book nine times, you will have nine understandings." Because this has been my experience, I will continue studying until the end of my life and recommend that others do likewise.

Often my study is interrupted because I am needed in the office. Lunch is just before noon, and after that I go to the office to work. My afternoons are filled with appointments, one right after the other. As a Buddhist monk, I don't eat dinner, and around 8:30 p.m., I go to sleep. I sleep very soundly, without any sleeping pills, and enjoy very peaceful meditation.

One teaching of the Kadam masters called the "four entrustments" especially touches my heart:

> Entrust your mind to Dharma practice;
> entrust your Dharma practice to a life of poverty;
> entrust your life of poverty to death;
> and entrust your death to an empty cave.[57]

These lines speak of completely giving ourselves to the cultivation of the two bodhicittas, conventional and ultimate, making this the most important activity in our lives, so much so that we are willing to give all our life's energies to it, from now until our death. Relinquishing attachment to the eight worldly concerns, our mind experiences so much joy and satisfaction with the freedom the Dharma bestows that money and reputation are of no concern to us. When I reflect on this verse, tears come to my eyes because this is my highest aspiration. It also reflects the greatest challenge in my life—balancing meditative cultivation with directly benefiting others in this life. Both are aspects of Dharma practice and our inner development. The pressing needs of people right now are very important, but meditative practice beckons, and the need to deepen my own practice in order to benefit others more is also essential. Perhaps some of you live with this tension in your lives, too.

Occasionally, I am able to do a retreat. During this time, I practice the visualization of deities and maṇḍalas and the recitation of mantras, but mainly I read and contemplate the great Indian texts. Being able to study and reflect on the meaning of these magnificent texts is a great treat for me.

Gradual Progress

Just as the Buddha was able to gradually transform his mind, we can as well. In my own life, I see progress from the time I was a child until now. Because I grew up in a Buddhist family and in a Buddhist country where everyone repeated, "I take refuge in the Buddha," I have had faith in the Buddha since

I was young. Although at that time I didn't have much understanding of the Dharma, I knew the Buddha was an extraordinary human being.

I came to the Potala Palace in Lhasa at age five, and my studies began when I was seven. My older brother and I studied together under the direction of our tutor, but as a young child I liked to play. The tutor had a whip, so I studied out of fear. Actually, the tutor had two whips, an ordinary whip and a gold whip that was for beating a holy person. But there was no holy pain!

When I was a little older, I began to study the lamrim, the stages of the path. This caused me to have a deep interest in the Buddhadharma and increased my confidence in the Three Jewels as authentic refuges. When I was fifteen or sixteen, my enthusiasm to practice the Dharma grew. Occasionally, when I received teachings or meditated, I felt very moved by the Dharma.

My education involved memorizing root texts and listening to my teachers' word-by-word explanations of them. I was tutored by seven debate masters from different monastic colleges. My Mongolian debate master was especially interested in emptiness, so in preparation for my geshe exams in 1958–59, I had to study many texts on that topic. We planned to visit southern Tibet on pilgrimage after my exams in March, 1959, and I would study Tsongkhapa's *Essence of Eloquence* (*Drang nges legs bshad snying po*) then. However, on March 10, everything changed, and we fled Tibet and became refugees in India. I took some texts with me—Śāntideva's *Engaging in the Bodhisattvas' Deeds*, Tsongkhapa's *Great Treatise on the Stages of the Path*, his *Essence of Eloquence*, and others—and studied whenever possible.

In my late twenties in Tibet and my early thirties in Dharamsala, I studied, contemplated, and meditated on emptiness more seriously. I became more convinced of the possibility of attaining nirvāṇa, and my confidence in the Dharma Jewel—true cessations and true paths—deepened. That led me to see the Saṅgha—those beings who have realized this Dharma directly—as magnificent and increased my admiration for them. This in turn helped me develop deeper, genuine faith in the Buddha as our teacher. At that time, the thought arose in my mind that if I could actualize nirvāṇa, I could then have a long, blissful rest!

Whereas I have high regard for bodhicitta and it is not difficult to understand, actually generating it seems challenging. My experience tallies with what the great masters say: emptiness is difficult to understand; it is especially challenging to maintain the tension between appearance and emptiness and to establish the efficacy of cause and effect in a world that is merely imputed and lacks any existence from its own side. However, when we think about emptiness and dependent arising over time, they become clearer, and we gain some feeling for them and confidence in them. Bodhicitta, on the other hand, is easy to understand but difficult to experience. But there is no other choice. We have to make the effort.

We Tibetans have the tradition of "students offering their realizations to the teacher," in which we share our understanding of the Dharma with our spiritual mentors. In the late '70s and early '80s I had several opportunities to meet with my senior tutor Ling Rinpoche, during which I spoke about my understanding of emptiness in particular. At one point, he listened very carefully and then said, "Soon you will become a yogi of space," which means someone who has realized emptiness.

Even in my dreams I would often discuss the Dharma with people or meditate on emptiness and bodhicitta. In the last few years, I have had more interest and enthusiasm in understanding emptiness, and that has brought deeper conviction and experience. Once I read in a text, "the person is mere designation," and a feeling like electricity shook me. I thought that perhaps this was selflessness. When I focused on the self, I could confirm that it was merely designated, but when I focused on the aggregates, the experience was not the same. That indicated that my experience was of the absence of a self-sufficient substantially existent person, not the emptiness of inherent existence.

Today my understanding of selflessness has improved, and that helps greatly to reduce the intensity and frequency of the afflictions, especially attachment and anger. Understanding emptiness has no adverse effect on the practice of authentic love and compassion because these are not driven by ignorance. In fact, understanding emptiness boosts our altruism by enabling us to recognize sentient beings' suffering more clearly. Contemplation of emptiness and compassion are the backbone of my daily practice.

I do not expect deeper understanding or experience to come within a short period of time. Ten, twenty, thirty, or more years of practice are necessary, but change will definitely occur when we make consistent effort. Some of you may not live another twenty or thirty years, but if you pay serious attention and make yourself familiar with emptiness and bodhicitta, you will put many positive imprints of these topics on your subtle consciousness. I have seen this in my own experience. Some Buddhist topics are easy for me to understand, but when I discuss these with some senior scholars, these topics sometimes appear difficult for them. This indicates some familiarity with these topics in my previous lives. So even if you are old now, whatever positive imprints you put on your mindstream from studying and contemplating for even a few months or years will carry on to your next life and benefit you.

All the virtuous actions you do now will certainly enable you to have a human rebirth and live in a conducive environment where there is more opportunity to learn and practice the Buddha's teachings. Those who are old like me should not excuse themselves by thinking that now they're very old and nothing can be done. The result of thinking like this will be not achieving anything. So please make as much of an effort as you can while you have this precious life.

Those of you who are young have more time to study and practice. Think seriously about what is important in your life, and put effort into the Dharma. Of course, whether you practice is up to you. If you have genuine interest, practice is very worthwhile. Please give this serious thought.

Some followers of other religions or spiritual traditions may read this book out of curiosity. Please continue with your current practice. The Buddha never imposed his beliefs on anyone. Each individual has complete freedom to follow whatever religion he or she chooses or to follow no faith at all. But whatever you do, be a kind human being.

In Montserrat, Spain, I met a Catholic monk who spent five years as a hermit meditating in the mountains behind the monastery. He told me that his main practice was meditating on love. When I looked into his eyes, there was some special feeling there. I admire and respect him greatly. His life shows that if we meditate for five years, some result will definitely come. Similarly, if we make daily effort to train our mind, the wild monkey of our mind will be subdued.[58]

Cultivating Bodhicitta

In 1959 Khunu Lama Rinpoche[59] came to visit me. At that time, he told me that his practice centered on bodhicitta, especially Śāntideva's *Engaging in the Bodhisattvas' Deeds.* Around that time, I also learned about a short text Khunu Lama Rinpoche authored, *The Jewel Lamp: A Praise of Bodhicitta (Byang chub sems kyi bstod pa rin chen sgron ma)*, and knowing that my guru Ling Rinpoche had already received teachings from him, in 1967 I requested him to give me the oral transmission of that text. While he was reading *The Jewel Lamp*, I was overwhelmed with tears.

In my twenties, I appreciated bodhicitta, but it seemed far away. In 1967, with Ling Rinpoche's permission, I requested teachings from Khunu Lama Rinpoche on *Engaging in the Bodhisattvas' Deeds.* He accepted and gave the teaching in Bodhgaya. After that, bodhicitta felt closer, and it became obvious that self-centeredness is the basis for fear and distrust. Conversely, if we genuinely care about others, even ghosts and spirits will eventually show appreciation. When our basic attitude is altruistic, then even if anger arises, it leaves quickly. It's like our mind has a strong immune system that protects it from the illness of the afflictions.

Around that time, I also studied another marvelous text, Nāgārjuna's *Precious Garland,* and a few other supplementary books, and every day I thought about and meditated on them. Because I already had strong admiration and faith in Nāgārjuna from contemplating his teachings on emptiness, even reading a short passage from his writings has a profound impact on me.

Of the thirteen great classical texts,[60] I received the oral transmission on Maitreya's *Ornament of Clear Realizations* and Candrakīrti's *Supplement to the Middle Way* from Ling Rinpoche. The oral transmissions of the other eleven treatises I received from Khunu Lama Rinpoche. In addition to being a great, yet humble, practitioner, he was a remarkable scholar and teacher. His teachings were very precise, and he could easily cite many passages from the scriptures. When I asked him how he received his training, he told me that when he was in Kham, Tibet, he thought that texts were to be "left behind" in the sense of not clinging to the physical books, although he was definitely immersed in their meaning and it touched his heart. His translations from both Tibetan and Sanskrit were impeccable. When I received teachings on Śāntideva's work, he often mentioned, "Here the Tibetan translation is wrong. The original Sanskrit says this . . ." I made these corrections in my own copy and incorporate them now when I teach that text.

My teacher Ling Rinpoche was very kind to me. He would encourage me in my practice, telling me that if I put in effort, I could gain realizations. But if I were to see Ling Rinpoche now, I would have to confess that I still have not attained those realizations, even though many years have passed.

Around 1970, my feeling for bodhicitta became more intimate. After some time, I became convinced that if I had enough time to meditate, I could become a bodhisattva within this life. However, I don't have sufficient time. That is my excuse. But for those with sufficient time, there is no excuse!

I continue receiving teachings on bodhicitta and doing analytical meditation on it. Sometimes when I meditate on bodhicitta in my room, I am so deeply moved that tears come. During one period of my life, I would do lengthy meditation sessions on bodhicitta and emptiness, and almost every day I would have strong experiences and be very touched. At the end of his *Essence of Eloquence,* Tsongkhapa says that when he reflects deeply on what he has learned, his faith in the Buddha increases even more. Sometimes his recollection of the kindness of the Nālandā masters overpowers him with appreciation for the teachings on emptiness, and other times reflecting on the suffering of sentient beings overwhelms him with compassion. He comments that it is almost as if these two feelings were competing with each other. While I do not have Tsongkhapa's realizations, at times I too am affected in the same way as he was when reflecting on emptiness and bodhicitta.

Now when I teach about bodhicitta, I feel very moved. That means my mind is more receptive and has grown closer to bodhicitta. Compared to when I was fifteen, my understanding of these topics has changed considerably. This confirms that the possibility of attaining awakening exists. Due to knowledge, examination, and some experience, my faith in the Three Jewels is firm and deep. The Buddha's marvelous teachings on infinite altruism and the wisdom of reality is indeed a living tradition. However, my experience of Tantrayāna is lacking.

During one period, when meditating on tantric practices such as Guhyasamāja, I focused on the generation stage, which involves dissolving oneself into emptiness and reemerging as the deity. I would try to maintain a stable continuity of this visualization and develop single-pointed concentration on it. When reflecting on the self, I would train to immediately think of myself as the deity, without any thought or appearance of the ordinary I. This is the practice of cultivating divine appearance and divine identity.

But in the late 1970s, I became very busy with my responsibilities to my students and the Tibetan community. Due to lack of time, I had to discontinue my long meditation sessions, and now I have fallen back to my previous level of experience. Born in 1935, I am becoming old; maybe it is too late to practice much more. The Tibetan community in exile now has an elected government, and I want them to carry out all the governmental and administrative responsibilities. Finally, in 2011, I was able to resign my post in the government in the hope of having more time for practice.

But I still have many visitors and appointments. I can't refuse to meet the Tibetans who have endured so much hardship to come from Tibet to see me. I can't ignore them and say "I am in retreat" when they have risked their lives to come all this way to see me. The purpose of doing retreat is to benefit others. Meeting these people brings some benefit to them, so this is part of my practice. I think the rest of my life will go like this. Although I'm sad not to have the chance to do more retreat, my greatest source of inspiration is Śāntideva's verse (BCA 10.55):

> As long as space endures,
> and as long as sentient beings remain,
> so too will I abide
> to dispel the misery of the world.

Whether I attain buddhahood or not in this one simple existence is not important; I must at least benefit others, especially when they have problems. Bodhicitta compels me to do this.

The First Dalai Lama, Gendun Drup, spent a long time in retreat. During this time, he had visions of White Tārā and Green Tārā and wrote very moving and meaningful praises to them. After his retreat, he voluntarily began to do more work, some of it difficult and time-consuming: he gave daily teachings on different texts to his students, and he established Tashi Lhunpo Monastery in Shigatse. By that time, he was already an old monk with white hair and a cane, but he was the architect and foreman who oversaw the construction of the monastery. He also sent people out to collect donations so the monastery could be built. Then, despite his age, as the manager of the monastery, he gave instructions on the daily operation of the monastery and the monks' discipline.

Naturally, some of his students created trouble. On one occasion, Gendun Drup became exasperated with them and said, "If I had remained in Kangchen Monastery, I would have developed some high spiritual attainments by now. But I sacrificed that to come to this place to help you, to help the larger Buddhist community and a greater number of people." Although this may have sounded boastful, he was cautioning his students to be careful, to look at the big picture, and to appreciate that their opportunity to learn the Dharma depended on others.

One day toward the end of his life, Gendun Drup said, "Now I am very old." He said it just like that.

One of his main disciples then reminded him, "It was prophesized that you would go directly to a pure land. Will you do that?"

Gendun Drup replied, "I have no wish to go to these higher places. My only wish is to go to troubled areas where I can serve." That is very wonderful! That truly inspires me!

The Buddha's tradition is a living tradition. If we practice, we can transform ourselves. This occurs not through merely praying but through meditating, principally doing analytical meditation. Buddhist practices use our human intelligence in the greatest way to develop the maximum potential of a good heart.

Willingness to Undergo Hardship

When we look at the life of our teacher, Śākyamuni Buddha, we notice that he went through a process of spiritual development. Born as a prince, he later gave up the comforts of royal life and became a monastic in order to pursue his spiritual practice. He endured the disapproval of his father and the poor living conditions that his wandering lifestyle entailed. He also did six years of severe, ascetic spiritual practice. After all this, he displayed the act of attaining full awakening.

His life exemplifies the necessity to be able to bear hardship in spiritual pursuit. This is true of the lives of the teachers of many other spiritual traditions as well. The message we receive from the examples of their lives is that we, as the followers of these teachers, must be willing to go through hardship and persevere in order to realize our spiritual aspirations.

Sometimes the thought remains in the back of our minds, "Yes, the Buddha went through so many hardships to attain awakening, but I don't need to do this. Somehow I'll be able to attain awakening without having to give up the comforts and luxury that I'm attached to." Although we may not say it, thinking in this way indicates we believe that we are more fortunate than the Buddha. While he had to go through so many hardships, we feel we can attain the same spiritual realizations without having to live ascetically and endure difficulties as he did. This is mistaken.

The Buddha taught the middle way, a path avoiding the extremes of severe asceticism and heedless indulgence. Nevertheless, we must be willing to give up the pleasures to which we are attached if we are to penetrate the nature of reality and open our hearts with bodhicitta toward all beings. Our priorities must be clear: Which do we value more, our present comfort and security or spiritual liberation? Are we willing to undergo the physical and emotional hardships of relinquishing our attachments in order to practice the spiritual path? These are questions on which we must reflect deeply.

Each of us will face different hardships along the path. For some people, the challenge will not be living a simple lifestyle but enduring the criticism of family and society. Others will face having to practice despite health issues, while some must deal with strong sexual cravings. We must develop the internal fortitude to persevere in our practice no matter what suffering—physical, emotional, or mental—comes our way.

Keeping a Happy Mind

It is important to keep a happy mind when practicing Dharma. Buoyancy, enthusiasm, and joy are needed to maintain our practice; these cannot exist in a mind weighed down by depression. People ask me how I maintain a happy mind and relaxed demeanor even though I have been a refugee for over fifty years. One time a news reporter was interviewing me and asked me why I wasn't angry given the fact that I have witnessed so much destruction in my native land and to my people. I looked at her and replied, "What good would it do to be angry? I wouldn't sleep well or be able to digest my food. Plus my anger wouldn't change the situation at all!" I suppose she assumed I would take the opportunity to tell the world about the sufferings of the Tibetans under the Communist Chinese and was astonished when I didn't.

While we may sometimes experience happiness when the mind is non-virtuous—for example, the pleasure that arises when our craving is satisfied or when we have exacted revenge on someone who hurt us—that happiness does not help us on the path to awakening and should be abandoned. In any case, deep down, I don't think we are really happy then.

Other experiences of happiness are rooted in virtuous mental states. When I am generous and can relieve the poverty of others, I feel good inside. The ability to live ethically with a nonviolent attitude makes me rejoice and generates a sense of well-being. Having lovingkindness toward others brings pleasure in the mind, and doing my daily meditation practices, which deepens my refuge in the Three Jewels, brings great inner satisfaction. It is also said that gaining meditative stabilization suffuses the mind with bliss.

We are often distracted from the Dharma by sensory stimuli—attractive or repulsive sights, sounds, smells, tastes, or physical sensations. But when our mind of attachment doesn't have enough sense stimuli, we are bored. People who are very involved with the external world of the five senses often find themselves in this predicament and are frequently dissatisfied, whereas those who derive happiness from internal qualities—faith, love, compassion, wisdom, and so forth—experience much joy and contentment. They are not swept away by the goings on of people in the environment around them. Too much sensory input makes us exhausted, and our mental potential declines. For that reason, it is better to watch our mind. I don't watch television or explore the Internet, although I do listen to BBC news on the radio so I know what is going on in the lives of other sentient beings. Listening to the news becomes a kind of meditation on karma and its effects and inspires me to cultivate compassion.

In my own practice, I weed out the unwholesome states that bring some sort of temporary, polluted pleasure and instead put energy into cultivating wholesome mental states. That enables me to keep a happy mind—which is important to continue practicing the Dharma—even in difficult situations.

Realized Beings

Some people have asked me whether I know people who have attained full awakening. The Buddha stipulated that unless there is great purpose in revealing one's realizations, one should not do so. Speaking of one's own spiritual attainments is an infraction of the monastic precepts, and proclaiming realizations that one does not have is a root downfall, such that one is no longer a monastic. Falsely proclaiming one has realized emptiness is a root downfall of the bodhisattva ethical code. Thus proclaiming one's realization publicly is unheard of among true Buddhist practitioners.

Nevertheless, I have had the opportunity to meet some people who have experienced extraordinary development and may be near buddhahood. Meeting these people demonstrates that the teachings are alive and gives us great inspiration and determination. For this reason, refuge in the Saṅgha—the highly realized beings—strengthens our practice.

In the remainder of this section, I (Chodron) would like to explain further why realized beings do not discuss their attainments, especially nowadays when people make great effort to proclaim their good qualities and accomplishments. First, speaking about attainments has a deleterious effect on our practice. As soon as someone begins to talk about spiritual experiences publicly, words begin to replace experience. The actual feeling of the experience fades in the mind, and we become expert in telling a fascinating story. It is easy to become arrogant and complacent if we attain celebrity as a spiritual luminary. For the sake of our personal practice, remaining humble and modest is best.

Furthermore, spiritually immature people easily confuse an unusual meditation experience for spiritual realization. Even if their intentions are good, if they proclaim their spiritual prowess and begin to instruct others, naive people can easily be led astray and follow an incorrect path. Then, if that teacher's veneer cracks, the followers will be deeply disillusioned and may even abandon following a spiritual path altogether. Teachers who make no special claim to greatness avoid being transformed into false idols by their followers.

Say someone with actual attainments were to announce them publicly, what would come of it? Many people would worship that person instead of listening to their teachings. Imagine if the Buddha appeared in New York with a body of radiant, golden light. People would be so struck by amazement that they would stare at him and wait for him to perform miraculous feats. The media would want to interview him, and soon there would be a new line of apparel named after him.

244 | APPROACHING THE BUDDHIST PATH

If someone has genuine and stable realizations, people with merit who are receptive will discern this and have faith in that person. It is not necessary to advertise one's qualities. Someone who is a good cook does not need to proclaim his culinary feats to all. When he cooks a meal, people will know for themselves.

Humble behavior is a sign of spiritual attainment. People with genuine realizations have no need for praise, reputation, and the glamour and perks that they bring. Their main interest is in stabilizing and enhancing their realizations and benefiting others.

In special cases, a teacher with close connections to a few students may reveal his or her spiritual experiences in a confidential manner and in a private setting. This may be to inspire those students who are already dedicated to the path, so that they will put more energy into their practice. These students should be discreet with regards to what they have heard.

While publicly discussing our attainments does not serve a good purpose, consulting with our spiritual mentor when engaging in intense spiritual practice is important. During a meeting, we relate our spiritual insights and experiences to the spiritual mentor, who will help us evaluate and understand them and will give us further guidance and instructions. If a practitioner is in strict retreat and her spiritual master is not nearby, she may discuss her meditation experiences with a trusted and experienced fellow retreatant to clarify and refine her understanding and avoid misinterpreting an experience. As such it is important for spiritual progress.

What I Have Learned in Life

Someone once asked me, "You have lived many decades now. Please sum up the most important things you have learned in life." I paused to reflect. Of course, I have had many different kinds of experience—as a citizen in my own country and as a refugee, as a young person and now as an older one, as a student and as a leader. In Buddhism we always pray for the welfare of all sentient beings no matter their life form; this has had great impact on me. In all situations and with a wide variety of people, I regard everyone as being fundamentally the same: each of us wishes to be happy and to be free from suffering. Thinking like this, I immediately feel close to others wherever I go; there is no barrier between us.

As a result of meeting many different kinds of people and also due to the experience that age brings, I act in an informal manner with everyone and talk to others as one human being to another. This attitude and behavior eliminate any ground for anxiety. On the other hand, if I thought, "I am the Dalai Lama and a Buddhist monk, so I should act a certain way, and people should treat me in a particular way," that would foster anxiety and resentment. So I forget about such distinctions and see that I am just a human being who is meeting another human being. On the emotional level, we are the same. On the mental and physical levels, we are also the same. It is helpful for me to think in this way, and it also puts others at ease. Sometimes at the beginning of a meeting or a conversation, people are very reserved and stiff, but within a few minutes that is gone and we feel very close.

12 | Working in the World

A s Buddhists, and particularly as practitioners of the Mahāyāna path, we are part of the human community and have the responsibility to benefit that community. We should take a more active role in helping society by employing whatever talents and abilities we possess to help others, whether or not they are Buddhist. If the human community is happy and at peace, all of us automatically benefit.

People's differing temperaments are reflected in two types of compassion. The first wants others to be free of their suffering and problems but still prioritizes happiness for oneself. The second not only wishes others to be free of suffering but is also prepared to act to bring this about. The experience of compassion is similar in the two, but due to focusing more on the well-being of others and the disadvantages of self-centeredness, the second compassion is courageous and actively engages with others.

There are many ways for those who wish to alleviate misery to apply Dharma principles to their interactions with family, society, and the surrounding world. As we actively help others, we must continue to meditate on the two methods to generate bodhicitta, using reason and concrete examples to increase the strength and scope of our compassion and to prevent it from degenerating.

Good health and a positive attitude are assets when we work to benefit others, so we will turn to these topics first. Reflections have not been included in this chapter, so please pause at the end of each section to reflect on its main points and how they relate to your own experience and aspirations.

Good Health and Dealing with Illness and Injury

Everyone desires good health, and for Dharma practitioners, it facilitates our ability to practice. For this reason we should do our best to maintain our health by eating nutritious meals, exercising and sleeping enough (but not too much!), and maintaining good standards of cleanliness. Here our motivation is not attachment to pleasure or fear of pain; it is the opportunity good health provides to use our precious human life for Dharma practice, and specifically to cultivate bodhicitta and wisdom in order to benefit all sentient beings.

Balance is important. One meaning of the "middle way" is to avoid the extremes of self-mortification and self-indulgence. Physical suffering comes naturally, simply because we have a body. Deliberately inflicting pain on our body does not purify our mind. In fact, severe ascetic practices could become another form of self-centeredness if the motive is to gain a good reputation for having the ability to tolerate pain.

Self-indulgence hinders Dharma practice by consuming our time. Instead of practicing the Dharma to go beyond the saṃsāric situation of having a body under the influence of afflictions and karma, we spend inordinate energy and time pampering our body and worrying about its health and comfort. It is wiser to accept that as long as we are human beings in cyclic existence, we will have a body that is prone to illness. Falling ill is not some unusual or unique fate that we alone suffer, nor is it a punishment or indicative of failure on our part. Accepting the limitations of having a samsaric body and understanding it is the basis of our precious human life, we must use it wisely without fussing over it.

People often write to me for advice regarding illness. Although my responses vary according to the illness and the person's disposition, I will share some general advice to help others.

When you are ill, you should consult a doctor and follow his or her advice. Do not abandon conventional medicine in favor of faith healing.

It happens that someone comments to a cancer patient, "Your anger caused the cancer." Such comments not only lack compassion, they are mistaken. Diseases come about due to many causes and conditions, and blaming someone who is ill for their disease is heartless.

The mind-training practice of seeing our illness as a result of destructive actions we have done in previous lives or earlier in this life is very different than blaming the victim. Seeing illness in this way does not mean that we deserve to suffer: no one *deserves* to suffer. Rather, we act and experience results that accord with those actions. Daisy seeds grow into daisies; they don't produce chilies. Thinking in this way enables us to release our anger and sense of injustice and accept the situation. Doing this transforms a bad situation into a learning experience, because we understand that if we do not like suffering results, we should abandon creating their causes in the future. This gives us great impetus to let go of destructive actions and negative habits.

Thinking that the karma that caused the illness could have instead ripened in a far worse suffering helps put our misery in perspective. Cancer is not at all pleasant, but if that karma had ripened in an unfortunate rebirth, we would have been in an even worse situation. Reflecting in this way helps us to realize that we can in fact endure our present misery. In addition, because that karma has now ripened, its energy has been consumed and cannot afflict us again.

Distinguishing between physical pain and mental suffering is crucial. Even if your body is ill, your mind can remain peaceful, and a relaxed mind will lessen your suffering and help the body heal. Sit quietly and observe the difference between the actual physical pain of the illness or injury and the mental suffering caused by fear and anxiety. By letting our preconceptions proliferate and imagining all sorts of horrible things that could happen due to our illness or injury, our mind can cause us more misery than our physical condition. Instead of indulging the anxiety, bring your attention to a wholesome way of viewing the situation: contemplate the kindness of those who are taking care of you. By doing so, you will be filled with strong gratitude.

Remembering that tragedy is not unique to ourselves also helps to broaden our view and prevents us from falling into self-pity, which only increases misery. We can contemplate, "At this very moment, many others are experiencing far worse miseries, and many of them have no protector, no refuge, and no friends to help them. I am more fortunate for I can rely on the Three Jewels, and so many friends, relatives, and even strangers—such as the hospital staff—are helping me. For someone who is ill, my situation is quite good." Then send love and compassion to others who are ill, injured, or unjustly imprisoned by wishing them to be free of misery and to have all happiness. You can combine this with the taking-and-giving meditation described in chapter 7.

Remembering that such problems are characteristic of cyclic existence helps us generate the determination to be free and to attain liberation. This gives our Dharma practice a big boost by helping us to make Dharma, not the eight worldly concerns, our priority in life. In addition, suffering has some benefits: it makes us humbler and helps us to open our heart in compassion for others.

Visualization practices can also be useful. At the place where you experience pain, visualize the syllables of a mantra or a ball of light. Its brilliant yet gentle white light radiates and fills the painful or diseased area, purifying all illness and pain and filling the area with bliss.

Alternatively, imagine the Buddha (or a meditational deity such as Avalokiteśvara or Tārā) in front of you or on the crown of your head. Light and nectar flow from the Buddha or deity into you, purifying and healing your body and restoring the balances of the elements.

Doing purification to cleanse the karma causing the illness is also helpful. Purifying karma that has already ripened or is presently ripening isn't possible, but the karma that perpetuates the illness in the future can be purified. However, when karma is extremely heavy, preventing it from ripening altogether is difficult, although purification can make the result shorter or less severe. It also makes the mind more peaceful and thus better able to handle the illness.

Maintaining a Positive Attitude

Except for a few rare individuals who can devote their full energies to meditation twenty-four hours a day, the majority of Buddhists should remain active in helping their communities. Social engagement is vital, but without meditation our work in society may not become a genuine Dharma activity. On the other hand, without a social component, our practice of benefiting others may not be truly effective. Balance is important.

Whenever you can offer direct help to others, do so. In Tibet, when I saw animals on the way to be slaughtered, I would send someone to buy them, and we gave the animals shelter. In India, seeing animals in cages on trucks pains me a lot. However, I cannot pull over the trucks and buy the animals.

Instead I recite mantras and prayers for them, reflect on karma, and generate compassion.

Countless sentient beings toil in cyclic existence. All of them are caught up in the three types of duḥkha: obvious physical and mental suffering, suffering because happy circumstances are fleeting, and suffering by being under the influence of afflictions and karma. Of course we cannot solve all of these problems. Cyclic existence remains; things will never be perfect. But making even a small contribution to one person or to ten people to help them have peace of mind is worthwhile. We have done something. Giving up hope, withdrawing, and doing nothing is senseless. We are all tourists here on Earth; we stay just a short time. So let's not be troublemakers while we are here! Every being wants to be happy and has the right to be. It is our responsibility to make a contribution toward their well-being, and we must do what we can. That is the purpose of our life.

From a Buddhist viewpoint, cyclic existence has been faulty since beginningless time. Because all sentient beings are under the influence of afflictions and karma, trying to create a perfect world by rearranging external conditions is impossible. Because of this worldview, Tibetans do not expect so much from external situations. They accept difficulties more readily and are more easily satisfied. If we cultivate a view that does not expect fantastic happiness and magnificence in cyclic existence, we will be more content with what we have. Rather than leading to apathy or complacency, having modest expectations makes our minds more stable and prevents discouragement.

People ask me how I can bear the suffering in Tibet. When I compare the suffering in Tibet with the suffering of cyclic existence, the latter is much worse. We can't close our eyes to suffering of any kind. Looking at our own suffering, we generate the determination to be free—this is compassion for ourselves. When seeing the suffering of others, we generate great compassion and bodhicitta and engage in practices that directly or indirectly contribute to their well-being.

Sometimes we may want to help, but the situation may not allow it. People who do humanitarian work in war zones speak of the danger they face in places where human beings have many disturbing emotions and cannot think clearly. These aid workers have one foot there and one foot ready to run, because there is no value in their getting killed. Even if the Buddha were to go to some of these places, he could not do much to help. Under these circumstances, we may have to leave the situation physically but can continue to send our compassion and pray for the well-being of those trapped there. We can actively work to educate people in danger of being drawn into the conflict. Although we may not be able to extinguish the fire, we can at least prevent it from spreading. Do not ignore the value of this.

Well-meaning individuals ask me how to develop the courage to keep trying to make a difference in a world that seems so chaotic. No matter how numerous the difficulties and no matter how large the obstacles, if our aim is reasonable and beneficial, we must keep our determination and maintain constant effort. If something is good for the larger community, it doesn't matter whether that goal materializes during our lifetime; we must keep working toward it. The next generation can build upon the good work we have done, and with time things will change.

Using Diverse Methods to Benefit Others

As limited beings, we may find it difficult to know what is beneficial for others. Sometimes our prejudice, attachment, and anger color the situation. We have preconceived ideas about how others should live their lives. The first step in helping others is clearing away the afflictions and self-preoccupation from our own minds.

Second, we actively cultivate love, compassion, and courage in order to have the inner strength to be of assistance.

Third, we develop the wisdom to determine the most skillful way to help. At this point, we may practice the four types of awakening activity: peace, increase, control, and wrath. Initially, we practice these in meditation, first imagining *pacifying* the afflictions of others by encouraging them to purify their negativities, then imagining *increasing* their lifespan, wisdom, and merit by inspiring them to act constructively. Next we imagine being able to influence or *control* their afflictions through the force of our wisdom and compassion. Finally, for those who are intractable, we imagine employing *wrathful* means to destroy their ability to harm others.

To apply these four to an actual situation, let's take the example of someone who is about to perform some act of cruelty. A bodhisattva who lacks clairvoyant powers, and thus doesn't know exactly what is best to do in the situation, begins with peaceful means. She uses gentle measures to intercede, pacifying that person by giving comfort, verbally addressing his concerns, or using reason to dissuade him from harming someone.

If that doesn't work, she tries increasing his well-being. She may give him medicine or a gift, or teach him a topic that interests him. If this too doesn't work, she will use strong pressure or influence to try to steer him in a good direction. Should that too fail, she may intimidate the person through aggressive means or destroy his ability to harm others. Such forceful action must be motivated by compassion, not by vengeance, and is used only as a last resort.

The basic approach here is to apply whatever techniques are most effective to relieve our own or others' difficulties. This is consistent with the advice that there is nothing a bodhisattva should not learn. We don't use just the Dharma to prevent or solve our own and others' problems but also eat a healthy diet, exercise, and use whatever type of medical treatment is suitable. Complementing Buddhist practice with other methods is fine, although it is wise to remember they are distinct fields. For example, if Buddhists have issues that psychotherapy can help solve, they can and should enter therapy. Dharma centers could have counselors who are also Dharma students. Students would not regard the counselors as spiritual teachers but could discuss psychological issues with them. I am happy to hear that some Buddhists are developing Buddhist-based psychotherapeutic methods.

From one viewpoint, anything can be considered Buddhist if it is motivated by bodhicitta. However, just because a practice is done by a Buddhist does not necessarily make it a Buddhist practice. For example, to attain liberation, a Buddhist must practice serenity meditation. But this in itself is not a Buddhist practice because practitioners of other traditions do it as well. Similarly, except for insight into impermanence and selflessness, insight in itself cannot be called Buddhist because non-Buddhists also practice it. Techniques from disciplines such as psychotherapy can be adopted by Buddhists, but that does not make these techniques Buddhist. From this viewpoint, the only techniques or practices that can specifically be called Buddhist are those directly relating to the goal of liberation from cyclic existence, for example, the meditation on selflessness.

If other disciplines, such as psychology or yoga, do not entail believing in a permanent soul or a creator, and if they make us a kinder or healthier person, we may use them. If other disciplines teach beliefs that conflict with Buddhist views or create difficulties in our practice, it is wiser to leave them aside. This is the general position, but there may be some exceptions. For instance, to help people with low self-esteem have a better view of themselves, teaching them there is a permanent soul may be helpful. Even the Buddha taught a permanent self in some scriptures as a skillful means to benefit a particular audience.

Any Buddhist teaching, such as mindfulness, compassion, or the taking-and-giving meditation can be taught to others to help them. People doing so should not consider themselves Buddhist teachers, nor should they call secularized versions of Buddhist practices "Buddhism." They may simply say the technique they teach has its source in Buddhism. Although mindfulness is very popular now and is rooted in Buddhadharma, the way it is taught and practiced in secular society differs from in a Buddhist context. The purpose of secular mindfulness is to help people live better in the present, while Buddhists meditate on the four establishments of mindfulness to attain liberation and awakening. Secular mindfulness simply observes sensation and thoughts as they arise in the body and mind; Buddhist mindfulness has an element of wisdom and leads to insight into impermanence, the nature of duḥkha, and selflessness.

If a person has faith in both Christianity and Buddhism, she may view Jesus as a bodhisattva and visualize him as a symbol of love and compassion. However, we can't say this is a Buddhist practice. We can teach Buddhist principles to the general public without using specifically Buddhist language and without calling these concepts Buddhist. However, we should not incorporate non-Buddhist practices or concepts into Buddhism and call them Buddhism. This harms the existence of the pure Dharma.

Engaged Buddhism and Political Involvement

I have some reservations speaking about politics, the business world, and so forth because I don't want it to appear that I have advice regarding each and every field, especially those in which my knowledge is limited. I also do not want my personal opinions on these topics to be seen as "the Buddhist view" to which all Buddhists must adhere, so I will simply discuss general points about motivation and so forth and leave their application to the reader.

If someone can make significant spiritual progress, remaining isolated in retreat and spending most of her energy in deep meditation is worthwhile. However, this is difficult for most people, who wish to have a family and a job. In this case, live in a balanced way: maintain a daily meditation practice of whatever length is practical for you, earn your living through right livelihood, and contribute to the benefit of society in general or to specific individuals in it. You will have to determine a good balance of time and energy, given your own situation.

We need education to help others most effectively. The purpose of education is not just to learn more about the world or the living beings in it; it is to build a happier human community and to benefit animals as well. With that motivation, study whatever field interests you and seek employment that does not involve harming others or living unethically. In this way, right from the beginning, your whole life will be involved in benefiting others.

I see three ways the Buddhist community can serve society. First, we can be more active in projects that directly benefit others. Dharma centers and monasteries can either set up their own projects or participate in already existing organizations that help the homeless, provide hospice care for the terminally ill, educate children, reach out to refugees, counsel prisoners, provide healthcare and food to the poor, protect endangered species, care for the environment, and so on. Some centers are already engaged in such works, and I am very pleased with this.

Baba Amte (1914–2008), a follower of Mahatma Gandhi and an Indian social worker, established an ashram for thousands of lepers, who are ordinarily neglected by society, and trained them in various skills. When I saw them working with tools, I was concerned that they would hurt themselves, but the lepers worked diligently and with self-confidence. I offered part of the money from my Nobel Peace Prize to his ashram.

I have also met residents of a slum in a large Indian city. Since they are from a low caste, they feel demoralized. If we treat them with kindness, respecting them as human beings like us, they feel more confident. Once, some laborers were repairing my residence in Dharamsala. At first they were shy and timid, but when I shook their hands and chatted with them, they smiled and laughed. We should not think we are special and look down on others; we have been in that situation in past lives and may be in future lives if we act recklessly now.

We should also help individuals directly. Often there are many severely disabled beggars outside the monasteries where I teach in India. Some of them drag themselves on the ground. I feel very sad looking at them and encourage people who attend teachings to help them.

Second, we can use Buddhist principles and techniques to promote compassion, altruism, self-confidence, fearlessness, fortitude, and tolerance in society. Many concepts and techniques found in Buddhism for working with the mind can help others, both secular people and those of other faiths. Social activists may want to learn methods to overcome anger. Teachers may want to introduce exercises to cultivate empathy, compassion, and good communication among students. We should explain these methods to others in a secular setting without speaking about Buddhist doctrine or encouraging people to become Buddhists.

Childhood is a crucial time, yet many children grow up in an atmosphere with little compassion. Their parents quarrel and divorce; their teachers do not care for them as individuals. When these children become adults and act without conscience or compassion, who can blame them? They never experienced deeper human affection. The Buddhist community can make significant contributions in schools and families by helping people build families with more warmth and affection, and by showing teachers how to be involved, patient, and compassionate with their students. Parents and teachers—and society in general—need to learn that teaching children to be good human beings is more important than helping them become rich or famous.

Third, we can present Buddhist ideas and practices to help those who are interested. Someone who is terminally ill may want to hear about rebirth. Healthcare professionals may be interested in the stages of dying as described in Buddhist texts. Buddhist teachings may help young people who are spiritually lost, and teaching buddha nature and compassion to the incarcerated can give them a new vision of life.

Representatives from various Buddhist groups could meet to consider taking a united stand on some issues. In that way, Buddhists can participate with concerted effort to preserve the environment and protect the beings in it, including animals. In our world many life forms that do not create problems are sacrificed to serve the purposes of human beings, who are the troublemakers. We cannot change these things at once, but it is worthwhile to voice our concerns and do whatever is possible.

Some people believe that religious practice and political involvement are contradictory and that a truly spiritual person should not be involved in politics. Several factors must be taken into consideration here. Although politics itself is not inherently corrupt or evil, a person's motivation can make it so. A person using politics to convert people to his religion or impose beliefs unique to his religion on all of society lacks respect for all beings. However, political action taken with a compassionate motivation can be another method to solve human problems, just as engineering, teaching, farming, healthcare, and factory work can benefit humanity.

It is especially important for politicians to behave ethically and develop compassion, and their personal spiritual practice may help them to do so. I sometimes tell Indian politicians that they should be genuinely religious because their actions have a strong effect on society. If a hermit in the mountains lacks proper ethical restraint, few people are harmed; but if a politician does, an entire nation and even the world can be adversely affected. In the *Precious Garland*, which Nāgārjuna wrote for the Śātavāhana king, he penned many verses with instructions on how to govern effectively and fairly. Here are some examples (RA 399, 256, 134):

At that time [as a ruler] you should internalize firmly
the practices of generosity, ethical conduct, and fortitude
that were especially taught for householders
and have as their essence compassion.

Just as you are intent on thinking
of what could be done to help yourself,
so you should be intent on thinking
of what could be done to help others.

Just as by themselves the true words
of kings generate firm trust,
so their false words
are the best means to create distrust.

Nāgārjuna also encouraged the king to tax citizens fairly, fund a system of public education that ensures teachers are well compensated, and construct public roads with rest stops and parks where people can relax and enjoy themselves.

In recent years many people have turned to Buddhist scriptures for guidance on current issues. Other people have sought confirmation of their political or social views in the Buddhadharma. Quotations to support this or that view may certainly be found in the scriptures. However, we must be open-minded and avoid thinking that everyone who calls themself a Buddhist should agree on all political and social issues. The Buddha principally taught the path to liberation from cyclic existence. When he gave advice on social, family, political, and other issues, he spoke in the context of Indian culture of the fifth century BCE. Some, but not all, of this advice can be applied and adapted to present contexts.

Some people regard the Tibet issue as political, and as Dharma practitioners they do not want to get involved. However, if we want Tibetan Buddhism to flourish and remain in our world, we need freedom in Tibet. Without having autonomy in our country, we Tibetans will have great difficulty in preserving our form of Buddhadharma. This, in turn, will adversely impact the rest of the world. Although I do not expect all Dharma practitioners to actively work for human rights and freedom in Tibet, your sympathy and moral support does have an effect.

Consumerism and the Environment

Peace and the survival of life on Earth as we know it are threatened by human activities that are bereft of humanitarian values. Destruction of nature and natural resources results from ignorance, greed, and disregard for sentient beings who depend on the earth for survival. Environmental degradation also cheats future generations, who will inherit a vastly degraded planet if the destruction of the natural environment continues at the present rate. Protecting the planet is an ethical issue.

While environmental destruction in the past could be attributed to ignorance, today we have more information. We must learn to work together for something we all care about—the survival and flourishing of our planet and the beings living on it. While science, technology, and industrialization have brought much benefit, they have also been the source of many current tragedies, including global warming and pollution. When we are able to recognize and forgive ignorant actions of the past, we gain strength to constructively solve problems in the present.

Scientific predictions of environmental change are difficult for ordinary human beings to comprehend fully. We hear about global warming and rising sea levels, increased cancer rates, depletion of resources, extinction of species, and overpopulation. The global economy may grow and with it extreme rates of energy consumption, carbon dioxide production, and deforestation. We must consider the prospects in the near future of global suffering and environmental degradation unlike anything in human history. Then we must do our best to prevent what is preventable and to prepare for what isn't.

Human activity driven by the wish for present pleasure and convenience without care for future living beings and their environment cannot be sustained. Our greed needs to take the backseat to practical methods to care for nature and natural resources. More equal distribution of wealth among nations and among groups of people within each nation is essential, as is education about the importance of caring for the environment and for each other.

Remembering our mutual dependence is a key to counteract harmful practices. Each sentient being wants happiness, not suffering. Developing a genuine, compassionate sense of universal responsibility is crucial. When we are motivated by wisdom and compassion, the results of our actions benefit everyone, not just ourselves.

Consumerism is closely related to the plight of our environment. Although advances in science and technology may be able to offset some deleterious effects of the overconsumption of natural resources, we should not be overly confident and leave it to future generations to resolve the problems we create. We human beings must consider the prospect that one day science and technology may not be able to help us in the face of limited resources. This earth we share is not infinite.

As individuals and as a society, we must practice contentment to counter our greed for more and better. No matter what we do to try to gratify our desires, we will not find total satisfaction; external goods are not capable of providing this. Real fulfillment is found by adopting the inner disciplines of self-restraint and contentment as well as the joy of love, compassion, and inner freedom.

Every person and each nation wants to improve its standard of living. If the standard of living of poorer countries were raised to that of wealthier countries, natural resources would not be able to meet the demand. Even if we had the resources to provide a car to every person on the planet, would we want to? Could we control the pollution they produce?

Sooner or later the lifestyle of wealthier nations will have to change according to new imperatives. While people expect a successful economy to grow each year, growth has its limits. Rather than being unprepared and colliding with the problems these limitations entail, we should cultivate a sense of contentment and voluntary restraint. Then we may be able to avoid or at least reduce the disastrous results of overconsumption. With a good heart and wisdom, we will be motivated to do what needs to be done to protect each other and the natural environment. This is much easier than having to adapt to the severe environmental conditions projected for the future.

The World of Business and Finance

Every human being has an ethical duty to humanity, a responsibility to consider our common future. In addition, each person has the potential to contribute to the common good. People in the world of business and finance are no exception; they have great potential and great responsibility for global welfare. If they think only of immediate profit, all of us will suffer the consequences. This is already evident in the environmental destruction that has occurred due to the unregulated pursuits of big business.

At the global level, a huge gap exists between wealthy industrialized countries and other nations in which people struggle to fulfill their basic needs for survival. While children in wealthy countries complain when they cannot get the latest technological device, children in impoverished countries face malnutrition. This is very sad. Within each country, too, the rich increase their wealth, while the poor remain poor, and in some cases become even poorer. This is not only ethically wrong, it is a source of practical problems.

Even though governments may theoretically ensure equal rights and opportunities, this great economic disparity places the poor at a disadvantage in terms of obtaining good education and jobs. As a result, they feel discontent and discouraged, which feeds resentment toward the privileged. This, in turn, entices them to become involved in legitimate protest as well as gangs, crime, and terrorism. Social discord affects the happiness of both the wealthy and the poor.

Each person wants to leave the world having made a positive contribution; everyone wants to ensure that their children and grandchildren have good lives. Therefore I ask those involved in business and government to keep future generations in mind as you make decisions in the present.

Human activities in all fields are constructive when done with regard for the interdependence of all beings. An awareness of the profound interconnection among all beings and the planet we share inspires a sense of responsibility and concern for others, a commitment to the welfare of society, awareness of the consequences of our actions, and restraint from harm. When we act with concern for only short-term interests or the welfare of only a select group or when our intention is simply to accrue money or power, our actions inevitably bring unpleasant results for everyone.

Our motivation is pivotal; for any human endeavor to be constructive, we must first check our motivation and purify it of ignorant and self-centered intent as much as possible. The most important element in a healthy and productive motivation is a sense of caring for others, an awareness of the big picture and long-term results. With such a motivation, doing business and making money are fine. These activities are not inherently flawed or corrupt.

Some businesspeople tell me that doing business honestly reduces their profit and bogs them down in bureaucracy. Because increasing their profits also benefits society and their employees, they say that cutting corners to facilitate business is beneficial. I have doubts about this line of reasoning.

Ethical standards and ethical behavior are neither a nuisance nor unrealistic when it comes to business matters. For me, ethics means doing what is right, and that means what is beneficial for self and others. There may be times when what is beneficial in the long-term and short-term conflict, but many other times they coincide. Overemphasis on short-term benefit often harms the long-term good, while wise attention paid to the long-term goals usually pays off.

If a company cheats its clients or customers, these stakeholders will become aware of the situation and stop doing business with that company. In addition, these customers and clients will tell others about the company's deceitful practices, and consequently, others will avoid doing business with that company. When clients are treated respectfully and charged fair prices, they will do business with that company over a long period and will refer their friends to it as well, thus increasing the company's profits over the long term.

When arrested for illegal business practices, CEOs and their families suffer disgrace and humiliation. Their behavior causes the public to lose faith in the stock market, which in turn harms those corporations and the national economy. Corporations spend an enormous amount on legal fees due to their malpractices, so even if we consider prosperity in this life, dishonest business practices ruin individuals and companies.

Buddhist practitioners have even greater reason to abandon illegal and deceitful business practices, for they understand the destructive karma involved and the three kinds of suffering effects that it produces. They know that truthful business dealings and kind interactions with others are constructive actions that bring prosperity and good relationships in future lives. Aware that happiness comes from having a contented mind, not from greedily grasping for more wealth, true Dharma practitioners conduct their business affairs honestly. Although in the short term they may not make as much profit as dishonest businesspeople, in the long term they have fewer problems and more mental peace.

In the business world compassion translates into cooperation, responsibility, and caring. Some companies now take more care of their employees, clients, and customers. They see that a pleasant working environment in which individuals are valued, respected, and have a voice increases productivity. Although their main motivation for caring for others may be financial gain, they nevertheless know that their success is dependent on others and that, therefore, kindness and fairness are important. In the end, this produces happier employees, a good working environment, and a better reputation for the company. This in turn wins public approval and support, which benefit the company.

Some people assume that compassion in business means being too soft, abandoning competition, and thus not being successful. These assumptions are not correct. There are two types of competition. One is negative; for example, actively creating obstacles for competitors or cheating customers in our efforts to reach the top. The other is beneficial: we want to improve ourselves and work hard to attain our goal, but not at others' expense. We accept that just like us, others also have the wish and the right to success.

Wanting to attain a goal is not necessarily selfish. In spiritual practice, our desire to become a buddha is not self-centered; it doesn't involve promoting ourselves at others' expense. Rather, to be more capable of benefiting others, we develop our abilities and talents and work toward our goal.

There's nothing wrong with wanting to be the best. That motivation gives us initiative and encourages progress. However, what makes us the best is not always money and status. If a company makes huge profits and earns a bad name, that's not being the best! A business that benefits more people and serves the community better than its competitors has become the best.

Each person in the business and financial world is responsible for his or her own goals and actions. At the end of the day, we have to be able to live with ourselves and feel good about what we have done. Human values are important, no matter our profession. I never heard of anyone who said on their deathbed, "I should have made more money," "I wish I had worked more overtime," or "I should have crushed that competitor."

The transformation of values in the business and financial worlds begins at the individual level. When one individual changes, the effects are felt within that person's sphere of activities. Through the ripple effect, this positive influence will spread to more people.

Media and the Arts

The media plays a vital role in investigating important issues and bringing them to the public's attention, and I appreciate their efforts in this direction. The freedom of press benefits society greatly. At the same time, those working in the media need to have compassion for the entire society and not sensationalize events in order to have larger sales. I find it frightening that people are constantly fed violence on the news as well as for entertainment. No wonder people report depression and despair, and children grow into violent adults.

Balanced reporting is essential. On one day in any large city, a few people receive great harm, whereas so many people receive help in the form of healthcare, education, friendship, and so on. Yet the headlines about the harmful events dominate. The tremendous amount of help that people give each other every day is overlooked. In this way, citizens get a skewed view of humanity, and their suspicion, fear, and distrust increase. If the media also reported the helpful activities that people do for each other and for the planet each day, people would have a more realistic perspective and would be aware of the great kindness human beings show each other. This in turn would cause the public to be more optimistic about the future, which will prompt them to work harder to create a good future for themselves and others.

The plots of movies and entertainment usually revolve around violence and sex. One of my American students told me that one day she heard a child suggest to his playmates, "Let's play divorce!" The children then proceeded to quarrel and argue, mimicking those on television programs they had seen. The media has great potential to influence others as well as the responsibility to use this potential wisely. Movies showing people developing skills to resolve their conflicts in a fair and mutually beneficial way can also be entertaining, in addition to teaching good communication skills.

The media, as well as the makers of video and online games, have some responsibility for the tragedies of mass shootings. When violence becomes entertainment, and when it is so normal that children see hundreds of instances of it each week on television or the Internet, it plants seeds in their minds that will affect their behavior. Those working in the media, game design, and advertising must have the well-being of the entire society in mind, not to mention the welfare of their own children. They should use their great creative powers and intelligence to influence youth in a constructive way and to teach them good human values, kindness, and respect for others.

Throughout history, the arts have been a medium for the expression of the highest human values and aspirations as well as of despair and depravity. Many people in the arts—painters, writers, actors, dancers, musicians, and others—ask me about the role of the arts in spiritual practice. As with other occupations, this depends on the artist's motivation. If art is created simply to make a name for oneself, with no concern for the effect it has on others, it has questionable spiritual value. On the other hand, if artists with compassion for the welfare of others use their talents to benefit others, their art can be magnificent artistically and spiritually.

Science

In general, the Buddha's teachings fall into three categories: Buddhist science, which involves the Buddha's description of the external world, the physical body, and the nature of consciousness; Buddhist philosophy, which contains the Buddha's theory of reality; and Buddhist religion, the practice of the spiritual path.

Interdependence and causality are central concepts in Buddhist philosophy and are now applied to all fields. Scientists in particular know that changing one thing produces ramifications elsewhere, and a fruitful dialogue between modern science and Buddhist science and philosophy has begun. Buddhists speak about Buddhist science and certain concepts from Buddhist philosophy such as subtle impermanence and interdependence. Some scientists are also interested in Buddhist assertions that ultimate reality lacks independent existence and phenomena exist by mere designation. We Buddhists do not discuss Buddhist religious practice or Buddhist concepts such as past and future lives, karmic causality, and liberation with scientists. Those topics are "our business" as the Buddha's followers.

In this interdisciplinary discussion, we are not trying to use science to validate the Dharma. Buddhists have a long history of realized spiritual practitioners who have validated the efficacy of the path through their personal experience. Buddhism has survived nearly 2,600 years without the support or approval of science; we will continue. However, our dialogue is good for society, as it is an example of the modern and the ancient learning from and complementing each other. Over the years, the dialogue has sparked many projects, for example, teaching mindfulness to help reduce physical pain and mental stress, and developing programs for teachers to instruct their students in compassionate thought and action. In addition, we Tibetans have begun science education in some of our monasteries and nunneries, and a few Tibetan monks are now studying science at Western universities, bringing their knowledge back to the debate ground.

I appreciate the scientific perspective very much. Scientists are looking for truth, for reality. They approach their investigation with an open mind and are willing to revise their ideas if their findings do not correspond to their original theories. As the Buddha's followers, we too are looking for truth and reality. The Buddha wanted us to test his teachings, not to accept them blindly. This accords with the scientific way. If scientists can disprove points in the Buddhist scriptures, we must accept their findings. Because of the similarity of our approach, I do not think there is any danger in discussion with scientists. Their attitude is objective, they are open to the investigation of new things, and they are intelligent.

Within Buddhist science, as we saw in chapter 8, there are three categories of phenomena: evident, slightly obscure, and very obscure. Up until now, common topics of dialogue with scientists have focused on evident phenomena and a little bit regarding slightly obscure phenomena, such as subtle impermanence and emptiness. Within the category of evident phenomena, we have discussed topics found in physics, neurology, cognitive science, psychology, and so forth.

It is useful for Buddhists to study scientific findings. For example, while Buddhist literature speaks about subtle particles, scientific knowledge of that topic is more advanced. Learning about the brain's role in cognition and emotion is new and interesting for Buddhists. However, regarding perception and psychology, Buddhist literature is much richer, and psychologists and neurologists find Buddhist findings and experiences regarding attention and emotion very helpful.

Both Buddhadharma and science can benefit humanity, and both also have limitations. Science helps us understand the physical basis upon which the mind depends while we are alive. However, because scientific research requires physical measurements of external phenomena, it lacks the tools to investigate things beyond the scope of our physical senses. Although science has contributed greatly to human knowledge about some topics, it lacks the tools necessary to fully understand every aspect of human beings. Scientists can benefit from learning the vast knowledge Buddhism possesses about the mind: for example, distinguishing sensory and mental consciousness, and differentiating between minds that directly perceive their object and conceptual consciousnesses that know their objects via conceptual appearance. Buddhism also describes various levels of consciousness and how they function, as well as the power the mind gains through developing single-pointed concentration. Buddhist psychology describes mental states conducive to human happiness and those that are unrealistic and bring suffering.

I believe that in this century many new ideas and findings will come, enlarging science's field of investigation. Continuing dialogue between Buddhists and scientists is important, so both can expand their knowledge, methodologies, and ways of thinking. Dialogues with scientists have been fruitful, and some of the perspectives I have gained from them are included in this book.

I encourage more Buddhist monasteries to introduce science into their curriculum. Studying scientific findings and dialoguing with scientists help us to cultivate faith based on analysis and investigation. In addition, for Buddhism to be taken seriously in the West and among the young Tibetans in India with a modern education, Buddhist practitioners and teachers must be conversant with scientific assumptions.

Similarly, I encourage scientists to stretch the field of their investigation. The ultimate laboratory is in our own mind and body, and for this meditation is important. Scientists who develop internal awareness of their own cognitive and emotional processes through meditation will bring new vigor to scientific exploration.

My main purpose in dialoguing with scientists is to bring a deeper awareness about the value to society of living an ethical life. So many of our problems are due to people's lack of care for the ethical dimensions of their actions and the effect their behavior has on others. We need to make more effort to promote inner values, but doing that is difficult if they are based only on religious ideas that appeal only to people following a particular religion. Secular ethics that speak of universal values appeal to believers of all religions and to nonbelievers as well.

Scientists have found and continue to find connections between our mental states on the one hand and our physical health and the quality of our social interactions on the other. Scientific findings demonstrate the benefits of compassion, a peaceful mind, and ethical living. Since the results of scientific research are respected internationally, their findings can be used to support the advancement of secular ethics for the benefit of society.

Gender Equality

Women's right to have equal opportunity in all fields must be respected. I don't believe that in the past, society in general or Buddhist institutions in particular deliberately discriminated against women. Rather, they were negligent and simply assumed that men should lead because larger and stronger bodies made them more fit to lead. But this concept is no longer valid, and it was not even true historically. Napoleon was physically small but very clever, and he became a powerful leader.

In addition, men assumed they were intellectually superior and less dominated by their emotions. However, as the Buddha noted, men and women have the same afflictions, and men and women are equally bound in cyclic existence by these afflictions. For civilized society, intelligence is far more important than physical strength, and in this regard, men and women are equal. Everyone should have a good education and be able to use their talents and abilities to contribute to society. Equal opportunity means equal responsibility, and men and women should share these.

People tend to identify strongly according to their gender. But as Āryadeva points out (CŚ 226–27), there is no inherently existent "inner self" that is male, female, or other. The body is also not an inherently existent man or woman because none of the elements that compose the body have a gender. Although from the viewpoint of emptiness, no distinction can be made between men and women, that is no excuse to ignore sexual discrimination. The status of men and women in Buddhist institutions is not equal, and this has a deleterious effect on female and male practitioners as well as on the acceptance of Buddhism in Western society. Buddhist institutions, teachers, and practitioners must treat everyone equally. All forms of exclusivity are based on an attitude of "me versus them," which is not suitable for genuine practitioners. True practitioners are humble and regard everyone as their teacher; they work to benefit all beings.

Women must develop self-confidence and take every opportunity to make themselves equal in all fields. Some women are accomplished practitioners, but they are shy and therefore do not teach or take leadership positions. Especially those practicing the bodhisattva path should develop great self-confidence, inner strength, and courage. They must take the initiative, studying and developing their qualities, and not get discouraged by the defeatist resignation that society is simply sexist. If they encounter prejudice from social and religious institutions, they should speak up, and we must work together to tackle these problems.

In the past, there has been a shortage of well-known female role models in Buddhism. This is due in part to lack of knowledge about great female practitioners of the past. More books and articles that focus on past and present female practitioners are needed. In India, the Buddha's stepmother was an extraordinary nun praised by the Buddha himself. The Indian nun Bhikṣuṇī Lakṣmī had a vision of Thousand-Armed Avalokiteśvara and is the first lineage holder of this practice. Nāropa's sister Niguma was a great tantric adept, as were Machik Labkyi Dronma and Dorje Pakmo in Tibet. The reincarnation lineage of Dorje Pakmo began very early on, more or less at the same time as that of the Karmapa, and continues today.

The Vinaya records that when the Buddha began the nuns' order, he stated that women were able to attain liberation and become arhats, and many stories of liberated women exist in the scriptures. Sūtrayāna and the three lower tantras state that one has to have a male body in the final life before attaining buddhahood, but in Tibetan Buddhism highest yoga tantra is the final authority, and here females and males are equally capable of attaining full awakening. Highest yoga tantra emphasizes cultivating respect for women, and one of the root tantric precepts forbids disparaging women.

The discriminatory statements against women in the Buddhist scriptures were made due to societal circumstances at the Buddha's time and later, when the scriptures were actually written down. Since this prejudice arose due to cultural bias, it can and must be changed. Other things, for example bhikṣus being the preceptors of bhikṣuṇīs, seem like prejudice but are difficult for one person to change. A council of saṅgha elders from all Buddhist traditions would need to meet and agree in order to change that.

According to the Vinaya, bhikṣus sit and walk in front of bhikṣuṇīs. While bhikṣuṇīs are governed by more precepts, most of them are for their protection. Because women are more prone to being raped or bullied than men, to offset these risks the Buddha established precepts that prevent women from encountering dangerous situations.

However, in terms of rights, both men and women are equal. Just as a man has the right and opportunity to become a monk, so a woman has the right and opportunity to become a nun. The bhikṣuṇī saṅgha of fully ordained nuns is responsible for the screening and training of women who are candidates for novice and full ordination. They are responsible for running their own communities and teaching other nuns. Bhikṣuṇīs are ordained by a process involving both the bhikṣuṇī and the bhikṣu saṅghas,

270 | APPROACHING THE BUDDHIST PATH

and the monks must teach the Dharma to the nuns when requested. Since the full ordination lineage for women did not spread to Tibet, it is my hope that it will be established and the bhikṣuṇī ordination given in the Tibetan community. It is also my hope more nuns will become teachers in their own right and abbesses in the nunneries. This has happened to some extent in Tibetan Buddhist monasteries in the West and certainly is the case in the Chinese Buddhist community.

A story in the Pāli canon (SN 15.2) tells of Bhikkhunī Soma, who was meditating one day in the forest. Māra, the embodiment of evil, appears, and with the intention of making her lose her meditative concentration, says:

> That state so hard to achieve
> that is to be attained by the seers
> cannot be attained by a woman
> with her two-fingered wisdom.[61]

Bhikkhunī Soma immediately recognized that it was Māra who was trying to make her afraid, lose self-confidence, and fall away from her concentration. She firmly replied:

> What does womanhood matter at all
> when the mind is concentrated well,
> when knowledge flows on steadily
> as one sees correctly into the Dhamma?
>
> One to whom it might occur,
> "I'm a woman" or "I'm a man"
> or "I'm anything at all"
> is fit for Māra to address.

In this instance "knowledge" refers to the knowledge of the four truths in the continuum of an arahant. As an arahant Bhikkhunī Soma had eradicated all defilements preventing liberation. Only someone who adheres to craving, conceit, and views—the defilements that lie behind false conceptualizations—is a receptive audience for Māra's rantings. Those with knowledge and vision do not grasp onto a self or fabricate identities and will not fall prey to Māra. They continue their practice and virtuous activities undaunted.

Interfaith

Buddhists should try to create friendly and respectful relations with people of other faiths. For me, Buddhism is the best and it suits me perfectly. But it is not necessarily the best for everyone. Therefore I accept and respect all religious traditions.

Jains, Buddhists, and one branch of Hindu Sāṃkhyas do not believe in a creator God, while Jews, Christians, and Muslims do. If we look only at this, we see a big difference among religions. However, the purpose of the religious theories of no-God and of God is the same: to make better human beings. Human minds are so varied and different that one philosophy cannot suit them all. Many philosophies are needed to suit the many kinds of mentality.

All great religious leaders endeavor to lead their followers away from selfishness, anger, and greed. All emphasize relinquishing violence and rampant materialism. By understanding their common function and aim, we will see that the superficial differences in religious theology are due to differences in the spiritual needs of people in a particular place at that time. Knowing this, we can avoid sectarianism, partisanship, and disparaging any authentic religious teaching.

This variety in religions is a blessing, not a difficulty. Just as there is a tremendous variety of food, giving each person the opportunity to eat what suits their taste and constitution, the great variety in religion enables each person to choose the belief system most suitable for them. Trying to make everyone accept the same religion is impossible and would not be beneficial.

Some people find it more comfortable to believe in a creator. Being a God-fearing person, they are disciplined and careful in their actions. This approach benefits these people. Other people may be more conscientious regarding their motivations and behavior when they believe that the responsibility lies with them. Both of these approaches share the same purpose in encouraging people to live ethically and be kind to each other.

My Christian and Muslim friends weep with faith when they pray to

God, and their lives are devoted to service to others. I appreciate my Christian brothers and sisters who make great effort to educate others. Hindus also work in education and healthcare. Their selfless effort to help others is due to devotion to God. People of other religions who practice sincerely create good karma and will have good future lives. Virtuous actions alone will not lead to nirvāṇa, however, because that depends on realizing selflessness.

Although some individuals may misinterpret the teachings of their own religion or use religion to incite hostility, I have never encountered true religious teachings that preach hatred and violence. We should abandon all such actions in the name of religion.

Many centuries ago Buddhists suffered under Muslim invaders in India, but now the Muslims in Bodhgaya help the Buddhist pilgrims there. Each year when I go to Bodhgaya, they invite me and we share food. Sincere Muslim practitioners are very good human beings. It is important that we remember this and not generalize about all people of a certain faith based on the harmful actions of a few who misuse their religion to justify their destructive actions.

Although all religions have a similar purpose and similar values, we must not blur the distinctions. We do not need to say that our beliefs are the same in order to get along. We can note and respect the differences, knowing that due to the diversity of religions everyone will be able to find a faith that suits them.

In our interfaith discussions, investigating the meaning of words and concepts is important. Sometimes we hastily conclude that because the words are the same, their meaning is also. The meaning of "blessing," for example, is not the same in Buddhism as in theistic religions. Conversely, we may think that because traditions use different vocabulary, their meanings are unrelated, although that may not be the case.

More contact and communication among religious leaders as well as among their followers are needed to promote mutual understanding and harmony. I suggest four activities in this regard. First, religious and theological scholars should meet to discuss points of similarity and difference among faiths. This will promote awareness of the similar purposes of all religions and respect for their doctrinal differences. At an interfaith meeting in Australia, a Christian introduced me and concluded by saying, "The Dalai

Lama is a very good Christian practitioner." When I spoke, I thanked him for his kind words and commented that he was a good Buddhist.

In addition, practitioners of various faiths should meet to talk, pray, and meditate together. This will bring deeper experiences that lead to seeing the value of other religions. Furthermore, people can go on pilgrimages together, not as tourists but to visit and pray together at the holy places of different religions. In this way, they will experientially realize the value of other religions.

Last, religious leaders should come together to pray and speak about remedying problems in the world and allow the media to cover the event. When citizens of the world see religious leaders working harmoniously together, they will feel more hopeful and will become more tolerant themselves.

Bishop Tutu, whom I admire greatly, suggested a fifth practice: religions should speak in a united voice on issues of global concern such as wealth inequality, human rights, the environment, and disarmament. I support this as well.

An important element in religious harmony is mutual respect, which entails refraining from aggressive attempts at conversion. As mentioned in chapter 1, when I give lectures on Buddhist topics in the West, I tell people that they should follow their family religion unless it does not suit their needs. The same is true in countries that have traditionally been Buddhist: the people there should remain Buddhist unless it does not suit them. In Mongolia, China, Korea, and some other Buddhist countries, Christian missionaries have strongly promoted their religion. I heard that in Mongolia some churches give people fifty dollars when they convert. Some Mongolians are apparently quite savvy and get baptized multiple times!

Sometimes it is necessary to say frankly to others that their attempts to convert others are harmful. It causes friction in families, especially when one family member converts and then pressures others to do the same. On one occasion some missionaries came to see me, and I candidly told them not to try to convert people in traditionally Buddhist countries because it creates discord and confusion in society. Once, some Mormons invited me to their headquarters and arranged for me to give a public talk in Salt Lake City. Here too I frankly said, "Doing missionary work among people who do not follow a religion with a philosophical basis is fine, especially if they perform animal sacrifices or other harmful practices. However, in places where the population follows their own traditional religion that has an ethical and philosophical basis, it is not good to proselytize. Maintaining harmony in society is far more important."

Incorporating Practices from Other Religions

Changing religion is a serious matter that should not be taken lightly. Some people prefer to follow the religion of their birth yet find it helpful to incorporate certain methods from other traditions into their own spiritual practice. While remaining deeply committed to their own faith, some of my Christian friends practice techniques for cultivating meditative concentration that they learned from Buddhism. They also use methods such as visualizations that enhance compassion and meditations to strengthen fortitude and forgiveness. This does not interfere with their refuge in God.

Similarly, Buddhists may learn and incorporate some aspects of Christian teachings into their own practice. One clear example is in the area of community work. Christian monastics have a long history of social work, particularly in education and healthcare, areas in which the Buddhist community lags behind. One of my friends, a German Buddhist, told me after he visited Nepal, that over the last forty or fifty years Tibetan lamas have constructed many large monasteries. However, they have built very few hospitals and schools for the public. He observed that if Christians had constructed new monasteries, they would include schools and hospitals for the general population. In response to his observation, we Buddhists can only hang our heads and agree that he is right.

Some of my Christian friends have taken serious interest in the Buddhist philosophy of emptiness. I have told them that since the theory of emptiness is unique to Buddhism, it may not be wise for them to look into it deeply. Doing so may cause difficulties in their Christian practice, because if they pursue the theory of emptiness and dependent arising that underlies the Buddhist worldview, it challenges the worldview founded upon belief in an absolute, independent, eternal creator. Adopting the Buddhist idea of emptiness would harm their deep faith in God, and this would not benefit them.

When we are beginning spiritual practitioners, it is good to develop a sense of reverence for the teachers of all religious traditions. At the beginning of our spiritual path, we can be both a practicing Buddhist and a practicing Christian or Jew. However, as we go further into spiritual practice, we reach a point where we need to accept one philosophical view and deepen our understanding of that. This is similar to new university students benefiting from studying many subjects but at a later point choosing to major in one.

From the viewpoint of an individual who is going deeper into their spiritual path, practicing one religion is important. However, from the perspective of society at large, it is important to adhere to the principle of many religions and many truths. At first glance, these two concepts—one truth, one religion versus many truths, many religions—seem contradictory. However, if we examine them carefully, we see that each is correct in its own context. From the perspective of an individual spiritual practitioner, the concept of one truth and one religion is valid. From the viewpoint of wider society, the concept of many truths and many religions is cogent. There is no contradiction. Truth must be understood and defined in relation to the context. Even within one religion, such as Buddhism, we speak of two truths, veil and ultimate.

A Nonsectarian Approach

In the past, sectarianism has created many problems and harmed both individuals and the Buddhist community. It arose mainly due to lack of personal contact among practitioners of different Buddhist traditions, leading to lack of correct information about each other's doctrine and practices. Unfortunately, in recent years it has spread to international practitioners and Dharma centers as well. Now, with better means of transportation and communication, practitioners from diverse traditions can learn about each other and meet together easily.

Sectarianism can take many forms. Sometimes it is motivated by jealousy or conceit. Other times it is done with "compassion," telling students that they will get confused if they go to other teachings or that other traditions are preliminaries to their own, higher tradition. Sometimes sectarianism arises due to ignorance in which someone believes he understands another system but in fact does not comprehend it correctly. Some people are prejudiced against other traditions or teachers due to a misdirected sense of loyalty to their own teacher or tradition.

Misunderstandings that lead to sectarianism may arise when comments made in relation to a specific individual are generalized for everyone at all times. Milarepa's demeaning remarks about scholars were the former. He was speaking about specific people who lived at that time and did not mean that all scholars did not practice purely or that being a scholar was worthless. If people misunderstand and think that all study of the scriptures is a waste of time, that will create friction between Buddhists who study a lot and those who don't, harm the existence of the Buddhadharma in the world, and inhibit individuals who want to learn.

The only solution to sectarianism is to study and practice other Buddhist traditions in addition to our own and to develop a broad understanding of all of the Buddha's teachings. Instead of identifying with a specific tradition, we should consider ourselves simply Buddhists; after all, when we take refuge it is in the same Three Jewels, not in a specific Buddhist tradition or teacher. You may still principally follow one Buddhist tradition, but when you need clarification in specific areas, learn the details from whichever tradition gives the fullest presentation of that point and incorporate that explanation into your practice.

In the past, especially in the late nineteenth century in Tibet and now in India as well, many Tibetan masters in principle were nonsectarian. Dilgo Khyentse Rinpoche, his main teacher Khyentse Chokyi Lodro, and his main disciple Trulshik Rinpoche were all nonsectarian. They belonged to the Nyingma tradition, but from the time they were young, they received teachings from many different spiritual mentors. In the 1940s, a Geluk lama in Amdo invited Dilgo Khyentse Rinpoche to his area to give teachings, and Rinpoche also received teachings from this Geluk lama.

The previous Dalai Lamas have practiced in multiple lineages. According to their biographies, the first three Dalai Lamas were basically Geluk but had a nonsectarian approach and received teachings from all traditions. The Fifth Dalai Lama received teachings from Sakya and Nyingma teachers, although not as many from Kagyu masters. The Seventh Dalai Lama did not have much connection with Nyingma or Sakya, and the Thirteenth Dalai Lama was in principle nonsectarian. He received Nyingma teachings as well as Geluk and included in his writings is a text about Vajrakīlaya, a deity central to the Nyingma tradition. One of my debate teachers, Lodro Chonyi from Mongolia, was a great scholar and good practitioner. His main teacher also practiced Nyingma, principally Hayagrīva. He told Lodro Chonyi that the Thirteenth Dalai Lama mainly practiced two deities: Yamāntaka and Vajrakīlaya.

When I was young, I was a strict Gelukpa but later became nonsectarian. One reason I recommended that people not worship the spirit Shugden is because I value the nonsectarian approach and the freedom to receive teachings from various spiritual mentors, and this spirit is opposed to this. My understanding of clear light has been greatly enhanced by hearing teachings on Dzogchen and Mahāmudrā in addition to Tsongkhapa's explanation of the different levels of mind. Now I read texts of all traditions; studying explanations on the same topic from different perspectives helps me immensely to gain a fuller understanding. In these days when the Buddhadharma is degenerating, nonsectarianism is essential. Quarreling and fighting in the name of religion is foolish and wrong.

According to practitioners, the various explanations of a topic come to one point. For example, in Dzogchen, sometimes you meditate on emptiness as an affirming negative as taught in the text of a great scholar who has actual meditation experience. Although emptiness is a nonaffirming negative, due to this specific way of practice, it may be useful to see it as an affirming negative.[62] Knowing these different perspectives is helpful; one day we'll know for ourselves through our own experience.

Once an elderly monk requested me to teach bodhicitta according to a Kagyu text. I was not familiar with the text. Unable to fulfill his wish, I felt sad. Unfortunately, not many Tibetan lamas can teach all four Tibetan traditions. I hope in the future that both Tibetan and Western practitioners will remedy this. More knowledge about each other's tradition enriches our own practice. Practitioners should have as broad a perspective as possible, without being scattered or confused by the multiplicity.

Furthermore, Tibetan contact with the Zen, Pure Land, and Theravāda traditions has not been adequate. During the years I've lived in exile, my relationship with the Pope and other Christian leaders has seemed closer than that with Theravāda, Zen, and Pure Land masters. On a personal level, I would like to have more contact with other Buddhists, and for the good of Buddhism in the world, I would like all the Buddhist traditions to be closer.

One reason for writing *Buddhism: One Teacher, Many Traditions* was to give Buddhists from all traditions accurate information about one another's doctrine and practices. In doing so, it becomes clear that the foundation for all our traditions is the same. We take refuge in the same Three Jewels, we see the world through the perspective of the four truths of the āryas, and we all practice the three higher trainings and cultivate love, compassion, joy, and equanimity. All Buddhist traditions speak of selflessness and dependent arising. Although we may approach some of these topics from different perspectives, that is no reason to criticize one another.

Within Tibetan Buddhism, we find scholars refuting one another's position. We should examine why they are doing this and the reasons they use to support their positions. If we do not agree, we can respond with reasons backing our understanding. Doing this furthers our own and the other's understanding and is not disrespectful. When debating the view in *Recognizing the Mother*, Changkya Rolpai Dorje says, "I am not disrespecting you. Please pardon me if you are offended." Debating ideas is different from being arrogant regarding our own tradition and denigrating others. While we may disagree with others, it is important to respect them and their traditions.

Coming together as disciples of the same Teacher, we Buddhists will have closer relationships. We could speak with a common voice about difficult social and environmental issues and promote nonviolence and tolerance. This would definitely please the Buddha and benefit all sentient beings.

Notes

1. That is, the object is reflected in the mind. It is similar to, but not the same as, the image of an object forming on the retina when the visual consciousness sees it. Seeing the aspect—the representation—is the meaning of seeing the object.

2. *Duḥkha* (P. *dukkha*) is often translated as "suffering," but this translation is misleading. Its meaning is more nuanced and refers to all unsatisfactory states and experiences, many of which are not explicitly painful. While the Buddha says that life under the influence of afflictions and polluted karma is unsatisfactory, he does not say that life is suffering.

3. The Sanskrit term *āsrava* is translated as "polluted," "contaminated," or "tainted," meaning under the influence of ignorance or its latencies.

4. In this context, "self" does not mean a person but refers to inherent, independent, or true existence. "Selflessness" is the absence of independent existence, not the absence of a person.

5. The term *clear light* has different meanings depending on the context. It may also refer to the emptiness of inherent existence or to the subtlest mind.

6. Hereafter this title is shortened to *Commentary on Reliable Cognition*.

7. See Russell Kolts and Thubten Chodron, *An Open-Hearted Life* (Boston: Shambhala, 2014) for an in-depth explanation of working with disturbing emotions and cultivating beneficial communication skills.

8. Theravāda Buddhists place the Buddha as living 563–483 BCE, while many people following the Sanskrit tradition often date the Buddha as living 448–368 BCE. Having analyzed traditional historical records from a different angle, Richard Gombrich, professor of Sanskrit at Oxford University, has placed the Buddha's life at 485–404 BCE. "Dating the Buddha: A Red Herring Revealed," in *The Dating of the Historical Buddha*, vol. 2, ed. Heinz Bechert (Göttingen: Vandenhoeck & Ruprecht, 1992), 237–59.

9. This word is the root of the title *bhante*.

10. This date is according to the old way of dating the Buddha's life. According to the dates Gombrich proposed for the Buddha's life, this requires revision.

11. Some academic scholars say the Mūlasarvāstivāda school was located in Mathurā

in northern India and may have later moved to Kashmir, and from there to Tibet, where its vinaya became the dominant monastic code.

12. Some say Paiśācī is a literary, but not spoken, Prakrit. Others say it was an early name for Pāli.

13. Many modern scholars believe that the Vaibhāṣikas were a branch of the Sarvāstivāda because the Vaibhāṣikas' main text, the *Mahāvibhāṣā* (*Great Detailed Explanation*), is a commentary on the final book of the Sarvāstivāda Abhidharma, the *Foundation of Knowledge* (*Jñānaprasthāna*). For a few versions of the eighteen schools, see Jeffrey Hopkins, *Meditation on Emptiness* (Boston: Wisdom, 1996), 713–19.

14. Steven Collins, "On the Very Idea of the Pāli Canon," *Journal of the Pāli Text Society* 15 (1990): 89–126.

15. Jonathan Walters, "Mahāyāna Theravāda and the Origins of the Mahāvihāra," *The Sri Lankan Journal of the Humanities* 23.1–2 (Sri Lanka: University of Peradeniya, 1997).

16. Correspondence from Bhikkhu Bodhi to Bhikṣuṇī Jampa Tsedroen, February 21, 2010: "Theravāda refers to a modern school of Buddhism which derives from the old Sthaviravāda, but the latter has a much longer history and is the source of many of the old Indian schools that did not survive...it would be misleading to simply assume that Theravāda is identical with Sthaviravāda and the latter simply a Sanskritized form signifying exactly what the former means.

"I also don't think it is suitable to identify Theravādins as Mahāvihārans. The latter term was meaningful during the period in Sri Lanka when the schools of Buddhism were named after the vihāras (monasteries) where they were centered. In that era, Mahāvihārans referred to those based at the Mahāvihāra in Anurādhapura. They were distinguished by their particular attitude toward Buddhist texts and methods of interpretation, preserved in the Pāli commentaries. But nowadays all that is left of the Mahāvihāra are its ruins...and what we call Theravāda has evolved in more complex ways than the old Mahāvihārans could ever have foreseen."

17. Peter Skilling, "Theravāda in History," in *Pacific World: Journal of the Institute of Buddhist Studies* 3.11 (Fall 2009): 72.

18. Walters, "Mahāyāna Theravāda and the Origins of the Mahāvihāra."

19. Collins, "On the Very Idea of the Pāli Canon."

20. Walters, "Mahāyāna Theravāda."

21. One is a Mahāyāna sūtra from Pakistan dated to the first or second century CE. There is also a Prajñāpāramitā (Perfection of Wisdom) manuscript from Gandhāra from the first century CE. The content of another Prajñāpāramitā sūtra in Prakrit dating from the first century BCE affirms it was already well-developed literature. Also see the work of Dr. Richard Salomon and the Early Buddhist Manuscript Project. Several Mahāyāna manuscripts written in Gāndhārī date from the firsr or second century CE.

22. Some historians place Asaṅga in the fourth century, while others say his life spanned from the latter fourth century through the first quarter of the fifth century.

23. Peter Skilling, "Vaidalya, Mahāyāna, and Bodhisattva in India," in *The Bodhisattva Ideal: Essays on the Emergence of the Mahāyāna* (Kandy: Buddhist Publication Society, 2013), 151n178.

24. The Kangyur was translated into Mongolian in the seventeenth century, the Tengyur in the eighteenth century.

25. Three additional scriptures are found only in the Burmese canon, including the *Questions of King Milinda* (Milindapañha), a dialogue between the monk Nāgasena and the Gandhāran king Menander.

26. Nanjio, Bunyiu, *A Catalogue of the Chinese Translation of the Buddhist Tripiṭaka, the Sacred Canon of the Buddhists in China and Japan* (San Francisco, Chinese Materials Central, Inc., 1975). This contains a complete list of contents of the Chinese Tripiṭaka and specifies if each title has a Tibetan version.

27. The information in the above three paragraphs was provided by Dr. Lobsang Dorjee Rabling from the Central University of Tibetan Studies in Sarnath in personal correspondence.

28. The five works attributed to Maitreya in the Chinese canon are: *Treatise on the Stages of Yogic Practice* (*Yogācārabhūmi*), which the Tibetan canon attributes to Asaṅga; the *Ornament of Mahāyāna Sūtras* (*Mahāyānasūtrālaṃkāra*); *Middle Beyond Extremes* (*Madhyāntavibhāga*); a commentary on the *Diamond Sūtra* (*Vajracchedikā Sūtra*); and *Yogavibhāga*, which is reputed to be lost. In the Tibetan canon the five works of Maitreya are *Ornament of Mahāyāna Sūtras, Middle Beyond Extremes, Distinction Between Phenomena and Their Nature* (*Dharmadharmatāvibhāga*), *Ornament of Clear Realizations,* and *Sublime Continuum* (*Uttaratantra* or *Ratnagotravibhāga*). The last two works appeared in India a few centuries after the death of Asaṅga, and Xuanzang never mentioned them in his collection of Indian Yogācāra texts nor did he attribute them to either Maitreya or Asaṅga. The Chinese say the *Uttaratantra Śāstra* was authored by Sāramati or Sthiramati.

29. The Vaibhāṣikas say the Buddha spoke the Abhidharma in many places and it was later compiled by others.

30. The seven in the Pāli canon are the: (1) *Dhammasaṅgaṇi* (*Enumeration of Factors*), which lists the various factors, or *dhammas*, of existence; (2) *Vibhaṅga* (*Analysis*), which explains the aggregates, sense sources, elements, truths, faculties, dependent arising, establishments of mindfulness, awakening, *jhānas*, four immeasurables, noble eightfold path, types of knowledge, and cosmology, among other topics; (3) *Dhātukathā* (*Discussion of Elements*), which discusses phenomena in relation to the aggregates, sense sources, and constituents; (4) *Puggalapaññatti* (*Descriptions of Individuals*), which describes the various kinds of persons; (5) *Kāthavatthu* (*Points of Controversy*), which is a discussion of differing perspectives; (6) *Yamaka* (*The Pairs*), which resolves misconceptions related to technical terminology; and (7) *Paṭṭhāna* (*Foundational Conditions* or *Relations*), which speaks of the relationship of all phenomena. The *Kāthavatthu* is said to have been written by Moggaliputta Tissa in the third century BCE.

31. Yaśomitra lists the seven Sanskrit treatises as the *Attainment of Knowledge* (*Jñānaprasthāna*) by Kātyāyanīputra, *Topic Divisions* (*Prakaraṇapāda*) by Vasumitra, *Compendium of Consciousness* (*Vijñānakāya*) by Devaśarman, *Aggregate of Dharma* (*Dharmaskandha*) by Śāriputra, *Treatise on Designation* (*Prajñaptiśāstra*) by Maudgalyāyana, *Combined Recitation* (*Saṃgītiparyāya*) by Mahākauṣṭhila, and the *Compendium of Elements* (*Dhātukāya*) by Pūrṇa.

32. This is one of the oldest Abhidharma texts, now extant only in Chinese. There are varying opinions regarding which of the eighteen schools it is from.

33. The *Treasury of Knowledge* has eight chapters: examinations of the elements; faculties; world (the cosmos and the sentient beings abiding in it); karma; pollutants; paths and persons; exalted wisdom; and meditative absorptions. Vasubandhu's autocommentary on this text has a ninth chapter, which presents the Sautrāntika viewpoint.

34. Tibetans consider Asaṅga as being a Mādhyamika but explaining the Dharma according to the Cittamātra view for the benefit of people inclined to that view. His brother, Vasubandhu, held the Cittamātra view but wrote some texts according to the Vaibhāṣika and Sautrāntika tenets to benefit people who appreciated those views.

35. Interestingly, in the Tibetan canon, the *Bhaiṣajyaguru* is in the tantra section of the Kangyur, while the *Sukhāvatīvyūha* is in the sūtra section.

36. There are divergent opinions among modern scholars regarding the tenet systems, when and where they flourished, the details of their philosophical positions, and to what extent the tenets were systematized in India before arriving in Tibet.

37. Scholars do not know when writing first became popular in India and have diverse theories about this, but by the time of King Aśoka in the third century BCE, writing was widespread. The Indus Valley civilization used writing since 2000 BCE, and some scholars believe that the Brahmi script used in Aśoka's time descended from it. K. R. Norman, *Buddhist Forum Volume V: Philological Approach to Buddhism* (London: School of Oriental and African Studies, 1997), 78. Norman also comments (p. 81) that it would be surprising if monks from the ruling and merchant castes, who were familiar with writing by the time of Aśoka in the third century BCE, did not write down, if not whole texts, then at least notes that would be helpful for their own practice and for teaching others.

38. It is wise to investigate all spiritual claims and not naively accept them. Some people misinterpret experiences they have in meditation.

39. See Khensur Jampa Tegchok, *Practical Ethics and Profound Emptiness* (Boston: Wisdom, 2017), verses 367–93.

40. John Benedict Buescher, *The Buddhist Doctrine of Two Truths in the Vaibhāṣika and Theravāda Schools*, PhD dissertation (University of Virginia, 1982), 44. His footnote on the citation credits a translation published by the Pali Text Society and reads, "P. Maung Tin, *The Expositor*, pp.5ff. The scriptural precedent that Buddhaghosa gives for this is an incident in the Madhupiṇḍika Sutta."

41. The Tibetan titles of these texts are respectively *Sems nyid ngal gso, Shing rta chen po, Kun bzang bla ma'i zhal lung, Thar pa rin po che'i rgyan, Thub pa'i dgongs gsal,* and *Lam rim chen mo.*

42. The seventeen Nālandā adepts are Nāgārjuna, Āryadeva, Buddhapālita, Bhāvaviveka, Candrakīrti, Śāntideva, Śāntarakṣita, Kamalaśīla, Asaṅga, Vasubandhu, Dignāga, Dharmakīrti, Vimuktisena, Haribhadra, Guṇaprabha, Śākyaprabha, and Atiśa.

43. These are being generous and giving material aid, speaking pleasantly by teaching

the Dharma to others according to their dispositions, encouraging them to practice, and living the teachings through example.

44. The above outline of the topics pertaining to each level of spiritual development may differ slightly according to the presentation. For example, meditation on the law of karma and its effects is included in the path in common with the initial level of spiritual development in the lamrim, but in the presentation in the three principal aspects of the path, it is subsumed in the practice in common with the person of medium spiritual development.

45. *Mind Training*, trans. Thupten Jinpa (Boston: Wisdom, 2006), 517.

46. The eight clear realizations are exalted knower of all aspects (omniscient mind), knower of paths, knower of bases, complete application of all aspects, peak application, serial application, momentary application, and the resultant truth body (dharmakāya).

47. The ten points that characterize the exalted knower of all aspects are mind generation (bodhicitta), spiritual instructions, four branches of definite discrimination, natural abiding lineage that is the basis of Mahāyāna attainments (buddha potential), the observed object of Mahāyāna attainment, the objective of practice, attainment through the armor-like practice, attainment through engagement, attainment through the collections, and definite emergence.

48. The Kadam great text tradition (*gzhung*) principally studied six Indian texts: Āryaśūra's *Garland of Jātaka Tales* (*Jātakamālā*) and the *Collection of Aphorisms* (*Udānavarga*) to cultivate devotion and take refuge; Asaṅga's *Bodhisattva Grounds* (*Bodhisattvabhūmi*) and Maitreya's *Ornament of Mahāyāna Sūtras* to learn meditation and the bodhisattva paths and stages; and Śāntideva's *Engaging in the Bodhisattvas' Deeds* and his *Compendium of Instructions* (*Śikṣāsamuccaya*) to learn the bodhisattva practices. From another perspective, the first two texts are studied in order to learn and observe karma and its effects, the second two to cultivate bodhicitta, and the last two to understand the correct view and realize emptiness. In addition to Potowa's great text tradition, there are two other Kadam traditions: the stages of the path tradition and the pith instructions tradition. The former principally studied lamrim texts, while the latter relied heavily on practice manuals and the oral instructions of their teacher.

49. Pith instructions (*man ngag*) and "ear-whispered" teachings (*snyan brgyud*) are types of oral instructions (*gdams ngag*) transmitted directly from teacher to student, though this style of advice now forms its own genre of texts. These teachings tend to be concise and practical, pointing to the heart of the practice and the nature of the mind. Such teachings are present in all the Tibetan Buddhist lineages but are more explicitly central to the Nyingma and Kagyu schools.

50. Gavin Kilty, trans., *Splendor of an Autumn Moon: The Devotional Verse of Tsongkhapa* (Boston: Wisdom Publications, 2001), 231–33.

51. Thupten Jinpa, trans., http://www.tibetanclassics.org/html-assets/In%20Praise%20of%20Dependent%20Origination.pdf.

52. Access concentration is the level of concentration attained with serenity; full concentration is deeper.

284 | APPROACHING THE BUDDHIST PATH

53. The five paths and ten bodhisattva grounds are stages that demarcate a bodhisattva's step-by-step journey to full awakening. On the first two paths—the paths of accumulation and preparation—one creates the causes to realize emptiness directly on the third path, the path of seeing. The ten grounds commence at the path of seeing and occur concurrently with the next path—the path of meditation—until the attainment of the path of no-more-learning, buddhahood.

54. Guy Newland, *Introduction to Emptiness* (Ithaca NY: Snow Lion, 2008), 112.

55. See the *Seven-Point Mind Training* by Geshe Chekawa and *Mind Training Like Rays of the Sun* by Nam-kha Pel.

56. Tibetans pronounce this *Om ah ra pa tsa na dhi.*

57. Thupten Jinpa, trans., *Wisdom of the Kadam Masters* (Boston: Wisdom, 2013), 5.

58. Thubten Chodron: In 1984 or 85 I visited Montserrat and together with two or three other nuns, I went to visit this monk at his hermitage in the mountain. We arrived unannounced, and he invited us in. On his altar was a long white *khatak* (Tibetan ceremonial scarf) and a picture of Avalokiteśvara that His Holiness had given him. As the sunlight streamed in and lit up his altar, he invited us to meditate with him. We did and after some time quietly departed. That same exceptional look in his eyes that His Holiness had noticed was still there.

59. Khunu Lama Rinpoche Tenzin Gyalsten (1894/95–1977) was born Kinnaur, India, studied in Tibet, and in the late 1950s went to Varanasi, where he was based for the remainder of his life. A story that illustrates the depth of his practice: in the mid-1970s some Westerners went to meet him and asked if he needed anything. He said, "No, I have all I need because I have bodhicitta." The next day he sent a one-rupee offering to each of the Westerners.

60. These are the *Prātimokṣa Sūtra*, *Vinayasūtra* by Guṇaprabha, *Treasury of Knowledge* by Vasubandhu, *Compendium of Knowledge* by Asaṅga, *Treatise on the Middle Way* by Nāgārjuna, *Four Hundred* by Āryadeva, *Supplement to the Middle Way* by Candrakīrti, *Engaging in the Bodhisattvas' Deeds* by Śāntideva, and Maitreya's five treatises.

61. "Two-fingered" indicates a woman's wisdom, because as the cook in a household, she tests the rice between two fingers to see if it is cooked. She also cuts thread while holding the ball of cotton between two fingers.

62. As a nonaffirming negative, emptiness is the absence of inherent existence; it doesn't establish anything positive. An affirming negative will negate one thing while establishing another. "The emptiness of the mind" negates inherent existence in terms of the mind. "The mind's emptiness" establishes the mind as having the attribute of emptiness.

Glossary

Abhayagiri. An early Buddhist monastery in Sri Lanka that was rooted in the teachings of early Buddhism and influenced by the Mahāyāna and later tantric teachings; a sect with that name.

Abhidharma. The branch of the Buddhist teachings dealing with wisdom that contains detailed analysis of phenomena; one of the three collections in the Tripiṭaka.

absolutism. Believing that phenomena exist inherently.

access concentration. The level of concentration attained with serenity.

affirming negative. A negation that implies something else.

afflictions (kleśa). Mental factors such as disturbing emotions and incorrect views that disturb the tranquility of the mind.

afflictive obscurations (kleśāvaraṇa). Obscurations that mainly prevent liberation; afflictions, their seeds, and polluted karma.

Āgamas. The anthologies of scriptures in the Chinese canon that correspond to four of the five Nikāyas in the Pāli canon.

aggregates (skandha). (1) The four or five components of a living being: body (except for beings born in the formless realm), feelings, discriminations, miscellaneous factors, and consciousnesses. (2) In general, the aggregates are a way to categorize all impermanent things. Here form includes the five sense objects, their five cognitive faculties, and forms for mental consciousness.

analytical meditation (*vicārabhāvanā, T. dpyad sgom*). Meditation for comprehending an object.

arhat. Someone who has eradicated all afflictive obscurations and is liberated from saṃsāra.

ārya. Someone who has directly and nonconceptually realized the emptiness of inherent existence.

basis of designation. The collection of parts or factors in dependence on which an object is designated.

bhāṇakas. A group of monastics whose duty it was to memorize and recite the scriptures.

bhikṣu and *bhikṣuṇī.* Fully ordained monk and nun.

bodhicitta. A primary mental consciousness induced by an aspiration to bring about others' welfare and accompanied by an aspiration to attain full awakening oneself. This is conventional bodhicitta. *See also* ultimate bodhicitta.

bodhisattva. Someone who has generated the spontaneous wish to attain buddhahood for the benefit of all sentient beings.

bodhisattva ground (*bodhisattvabhūmi*). A consciousness characterized by wisdom and compassion in the continuum of an ārya bodhisattva. It is the basis of development of good qualities and the basis for the eradication of ignorance and mistaken appearances.

cessation (*nirodha*). The cessation of afflictions, their seeds, and the polluted karma that produces rebirth in cyclic existence; liberation.

clear light. A mind that has always been and will continue to be pure; emptiness.

cognitive obscurations (*jñeyāvaraṇa*). Obscurations that mainly prevent full awakening; the latencies of ignorance and the subtle dualistic view that they give rise to. *See also* afflictive obscurations.

collection of merit. A bodhisattva's practice of the method aspect of the path that accumulates merit.

compassion (*karuṇā*). The wish for sentient beings to be free from all duḥkha and its causes.

conceptual appearance. A mental image of an object that appears to a conceptual consciousness.

consciousness (jñāna). That which is clear and cognizant.

conventional existence. Existence.

corrupted intelligence. An analytical mental factor that reaches an incorrect conclusion.

cyclic existence. See saṃsāra.

ḍākinī. A highly realized female tantric practitioner.

definitive teachings (nītārtha). Teachings that speak about the ultimate nature of reality and can be accepted literally (according to the Prāsaṅgikas). *See also* interpretable/provisional teachings.

dependent arising (pratītyasamutpāda). This is of three types (1) causal dependence—things arising due to causes and conditions, (2) mutual dependence—phenomena existing in relation to other phenomena, and (3) dependent designation—phenomena existing by being merely designated by terms and concepts.

Dhamma. The Pāli word for Dharma.

dhāraṇi. Mantra, a set of syllables expressing a spiritual meaning.

Dharmaguptaka. One of the eighteen early schools, whose Vinaya is practiced today in East Asia.

duḥkha. Unsatisfactory experiences of cyclic existence, which are of three types: the duḥkha of pain, the duḥkha of change, and the pervasive duḥkha of conditioning; the first truth of the āryas.

emanation body (nirmāṇakāya). The buddha body that appears to ordinary sentient beings in order to benefit others.

emptiness (śūnyatā). The lack of inherent existence, lack of independent existence.

enjoyment body (saṃbhogakāya). The buddha body that appears in the pure lands to teach ārya bodhisattvas.

evident phenomena. Phenomena that ordinary beings can perceive with their five senses.

exalted knower. A wisdom consciousness that realizes emptiness.

feeling (vedanā). One of the five aggregates; the experience of objects as pleasant, unpleasant, or neutral.

form body (rūpakāya). The buddha body in which a buddha appears to sentient beings; it includes the emanation and enjoyment bodies.

four truths of the āryas. The truth of duḥkha, its origin, its cessation, and the path to that cessation.

full awakening. Buddhahood; the state where all obscurations have been abandoned and all good qualities developed limitlessly.

functional phenomena. A thing that is produced by causes and conditions and produces an effect.

fundamental, innate mind of clear light. The subtlest level of mind.

Fundamental Vehicle. The path leading to the liberation of śrāvakas and solitary realizers.

gāthas. Short phrases used in the mind-training practice.

god (deva). A celestial being who is still born in saṃsāra.

highest yoga tantra (anuttarayogatantra). The most advanced of the four classes of tantra.

ignorance (avidyā). A mental factor that is obscured and grasps the opposite of what exists. There are two types: ignorance regarding reality that is the root of saṃsāra, and ignorance regarding karma and its effects.

inferential cognizer (anumāna). A conceptual mind that ascertains its object by means of a correct reason.

inherent existence (svabhāva). Existence without depending on any other factors; independent existence.

insight (vipaśyanā). A discerning wisdom conjoined with special pliancy induced by the power of having analyzed one's object within serenity.

interpretable/provisional teachings (neyārtha). Teachings that do not speak about the ultimate nature of phenomena and/or teachings that cannot be taken literally. *See also* definitive teachings.

Jetavana. An early Buddhist monastery in Sri Lanka that was rooted in the teachings of early Buddhism and influenced by the Mahāyāna and later tantric teachings; a sect with that name.

karma. Intentional action.

lamrim. Stages of the path to awakening; a text that teaches these based on the explanation of the three levels of practitioners.

latencies (vāsanā). Predispositions, imprints, or tendencies. There are latencies of karma and latencies of afflictions.

liberation (mokṣa). The state of freedom from cyclic existence. *See also* nirvāṇa.

Mahāvihāra. A monastery in Sri Lanka many centuries ago, whose teachings became prominent in Sri Lanka and the Theravāda world; a Buddhist sect in Sri Lanka.

Mahāyāna. The path to buddhahood; scriptures that describe this; a movement or type of practice within Buddhism that became prominent in India and spread to Central and East Asia.

meditational deity. A Buddhist deity that is a buddha or very high bodhisattva that is visualized in certain kinds of meditation.

meditative equipoise on emptiness. An ārya's mind focused single-pointedly on the emptiness of inherent existence.

mental factor (caitta). An aspect of a consciousness that apprehends a particular quality of the object or performs a specific cognitive function.

merit (puṇya). Good karma.

mind (cittajñāna). The clear, immaterial, and aware part of living beings that cognizes, experiences, thinks, feels, and so on.

mind training. A method to train the mind in conventional and ultimate bodhicitta. Mind training texts consist of short, pithy instructions.

mindstream. The continuity of mind.

monastic. Someone who has received monastic ordination; a monk or nun.

Mūlasarvāstivāda. An early Buddhist school that is a branch of the Sarvāstivāda school; the Vinaya lineage dominant in Tibet.

Nālandā tradition. The Buddhist tradition descendant from Nālandā Monastery and other monastic universities in India that flourished from the sixth to the late twelfth century.

nature truth body (svābhāvikadharmakāya). The buddha body that is the emptiness of a buddha's mind and that buddha's true cessations. *See also* truth body.

nihilism. Believing that our actions have no ethical dimension; believing that what exists—such as the Three Jewels, four truths, and the law of cause and effect—does not exist.

nikāya. (1) A collection of suttas in the Pāli canon, (2) a tradition within Theravāda Buddhism.

nirvāṇa. Liberation; the cessation of afflictive obscurations and the rebirth in saṃsāra that they cause.

nonaffirming negative. A negation that does not imply something else.

nonduality. The non-appearance of subject and object, inherent existence, veil truths, and conceptual appearances in an arya's meditative equipoise on emptiness

object of negation. What is negated or refuted.

Pāli tradition. The form of Buddhism based on scriptures written in the Pāli language.

parinirvāṇa. The Buddha's passing away.

permanent, unitary, independent self. A soul or self *(ātman)* asserted by non-Buddhists.

permanent. Unchanging moment to moment, static. It does not necessarily mean eternal.

person (pudgala). A living being designated in dependence on the four or five aggregates.

polluted. Under the influence of ignorance or the latencies of ignorance.

Prajñāpāramitā. The perfection of wisdom, which is the topic of a class of Mahāyāna sūtras by this name.

prātimokṣa. The different sets of ethical precepts that assist in attaining liberation.

pure vision teachings. The teachings stemming from the pure vision of a meditational deity seen by a realized master in meditation.

reliable cognizer (pramāṇa). A nondeceptive awareness that is incontrovertible with respect to its apprehended object and that enables us to accomplish our purpose.

samādhi. Single-pointed concentration.

saṃsāra. The cycle of rebirth that occurs under the control of afflictions and karma.

Sanskrit tradition. The form of Buddhism based on scriptures originally written in Sanskrit as well as other Central Asian languages.

Sarvāstivāda. One of the prominent early Buddhist schools in northern India.

scriptural authority. The authority of a scripture that has met three criteria that deem it reliable.

self (ātman). Depending on the context, (1) a person or (2) inherent existence.

self-centeredness. (1) In general, the attitude that believes our own happiness is more important than that of all others, (2) the attitude seeking only our own personal liberation.

self-grasping (ātmagrāha). The ignorance grasping inherent existence.

self-sufficient, substantially existent person. A self that is the controller of the body and mind. Such a self does not exist.

sentient being (sattva). Any being with a mind that is not free from pollutants; i.e., a being who is not a buddha. This includes ordinary beings as well as arhats and bodhisattvas.

serenity (śamatha). A concentration arising from meditation and accompanied by the bliss of mental and physical pliancy in which the mind abides effortlessly, without fluctuation, for as long as we wish, on whichever object it has been placed.

six perfections (sadpāramitā). The practices of generosity, ethical conduct, fortitude, joyous effort, meditative stability, and wisdom that are motivated by bodhicitta and sealed with the wisdom seeing them as both empty and dependent.

slightly obscure phenomena. Phenomena that can initially be known only by an inferential cognizer.

solitary realizer (pratyekabuddha). A person following the Fundamental Vehicle who seeks personal liberation and emphasizes understanding the twelve links of dependent arising.

śrāvaka. Someone practicing the Fundamental Vehicle leading to arhatship who emphasizes meditation on the four truths of the āryas.

stabilizing meditation. Meditation for developing concentration.

Sthavira. An early Buddhist school. The Theravāda is said to have descended from it.

Sūtrayāna. The path to awakening based on the sūtras.

sutta. The Pāli word for sūtra.

Tantrayāna. The path to awakeningdescribed in the tantras. To practice it one must have a firm understanding of the teachings in the Fundamental Vehicle and the general Mahāyana.

tathāgata. A buddha.

terma. Treasure teachings; teachings hidden in the environment or revealed as visionary teachings.

terton. A Buddhist teacher who discovers a terma.

Theravāda. The predominant form of Buddhism practiced today in Sri Lanka, Thailand, Burma, Laos, Cambodia, and so forth.

thirty-seven aids to awakening (bodhipakṣya-dharma). Seven sets of trainings—four establishments of mindfulness, four supreme strivings, four bases of supernormal power, five faculties, five powers, seven awakening factors, and the eightfold noble path—that together lead to the attainment of serenity and insight.

three higher trainings. The trainings in ethical conduct, concentration, and wisdom that are practiced within having taken refuge in the Three Jewels and that form the path to liberation.

Tripiṭaka. The Buddha's teachings in three branches: Vinaya, Sūtra, and Abhidharma.

true cessation. The cessation of a portion of afflictions or a portion of cognitive obscurations.

true existence. Inherent existence (according to the Prāsaṅgika system).

truth body (dharmakāya). The buddha body that includes the nature truth body and the wisdom truth body.

turning the Dharma wheel. The Buddha giving teachings.

ultimate bodhicitta. The wisdom directly realizing emptiness that is supported by conventional bodhicitta. *See also* bodhicitta.

ultimate truth (paramārthasatya). The ultimate mode of existence of all persons and phenomena; emptiness.

unfortunate rebirth. Rebirth as a hell being, hungry ghost, or animal.

veil truth (saṃvṛtisatya). That which appears true from the perspective of the mind grasping true existence. Also called conventional truth.

very obscure phenomena. Phenomena that can be known only by relying on the testimony of a reliable person or a valid scripture.

view of a personal identity (satkāyadṛṣṭi). Grasping an inherently existent I or mine (according to the Prāsaṅgika system).

Vinaya. Monastic discipline; the scriptures that present the monastic discipline.

wisdom truth body (jñānadharmakāya). The buddha body that is a buddha's omniscient mind. *See also* truth body.

Further Reading

Chodron, Thubten. *Don't Believe Everything You Think.* Boston: Snow Lion, 2012.

———. *Working with Anger.* Ithaca NY: Snow Lion, 2001.

Dalai Lama, H. H. Tenzin Gyatso, the Fourteenth. *Beyond Religion.* New York: Houghton Mifflin Harcourt, 2011.

———. *The Compassionate Life.* Boston: Wisdom Publications, 2001.

———. *The Four Noble Truths.* London: Thorsons, 1997.

———. *The Good Heart.* Boston: Wisdom Publications, 1996.

———. *Healing Anger.* Ithaca, NY: Snow Lion, 1997.

———. *How to See Yourself as You Really Are.* New York: Atria Books, 2007.

———. *An Open Heart.* New York: Little, Brown and Co., 2011.

———. *Transforming the Mind.* London: Thorsons, 2000.

———. *The Universe in a Single Atom.* New York: Morgan Road Books, 2005.

———. *The World of Tibetan Buddhism.* Boston: Wisdom Publications, 1995.

Dalai Lama, H. H. the, and Howard Cutler. *The Art of Happiness.* New York: Riverhead Books, 1998.

Dalai Lama, H. H. the, and Thubten Chodron. *Buddhism: One Teacher, Many Traditions.* Boston: Wisdom Publications, 2014.

Jinpa, Thupten. *Essential Mind Training.* Boston: Wisdom Publications, 2011.

———. *Wisdom of the Kadam Masters.* Boston: Wisdom Publications, 2013.

Rinchen, Geshe Sonam, and Ruth Sonam. *Eight Verses for Training the Mind.* Ithaca NY: Snow Lion, 2001.

Skilling, Peter. "Scriptural Authenticity and the Śrāvaka Schools: An Essay toward an Indian Perspective." *The Eastern Buddhist* 41–42. Kyoto: Otani University, 2010.

Salomon, Richard. *Buddhist Texts of Ancient Gandhāra*. Boston: Wisdom Publications, 2017.

Tegchok, Geshe Jampa. *Practical Ethics and Profound Emptiness: A Commentary on Nagarjuna's Precious Garland of Advice to a King*. Boston: Wisdom Publications, 2017.

———. *Transforming Adversity into Joy and Courage*. Ithaca, NY: Snow Lion, 2005.

Yeshe, Lama Thubten. *Becoming Your Own Therapist* and *Making Your Mind an Ocean*. Boston: Lama Yeshe Wisdom Archives, 2007.

———. *The Peaceful Stillness of the Silent Mind*. Boston: Lama Yeshe Wisdom Archives, 2004.

Zopa Rinpoche, Lama Thubten. *Cherishing Others*. Boston: Lama Yeshe Wisdom Archives, 2011.

Index

Note: Page numbers followed by "(2)" indicate two discussions. Page numbers followed by "n"/"nn" plus a number/numbers as in 281n29 and 281nn30,31 indicate endnotes.

About the Authors

THE DALAI LAMA is the spiritual leader of the Tibetan people, a Nobel Peace Prize recipient, and an advocate for compassion and peace throughout the world. He promotes harmony among the world's religions and engages in dialogue with leading scientists. Ordained as a Buddhist monk when he was a child, he completed the traditional monastic studies and earned his geshe degree (equivalent to a PhD). Renowned for his erudite and open-minded scholarship, his meditative attainments, and his humility, Bhikṣu Tenzin Gyatso says, "I am a simple Buddhist monk."

Peter Aronson

BHIKṢUṆĪ THUBTEN CHODRON has been a Buddhist nun since 1977. Growing up in Los Angeles, she graduated with honors in history from UCLA and did graduate work in education at USC. After years studying and teaching Buddhism in Asia, Europe, and the United States, she became the founder and abbess of Sravasti Abbey in Washington State. A popular speaker for her practical explanations of how to apply Buddhist teachings in daily life, she is the author of several bestselling books, including *Buddhism for Beginners*. She is the editor of Khensur Jampa Tegchok's *Insight into Emptiness*. For more information, visit sravastiabbey.org and thubtenchodron.org.

Also Available by the Dalai Lama from Wisdom Publications

Buddhism
One Teacher, Many Traditions

The Compassionate Life

Essence of the Heart Sutra
The Dalai Lama's Heart of Wisdom Teachings

The Good Heart
A Buddhist Perspective on the Teachings of Jesus

Imagine All the People
A Conversation with the Dalai Lama on Money, Politics, and Life as it Could Be

Kalachakra Tantra
Rite of Initiation

The Life of My Teacher
A Biography of Kyabjé Ling Rinpoche

Meditation on the Nature of Mind

The Middle Way
Faith Grounded in Reason

Mind in Comfort and Ease
The Vision of Enlightenment in the Great Perfection

MindScience
An East-West Dialogue

Practicing Wisdom
The Perfection of Shantideva's Bodhisattva Way

Sleeping, Dreaming and Dying
An Exploration of Consciousness

The Wheel of Life
Buddhist Perspectives on Cause and Effect

The World of Tibetan Buddhism
An Overview of Its Philosophy and Practice

ALSO AVAILABLE FROM THUBTEN CHODRON

Insight into Emptiness
Khensur Jampa Tegchok
Edited and Introduced by Thubten Chodron

"One of the best introductions to the philosophy of emptiness I have ever read."—José Ignacio Cabezón

Practical Ethics and Profound Emptiness
A Commentary on Nagarjuna's Precious Garland
Khensur Jampa Tegchok
Edited by Thubten Chodron

"A beautifully clear translation and systematic explanation of Nagarjuna's most accessible and wide-ranging work. Dharma students everywhere will benefit from careful attention to its pages.."— Guy Newland, author of *Introduction to Emptiness*

Buddhism for Beginners

Cultivating a Compassionate Heart
The Yoga Method of Chenrezig

Don't Believe Everything You Think
Living with Wisdom and Compassion

Guided Meditations on the Stages of the Path

How to Free Your Mind
Tara the Liberator

Living with an Open Heart
How to Cultivate Compassion in Daily Life

Open Heart, Clear Mind

Taming the Mind

Working with Anger

About Wisdom Publications

Wisdom Publications is the leading publisher of classic and contemporary Buddhist books and practical works on mindfulness. To learn more about us or to explore our other books, please visit our website at wisdompubs.org or contact us at the address below.

Wisdom Publications
199 Elm Street
Somerville, MA 02144 USA

We are a 501(c)(3) organization, and donations in support of our mission are tax deductible.

Wisdom Publications is affiliated with the Foundation for the Preservation of the Mahayana Tradition (FPMT).